EPWORTH PREACHER'S COMMENTARIES

★

THE GOSPEL
ACCORDING TO
ST JOHN

★

OWEN E. EVANS
M.A., B.D.

LONDON : EPWORTH PRESS

FIRST PUBLISHED 1965

© EPWORTH PRESS 1965

Book Steward
FRANK H. CUMBERS

SET IN MONOTYPE TIMES ROMAN AND PRINTED IN
GREAT BRITAIN BY THE CAMELOT PRESS LTD
LONDON AND SOUTHAMPTON

THE GOSPEL ACCORDING TO ST JOHN

To the memory of
MY MOTHER

General Introduction

WE are living in a day in which the authority and message of the Bible is being rediscovered and declared. Preachers are realizing afresh that their message must be based on the Word of God in Scripture. Many commentaries on the books of the Bible are already available, and give much space to the consideration of critical questions and historical and literary problems.

This new series of commentaries, as its name suggests, is written specifically for preachers, and particularly for those who feel themselves ill-equipped to study the more advanced works of scholarship. Its aim is to set forth the essential message of the Bible. Questions of authorship, date, background will be dealt with briefly, and only in so far as they are necessary for informed preaching. The main purpose of each commentary will be (*a*) to explain the original meaning of each biblical passage, and (*b*) to indicate its relevance to human need in the present situation. Bearing in mind this dual purpose, each author will have freedom to use what method of treatment he thinks most suitable to the book of the Bible on which he is commenting.

To save space, the biblical text is not printed, but the commentary is based on that of the *Revised Version*.

The author of this, the fifteenth of the *Epworth Preacher's Commentaries*, is the Rev. Owen E. Evans, who has been New Testament tutor at Hartley Victoria College since 1953, and is part-time lecturer at the University of Manchester.

In a brief Introduction, he accepts the conclusions of modern 'middle-of-the-road' scholarship as regards the more important issues of the Johannine 'problem'. Thus, keeping in mind the purpose of these Commentaries, he prepares the reader for the study of what is (he claims) pre-eminently 'the preacher's Gospel', and throughout his commentary he justifies and illustrates this claim, to the great benefit of the preacher.

GREVILLE P. LEWIS

Preface

IN the preparation of this commentary I have been helped by
the existence of three of the earlier volumes in the series—
namely, the commentaries of Dr C. L. Mitton and Dr A. M.
Ward on *St Mark* and *St Matthew* respectively, and that of
the General Editor on *The Johannine Epistles*. Wherever
possible I have tried to save space by referring to these works;
Mr Greville Lewis's many excellent notes on Johannine themes
have proved particularly helpful in this respect, and the reader
of this commentary is advised to have them constantly at hand
for reference. Even so, the necessity of relating the themes to
their contexts in the Gospel, of tracing the closely knit patterns
of the evangelist's thought, and of seeking to do justice to the
rich suggestiveness of the Gospel for the Christian preacher,
has resulted in the growth of the commentary to a size
somewhat larger than that originally intended for contribu-
tions to the series. I am grateful to the Editors for being so
sympathetic and accommodating in this respect.

The method adopted has been to divide the Gospel into its
natural sections (which inevitably vary considerably in length),
and for each section to provide, first, a more or less continuous
exposition aimed at bringing out the meaning of the text, and
secondly (printed in smaller type), a number of suggestions as
to how the material of the commentary may be used in preaching. It is not intended that all, by any means, of these suggestions should provide a theme for a sermon as such—though it
is hoped that many will. In many cases it is merely a matter of
indicating how a particular theme (on which a preacher may
be making a sermon) may be illustrated by reference to the
Johannine text.

Much of the material in the commentary on the first four
chapters of the Gospel has already been used, in a somewhat
different form, in my contribution to *The Preacher's Handbook,
Number Five* (ed. Greville P. Lewis, Epworth, 1957). To
possessors of that volume I apologize for this repetition, which
in the circumstances could hardly be avoided.

I would gratefully acknowledge my deep indebtedness to the works of many commentators and writers on St John's Gospel, and most especially to those of W. F. Howard, C. H. Dodd, and C. K. Barrett. To the General Editor and the New Testament Editors of the series I am most grateful for their patient understanding, their constant encouragement, and their many wise and helpful suggestions.

Hartley Victoria College,   OWEN E. EVANS
Manchester.
1964.

Abbreviations

AV.   Authorized Version
RV.   Revised Version
RSV.   Revised Standard Version
NEB.   New English Bible
CLM.   C. Leslie Mitton, *St Mark* (E.P.C.)
AMW.   A. Marcus Ward, *St Matthew* (E.P.C.)
GPL.   Greville P. Lewis, *The Johannine Epistles* (E.P.C.)
MHB.   *The Methodist Hymnbook* (1933)

N.B.   Text references printed in heavy type relate to chapters and verses in *John*.

Introduction

Authorship, Date and Place of Writing

THE Gospel according to St John is called *The Fourth Gospel*, not only because of its position in the NT but also because, by general consent, it was the last of the four canonical Gospels to be written. From the end of the second century until modern times it was universally believed to be the work of the Apostle John, the son of Zebedee, who according to an ancient tradition had eventually settled in Ephesus and lived there until the closing years of the first century, and who wrote the Gospel there at the end of his long life. Most modern scholars, whilst accepting the view that the Gospel was written at Ephesus at some time between AD 85 and 100, have abandoned —for reasons which may be found in any modern text-book on NT Introduction, or any critical commentary on the Gospel itself—the theory of direct apostolic authorship, in favour of the view that the actual writer was a *disciple* of the Apostle who based his work largely upon the testimony and teaching of his venerated master (see commentary on 19³⁵ and 21²⁴), to whom he referred in the Gospel as '*the disciple whom Jesus loved*' (see on 13²³). Some identify the author with John the Elder, a prominent figure in the Church at the end of the first century, who is mentioned by Papias, a writer of the mid-second century (for this view see *GPL*, pp. 1-2), and suggest that the fact that he shared the same name with the Apostle may have been responsible for the misunderstanding that later led to the authorship being attributed to the latter. It cannot be proved, however, that John the Elder wrote the Gospel, or even that he was associated with Ephesus, and all things considered it seems best not to attempt to attach a name to the evangelist, but to be content with noting his close relationship with the Apostle John. If, as is most likely, he was also the author of the Johannine Epistles, we have evidence that, whatever his name may have been, he belonged to the class of 'Elders' (see 2 Jn 1, 3 Jn 1, and *GPL*, p. 2). That he was a Jew is highly probable, but there is ample evidence in the Gospel that he was thoroughly familiar also with Greek ways of thought (see below on the character and purpose of the Gospel). For purposes of convenience, in the present commentary the evangelist will be referred to (without prejudice) as John, and the Gospel itself as *Jn*.

Relationship to the Synoptic Gospels

The traditional view is that John was acquainted with the works of his predecessors (or at least with those of Mark and Luke) and derived some of his material from them. A growing body of scholarly opinion in recent years has challenged this view, claiming that the parallels between *Jn* and the Synoptics —in contents, in order of events, and even in the occasional striking examples of verbal identity (e.g. at 5^{8-9} and 12^3)—can be adequately explained on the basis of John's acquaintance, not with the Synoptic Gospels as such, but with some of the tradition (whether oral or written) which was used in their composition. For the purpose of this commentary it does not greatly matter whether the material for which there are Synoptic parallels was drawn directly from the earlier Gospels, or from the same underlying tradition, or from some other parallel source of tradition which overlapped with the Synoptic tradition. More important is the question (see next section) of the manner in which John used the traditional material on the basis of which he composed his Gospel, including the large amount of material which has no Synoptic parallel and which was presumably unknown to any of the earlier evangelists.

Character and Purpose of the Gospel

It has often been assumed that, whereas the Synoptics are concerned with *history* (factual accounts of the life, teaching, and work of Jesus), the Fourth Gospel is a work of *theology* (the interpretation of the theological significance of the facts). It is being increasingly recognized nowadays that this is a considerable over-simplification of the issue. Each of the four Gospels, in varying degrees, combines the historical and theological elements, and a more accurate assessment of the difference between the Synoptics and *Jn* is to say that in the former the historical element, and in the latter the theological element, *predominates*. This does not mean, however, that the Synoptic account is always to be preferred when it differs from *Jn* on a point of history (e.g. the date of the Last Supper—see comment on 13[1]); each case must be treated on its merits. It is generally agreed today that John had access to historical traditions, independent of those used in the Synoptics, which deserve to be treated with the same respect, from the point of view of trustworthiness, as the latter. The vital question, as was mentioned above, concerns the use which John made of the historical tradition in the fulfilment of his purpose in writing. On this subject, see *Special Note* on pp. 123-6.

This purpose, which determined both the form and the contents of the Gospel, finds expression in the words with which the book originally concluded (20[30-1]). Here we learn that it was not the evangelist's intention to give an exhaustive account of the ministry of Jesus, but rather to treat a *selection* of the events thereof. The principle on which the selection was made was a theological one, each incident being regarded as a '*sign*' (see p. 22) which symbolizes a deep spiritual truth, and being recorded not for its own sake (simply to add to the reader's knowledge of the facts about Jesus) but for the sake of the truth it signifies. John is not content to relate bare facts; rather does he, under the inspiration of the Holy Spirit (cf. 16[13-14]), interpret the facts so as to bring out their abiding significance. The ultimate aim of the work is an evangelical one: '*that ye may believe that Jesus is the Christ, the Son of God; and that believing ye may have life in his name*'. That the Gospel is addressed primarily to Gentile rather than Jewish readers is evident from the trouble the author takes to translate Hebrew and Aramaic words (see 1[38], etc.) and to explain Jewish customs (see 2[6], etc.), and also from the many marks his thought reveals of Greek ideas and ways of thinking. If this Greek background of John's thought is marked, however, the Jewish background is even more prominent. The Gospel reveals a synthesis of Jewish and Greek ideas. This indeed is a measure of the evangelist's success, for his aim was to commend the Christian Faith—a Faith rooted in the soil of Jewish thought—to a pagan world that was under the dominance of Greek ways of thinking, in order to lead that world to believe in Christ. To achieve this end he transposed, so to speak, the Palestinian Gospel into a Hellenistic key, and succeeded in doing so without obscuring or distorting the original tune.

John was thus a prototype of all Christian preachers in that he sought to interpret, to his own age and environment, the eternal spiritual meaning and significance of those historical events in which Christianity is rooted and grounded. Accordingly it may well be claimed that the Fourth Gospel is pre-eminently 'the preacher's Gospel'.

The Original Extent and Order of the Gospel

As has already been indicated, the Gospel originally ended at 20^{31}, which forms a natural and impressive conclusion. It is generally agreed that Chapter **21** forms an Appendix subsequently added, the only question in dispute being whether it was added by the evangelist himself or by an editor or editors (see p. 219).

Readers of Moffatt's translation of the NT, and of certain commentaries on *Jn* written a generation or so ago, will be familiar with the theory that the Gospel, as we have it, has at some points suffered from transpositions of the original order intended by the author (e.g. in Chapters **13–16**). Such theories have lost favour in recent years. In view of the fact that there is virtually no manuscript evidence for any different order, coupled with the fact that the evangelist's purpose (see above) was primarily a theological one (and the theological sequence is natural and intelligible when the Gospel is read in its traditional order), there is no compelling reason for adopting any transpositions in the order of chapters or paragraphs.

Books for further study

The scope and purpose of this commentary make impossible a full discussion of the very complex problems of Introduction and criticism of the Gospel. For the treatment of such questions the reader is referred to the text-books on NT Introduction and to the many admirable commentaries and other books on Johannine thought, a short list of which is given below:

Introduction

V. Taylor: *The Gospels: a Short Introduction* (Epworth), pp. 84–109.

children of God, but it is only by faith in Christ that they become *actually* so (cf. Paul's teaching about adoption in Gal 4[4-6] and Rom 8[14-17]). A man is born into God's family, not by any physical or natural process of birth, but by a supernatural and spiritual rebirth (this theme is developed more fully in 3[17]; see also *GPL, Note 15*, p. 77).

1[14-18]. The final section of the Prologue explains in greater detail the significance of the Word's entry into the world. Verse 15 is best treated as a parenthesis, as in *RSV*. It interrupts the natural connection between *vv.* 14 and 16, and is probably inserted here to reassert, in the light of the great pronouncement of *v.* 14, the subordination of the Baptist to Jesus and his testimony to Him (cf. 1[6-8, 26-34]).

1[14]. '*the Word became flesh*'. John stresses the fact that a real incarnation is involved. The word 'flesh' in the Bible stands for human nature. It is usually associated with the idea of the frailty and sinfulness of that nature; that is why Paul shrinks from saying that Christ actually came 'in the flesh', and chooses rather, in Rom 8[3], to speak of His coming 'in the likeness of sinful flesh'. John is bolder and does not hesitate to attribute flesh to the Word. This is sufficient proof that, for him, the flesh is not necessarily and inherently sinful. The fulness and reality of the humanity of Christ is consistently emphasized in the Gospel and Epistles of John— a fact accounted for by his desire to refute the Docetic heresy, i.e. the claim that Christ only *seemed* to have a human body (see *GPL, Note 14*, p. 69).

'*and dwelt among us*'. The verb literally means 'pitched a tent' (cf. *RVm*), and so suggests a temporary sojourning. The use of the first person plural here and in *v.* 16 does not necessarily imply that the evangelist is claiming to have been an eye-witness of Jesus' ministry. It probably means simply that he is speaking in the name, not of himself alone, but of the whole Church, which is founded upon the testimony of the apostolic eye-witnesses (cf. *GPL*, pp. 8-9).

'*full of grace and truth*'. This phrase is to be linked to the primary subject of the sentence, '*the Word*', and the intervening words ('*and we beheld . . . Father*') treated as a parenthesis (so *RV*; cf. *RSV*). ' *Grace*' is not a characteristic word of John (as it is of Paul); outside the Prologue it is not found in the Gospel.

It means the free, loving favour of God towards the undeserving. '*Truth*', on the other hand, is one of the great Johannine words; behind it lies the idea of God's unwavering fidelity to His own nature and character (see *GPL*, *Note 4*, p. 25). The linking of '*grace and truth*', here and in *v.* 17, reflects the common OT phrase 'mercy and truth' (Ex 34⁶, etc.); in the OT these are attributes of God, and John applies them (as he does 'life' and 'light' in 1⁴) to the Word. It is this combination of divine attributes that constitutes His '*glory*'.

'*we beheld his glory*'. '*Glory*' is another of John's great words; it denotes all the richness of God's character and personal activity. In the Jewish mind the idea of God's glory was closely associated with that of the *shekinah*—the visible manifestation of the divine presence—and there seems to be a deliberate play on words in John's choice of the Greek word *eskēnosen* (translated '*dwelt*'), with its resemblance, both in sound and meaning, to the Hebrew *shekinah*.

'*the only begotten*'. This term occurs in reference to Christ four times in this Gospel (cf. 1¹⁸, 3¹⁶, ¹⁸) and also in 1 Jn 4⁹ (see *GPL*). The word means 'only one of its kind' or 'unique', and as used of Christ it describes His unique Sonship. His relationship to the Father is quite different from that of any other man (see comment on *vv.* 12-13). The intimacy of this relationship appears in the phrase '*which is in the bosom of the Father*' in *v.* 18 (cf. 13²³, where the same phrase again denotes a specially intimate relationship).

1¹⁶⁻¹⁷. '*his fulness*' is the fulness of grace and truth referred to in *v.* 14.

'*grace for grace*' means, literally, 'grace in place of grace'; not, however, the grace of the gospel in place of that of the law (*v.* 17 implies that grace does not belong to the law), but rather 'grace upon grace' (*RSV*, *NEB*). The Christian receives, as it were, wave upon wave of divine grace.

'*Moses . . . Jesus Christ*'. John asserts the superiority of Christ and the gospel over Moses and the law; the latter mediates law, which gives man knowledge of sin (cf. Rom 3²⁰, 7⁷), but the former mediates grace and truth, which give man deliverance from sin. Here for the first time in *Jn*, '*Jesus Christ*' is referred to by name, so that readers can be henceforth in no doubt that He is in fact the Word with whom the whole Prologue has been concerned.

1[18] reflects the characteristically Jewish belief that God is invisible (Ex 33[20], etc. Cf. 5[37], 6[46], 1 Jn 4[12, 20]). The Prologue, however, concludes with the assertion that the Unseen is no longer the Unknown; His only Son, who is His Word, has made Him known.

'*the only begotten Son*'. See on *v*. 14. The original text of *Jn* probably read 'God' (*RVm*) and not '*Son*' after '*only begotten*' here, the meaning being 'the only one, himself God' (*NEBm*). Read in this way, the verse re-emphasizes the fact of the divinity of Christ, already asserted in *vv*. 1-2.

In this majestic Prologue John has set forth the fundamental truth which underlies the whole Gospel, namely that Jesus Christ, the eternal, divine Word made flesh, the true Light, the only Son of God, is the Revealer of God to men. He is now ready to begin his account of the life, the works and the words of Jesus, in and through which this revelation is given.

The Prologue is full of material for the preacher. Among the themes which arise out of it we may note the following: (*a*) The God of the Bible is a God who speaks to men, making known to them His mind, His character and His purposes, and who has spoken His final and all-sufficient Word in the Incarnation of His Eternal Son (cf. Heb 1[1-2]). In Jesus Christ God has told men all that He wishes them to know, and all that they need to know, about Himself. (*b*) The invisible God has been made known by One who was supremely fitted (by virtue of His being united with God from all eternity in the most intimate personal relationship, and of His sharing fully in the divine nature) to reveal Him; and the revelation has been given in the only terms which men can fully understand— in terms of a human life lived out in this world of sense and time. (*c*) The true Light has shone into the darkness of the world—a fact which contains a message both of comfort and of challenge. The comfort lies in the fact that the Light can never be extinguished; the challenge in the fact that it is possible for men to remain in darkness in spite of the fact that the Light is shining upon them (cf. 3[19]). (*d*) The wonderful privilege of Christian believers is to be reborn into the family of God. (*e*) The Christian life is a matter of grace from beginning to end; each experience of God's grace that we accept leads on to a further and richer experience. (*f*) The contrast between the Old and New Dispensations: Moses offered men a law and bade them keep it, that they might live thereby (cf. Rom 10[5]); Christ offers men His own fulness of grace and truth, that they may find life in Him.

1¹⁹⁻³⁴: John the Baptist's Testimony to Jesus

Like the other evangelists, and following the pattern of the
apostolic preaching (cf. Acts 10³⁷), John makes the ministry
of the Baptist the starting-point of his account of the ministry
of Jesus. Unlike the others, however, John is not interested in
the Baptist's work as a preacher of repentance and leader of a
considerable religious revival in Judea and the surrounding
regions (see Mk 1⁴⁻⁸, Mt 3¹⁻¹², Lk 3¹⁻²⁰); he depicts him solely
as a witness to Jesus (cf. 1⁶⁻⁸, ¹⁵). The subordination of the
Baptist to Christ is a prominent feature of the account given in
this section of his conversation with the deputation sent by the
religious authorities at Jerusalem to question him about his
unorthodox preaching and practices.

1¹⁹. *'the Jews'* is the title generally given in *Jn* to the religious
authorities who were the constant opponents of Jesus. Verse
24 suggests that it was the Pharisees who were chiefly responsible for sending the deputation. On the Pharisees, see *CLM*
on Mk 2¹⁶.

'priests and Levites'—two classes of Temple officials.

1²⁰. *'I am not the Christ'*. This denial suggests that some at
least of the Baptist's contemporaries had entertained the
notion that he might be the Messiah (cf. Lk 3¹⁵).

1²¹. *'Elijah'*. The Jews expected Elijah to return as the forerunner of the Messiah (see Mal 4⁵). In the Synoptics Jesus
identifies the Baptist with Elijah (see *CLM* on Mk 9⁹⁻¹³), but
here he himself refuses to claim such identity. He did not fully
realize his own significance.

'the prophet' is an allusion to Moses' promise in Deut 18¹⁵.
The title appears again in 6¹⁴ (where it seems to refer to the
Messiah) and in 7⁴⁰ (where it seems to be distinguished from
'the Christ' of the following verse). It is uncertain whether the
Jews identified the expected prophet with the Messiah, but
the primitive Church seems to have regarded Jesus as the
fulfilment of Deut 18¹⁵ (cf. Acts 3²²).

1²²⁻³. After his threefold denial of a claim to any kind of
Messianic status, the Baptist is pressed to say something
positive about himself. He is content to describe himself in

words quoted from Isa 40³—a passage which is referred to the Baptist in all four Gospels (see *CLM* on Mk 1³). He claims to be no more than a '*voice*' calling on Israel to prepare for the Messiah's coming. 'It is not who he is, but what he says, that matters' (W. Temple).

1²⁵. '*Why then baptizest thou. . . .?*' The authorities, realizing that the baptism is in some way connected with the approach of the Messianic kingdom, imply that John has no authority to administer it, since on his admission he has no Messianic status.

1²⁶⁻⁷. The Baptist replies that the rite which he administers is an inferior and merely preparatory baptism. This implies that the successor of whom he speaks will administer a better baptism (see below on *v.* 33). On the significance of John's water-baptism and the Messianic Spirit-baptism, see *CLM* on Mk 1⁴⁻⁸.

'*in the midst of you standeth one. . .*'. The Baptist suggests to his questioners that the Messiah Himself is already present, though unrecognized.

'*the latchet of whose shoe . . .*'. The Baptist could hardly have expressed more emphatically his own subordination to Christ; there was a Rabbinic saying to the effect that a disciple might perform for his master any duty proper to a slave, except that of untying his sandals.

1²⁸. '*Bethany*' is much better attested than either of the variants noted in *RVm*. This is not the Bethany of **11¹**, but another place of the same name, not mentioned elsewhere, and whose exact position is not known, though it was clearly '*beyond Jordan*' (cf. **10⁴⁰**).

1²⁹. Here the historical figure of Jesus makes His first appearance in the narrative, and the Baptist's direct witness to Him commences.

'*the Lamb of God*'. The question of the background and significance of this title, which occurs in the NT only here and in *v.* 36, has been much discussed. There are four main theories: (*a*) that the reference is to the Passover lamb of Ex 12; (*b*) that the Suffering Servant is meant (cf. Isa 53⁷); (*c*) that the lamb of the sin-offering is in mind; and (*d*) that the title refers to the horned ram which in Jewish apocalyptic works represents the Messiah as the leader of the flock of God (cf. Rev 14[1], etc.). The most satisfactory solution to the problem would seem to be a combination of (*a*) and (*b*). It is difficult not to believe that the evangelist, in using the title of Jesus, had the Passover lamb in mind, for in **19[36]** Jesus is again identified with that lamb (cf. Paul's use of the same imagery in 1 Cor 5[7]). The Passover lamb, however, is nowhere spoken of as taking away sin, so that theory (*a*) hardly provides by itself an adequate explanation of the Baptist's phrase as a whole. Isa 53[12] describes the Suffering Servant as bearing 'the sin of many'. Thus it seems that John has combined the ideas of the Passover lamb and the Suffering Servant (and possibly other OT sacrificial ideas too), and compressed them into one richly significant description of Jesus as '*the Lamb of God, which taketh away the sin of the world*'. Jesus is the Servant whom God sent to offer Himself as a new Passover sacrifice in order to make an end of sin (cf. Heb 9[26]). This idea of the death of Christ as an atoning sacrifice is not prominent in *Jn*, but it was not strange to the author, for he develops it more fully in 1 Jn 2[1-2], 3[5] and 4[10] (see *GPL*).

1[30]. The Baptist explains that Jesus is the Messiah to whom he referred in *v.* 27 (cf. *v.* 15). Although subsequent in chronological order, Jesus precedes the Baptist by virtue of His pre-existence (see **1** [1-2, 6]).

1[31]. '*And I knew him not*'. This does not mean that the Baptist and Jesus were strangers to one another before this encounter (according to Lk 1 they were related), but rather that the Baptist did not realize that Jesus was the Messiah until he received the vision to be described in the following verses. Before describing this vision, however, he reasserts that the purpose of his own ministry of water-baptism is simply to prepare the way for the revelation to Israel of the Messiah (see above on *v.* 26).

1[32-4]. The Baptist explains how he came to recognize Jesus as Messiah. He is clearly referring to the occasion when Jesus came to be baptized (see Mk 1[9-11], Mt 3[13-17], Lk 3[21-2]). John, however, does not refer explicitly to Jesus' baptism; the reason for this is probably his desire to counteract the tendency to over-exalt the Baptist (see on 1⁶⁻⁸). The Baptist had received a warning from God of what was to happen (*v*. 33). It has already been implied in *vv*. 26-27 that the coming Messiah is to administer a baptism superior to his, and now this baptism is defined as being '*with the Holy Spirit*'. The Baptist's witness to the fulfilment of the divine warning is given in *vv*. 32 and 34.

'*I have beheld the Spirit* . . .'. In the Synoptic accounts it is Jesus alone who sees this, but here the Baptist claims to have shared the vision. On the significance of the Spirit's descent, see *CLM* on Mk 1¹⁰.

'*it abode upon him*'. John alone adds this significant phrase. The OT prophets were visited from time to time by the Spirit, but Jesus' possession of the Spirit was constant and unbroken. It was in this perfect communion with the Holy Spirit, and under His guidance and inspiration, that Jesus fulfilled his ministry (cf. Mk 1¹²).

'*this is the Son of God*'. A well-attested variant reading here is 'God's Chosen One' (*NEB*). For the idea of Christ's divine Sonship, see on 1¹⁴, ¹⁸. The Baptist's confession here suggests that, in addition to witnessing the Spirit's descent, he also heard the voice from heaven testifying to the Sonship of Jesus (Mk 1¹¹). It is unlikely, as a matter of history, that the Baptist recognized Jesus as Messiah at the time of His baptism (see *AMW* on Mt 11²⁻¹⁵). John, however, in line with his theological and evangelical purpose (see Introduction, pp. 2-4), sometimes describes events, not precisely as they appeared at the time, but as their significance was realized later. Thus the Baptist, throughout the present section, has been witnessing to the view of the Person and Work of Jesus which the evangelist himself holds, and which he wishes to bring before the minds of his readers right at the outset of his narrative.

(*a*) In his humble self-effacement, the Baptist stands as a shining example to everyone whose task it is, whether in the pulpit or out of it, to witness for Christ. It is Jesus who is '*the Word*' (1¹¹⁻⁸); the witness is a mere '*voice*', whose privilege it is to speak that '*Word*' and to make straight His way into the hearts of his hearers. (*b*) The Christian disciple is the bond-servant of Christ, and there is no task, however humble, that it is not his privilege to perform in his Master's service; we are not worthy to perform even the lowliest service for Him. (*c*) The new and unconventional is not necessarily right and commendable, but official Christendom (which has often been guilty—as was official Judalism in the case of the Baptist—of a conservative suspicion of new and unorthodox methods) should be wary of condemning out of hand the prophet who arises from outside its official ranks; the sure test is that advocated by Gamaliel in Acts 5³⁸⁻⁹. (*d*) No one can recognize Jesus as the Son of God save by divine illumination and inspiration (cf. Mt 16¹⁷, 1 Cor 12³). (*e*) The atoning significance of the death of Christ is the very heart of the gospel we are privileged to preach. *Why* such a sacrifice should have been necessary before men could be delivered from sin and reconciled to God is a question that no preacher will ever be able adequately to answer; he can, however, point out that when one considers 'of what great weight is sin', on the one hand, and the awe-full holiness of God on the other, one ought not to be surprised that atonement should have involved such costly sacrifice. Moreover, our own experience on the human level of the efficacy and fruitfulness for good of suffering sacrificially borne may afford some useful clue. In the final analysis, however, the privilege of the Christian is not to comprehend the 'Why?' of the Cross, but to experience its 'How?' We rejoice in, and proclaim the glorious news that the all-sufficient sacrifice has been offered on our behalf by our Lord and Saviour.

1³⁵⁻⁵¹: Jesus and His Disciples

As in the Synoptic narratives of the Ministry, one of the first things Jesus does is to call disciples (cf. Mk 1¹⁶⁻²⁰). John's account reveals that some members of the Twelve were formerly adherents of the Baptist, and that they first came into contact with Jesus at the scene of the Baptist's ministry. This does not contradict the Synoptic account, provided that the call related here by John is understood as being of a preliminary nature, and that the call to leave their occupations and become full-time disciples of Jesus came later in Galilee (cf. *CLM* on Mk 1¹⁶⁻²⁰).

1³⁵⁻⁷. The Baptist's humility appears again in the fact that he allows two of his own disciples to leave him and attach themselves to Jesus; indeed he encourages them to do so by pointing them to Jesus as '*the Lamb of God*' (see on **1²⁹**).

1³⁸. '*Rabbi*' is a Hebrew word meaning 'my great one', commonly used as a title of respect by disciples in addressing their teacher. As is his custom (see Introduction, p. 3), John translates the Hebrew for the benefit of his Gentile readers.

'*where abidest thou?*' There is more in this question than a mere request for an address. They wish to go home with Jesus to discuss matters at a deeper level than is possible by the wayside.

1³⁹. '*Come, and ye shall see*'. Similarly, there is more in this reply than the mere promise of a view of Jesus' lodgings. The verb translated '*see*' is one frequently used of spiritual vision (cf. *vv.* 50-1). Jesus' seemingly simple statement implies, for John, the far deeper truth that those who follow Him will have their eyes opened to spiritual realities. That this proves to be the case for the first two disciples is shown by the conviction they express in *v.* 41.

'*the tenth hour*'. This would be about 4 p.m. by our reckoning.

1⁴⁰. '*Andrew*'. We learn more about this disciple from *Jn* than from the other Gospels (cf. **6⁸⁻⁹, 12²²**). It is widely believed that the other, unnamed, disciple was John the son of Zebedee; this is possible, but cannot be proved (see next verse). If the theory is true, and if the personal testimony of the apostle John lies behind the Gospel (see Introduction, p. 1), the precise note of time in *v.* 39 becomes readily understandable. We may well believe that John, like many another Christian, never forgot the exact hour at which he first met his Master.

1⁴¹. '*He findeth first.*' The text here is uncertain. Three different readings are found: (*a*) 'In the morning he found' (*NEBm*); (*b*) 'He first findeth' (*AV*)—the adjective 'first' agreeing with the subject 'he', and thus implying that later the unnamed disciple emulated Andrew and in turn found *his* brother; (*c*) 'The first thing he did was to find' (*NEB*). Of these, (*c*) is the best attested; understood thus, the verse reveals Andrew as a missionary by nature, who begins to bear his witness among his own family. The reading (*b*), if correct, would support the identification of the unnamed disciple with John, since he in that case would find his brother James, thus completing the same group of four first disciples as appears in Mk 1¹⁶⁻²⁰.

'*the Messiah*'. John again translates the Hebrew term by the Greek '*Christ*' (cf. *v.* 38). Both words literally mean 'Anointed' (see *CLM* on Mk 1¹ and 8²⁹).

1⁴². '*Simon the son of John*'. For the name, cf. Mt 16¹⁷.

'*Cephas*' is an Aramaic word meaning 'rock'; '*Peter*' represents the Greek word of the same meaning. As in *vv.* 38 and 41, John provides the translation. It is by this name (in its Aramaic or Greek form), or by the double name '*Simon Peter*' (cf. *v.* 40), that Andrew's brother will henceforth be known. John does not explain why the nickname was given, and he differs from Matthew as to when it was given (see *AMW* on Mt 16¹⁸ and *CLM* on Mk 3¹⁶). We know how often Peter failed to live up to his name, but Jesus sees beyond the failures to the fulfilment of the great possibilities that lie in the man (cf. 21¹⁸⁻¹⁹).

1⁴³⁻⁴. Jesus decides to return from Bethany (see 1²⁸) to His home district of Galilee. Meanwhile He calls another disciple.

'*Philip*', like Andrew, is more prominent in *Jn* than in the Synoptics (cf. 6⁵⁻⁷, 12 ²¹⁻², 14⁸⁻⁹).

'*Bethsaida*'. A town on the N.E. coast of the Sea of Galilee. John claims it as the home-town of Andrew and Peter as well as of Philip, but Mk 1²⁹ indicates that the two brothers were resident at Capernaum, a town on the opposite shore.

1⁴⁵. '*Philip findeth*'. Like Andrew (*v.* 41), Philip immediately turns missionary. These two disciples seem to have had a good deal in common, and appear together in 6⁵⁻⁹ and 12²¹⁻².

'*Nathanael*'. Cf. 21², where we learn that he was a native of Cana in Galilee, a village some twelve miles to the West of the Sea of Galilee and not far from Nazareth. Nathanael is a Hebrew name, meaning 'God gave'. It occurs in none of the lists of the Twelve in the Synoptics, but he is probably to be identified with Bartholomew, whose name is found next to Philip's in those lists (see Mk 3¹⁸, etc.).

'*him, of whom Moses . . . did write*'. These words indicate that Philip, again like Andrew, has recognized Jesus as the Messiah who is to fulfil the OT prophecies (for the idea of the OT witness to Christ, cf. 5³⁹, and see *CLM* on Mk 1²⁻³).

'*Jesus of Nazareth*'. The home-town of Jesus (cf. Mk 1⁹, Mt 2²³, Lk 4¹⁶) is nowhere mentioned, let alone connected with the Messiah, in the OT— a fact which sufficiently explains Nathanael's scepticism in the next verse.

'*the son of Joseph*'. The use of this description here and at 6⁴² (cf. Lk 4²²) does not preclude the doctrine of the Virgin

Birth (which, however, is nowhere mentioned in *Jn*). Whether or not Joseph was physically Jesus' father, he was legally so and would certainly be so regarded by the contemporaries of Jesus (cf. Lk 3²³).

1⁴⁶. '*Can any good thing . . . Nazareth?*' See on previous verse.

'*Come and see*'. Cf. Jesus' invitation in *v*. 39. Philip's reply to Nathanael is not to argue the point, but to invite him to come and see for himself.

1⁴⁷⁻⁸. In greeting Nathanael, much to the latter's surprise, Jesus reveals that He already knows all about him. For this supernatural knowledge of men shown by Jesus, cf. 2²⁴⁻⁵.

'*an Israelite indeed, in whom is no guile*.' A high tribute to Nathanael's character (cf. Ps 32²); he is a true and worthy representative of Jewish piety at its best.

'*under the fig tree*'. The phrase symbolizes the peace and quietness of a man's house (cf. 1 Kings 4²⁵, Mic 4⁴). It was customary for devout and studious Jews, who longed for the coming of the Messiah, to sit under the fig tree to meditate upon and discuss the scriptures. Nathanael clearly belongs to this class (cf. the terms of Philip's message to him in *v*. 45).

1⁴⁹. Convinced by Jesus' supernatural knowledge of him, Nathanael realizes that his hopes have been fulfilled, and immediately confesses his faith in Jesus as the Messiah. This recognition by the disciples of Jesus as Messiah, from the very beginning of their association with Him (cf. *vv*. 41, 45), raises the same problem as the Baptist's testimony (see on 1³²⁻⁴), since the Synoptics represent the disciples as only gradually coming to recognize who Jesus is, and reaching the climax of confession at Caesarea Philippi (see Mk 8²⁹). Here again it is likely that the Synoptic account is more reliable historically, and that John is reading back to the beginning of their discipleship that faith to which the disciples eventually came.

'*Son of God*'. See on 1³⁴.

'*King of Israel*'. Another Messianic title associated with Jewish nationalistic hopes (cf. 12¹³, and the frequent reference to the kingship of Jesus in Chapters **18-19**).

1⁵⁰. Jesus implies that Nathanael's faith is as yet imperfect, because it is only a response to Jesus' supernatural knowledge, but that later he will find a firmer basis for his faith.

'*thou shalt see*' . On this verb (here and in *v.* 51), see on *v.* 39.

1⁵¹. '*Verily, verily, I say unto you.*' The repetition of '*verily*' in this formula is peculiar to the Fourth Gospel, where it occurs frequently to introduce solemn and important pronouncements of Jesus.

'*Ye shall see*'. The transition from the singular '*thou*' of the previous verse to the plural '*ye*' suggests that John means this promise to be understood as made, not simply to Nathanael, but to all who believe in Jesus. The promise itself clearly echoes the description of Jacob's dream in Gen 28¹². John seems to follow a well-known Rabbinic exegesis of that passage in which 'on it' (i.e. the ladder) was interpreted as 'on him' (i.e. Jacob). Just as Jacob's ladder joined earth and heaven (making two-way traffic between them possible), so believers are here assured that they will see in the Son of Man the true Mediator between heaven (now '*opened*') and earth. This promise may in part refer forward to the Last Day, when the Son of Man will come in glory with the angels (see Mk 8³⁸, etc.). But the primary reference, for John, is probably to the ministry of Jesus which he is to relate in the succeeding chapters. Thus the verse, strategically placed at the close of the first chapter of the Gospel, where Jesus is about to commence His public ministry, provides a valuable clue to the significance of that ministry. It is to establish a two-way traffic between heaven and earth, bringing God to man and man to God (cf. 3¹³⁻¹⁵, 14⁶).

'*Son of man*'. In *Jn*, as in the Synoptics, this title is Jesus' favourite self-designation. For the background and meaning of the title, see *CLM* on Mk 8³¹.

(*a*) Seeing Jesus first as a teacher, and being attracted to Him and willing to learn from Him, the first disciples soon came to believe in Him as the Son of God and the fulfilment of all God's promises to Israel. There are still those whose experience may follow similar lines, and part of the preacher's task is to invite those who regard and revere Jesus as the supreme Teacher, but have not yet seen anything more in Him than that, to follow Him obediently and learn of Him, that they may be led to a fuller understanding and experience of all that He is and means to men. (*b*) No text provides a better basis than 1⁴¹ for an appeal for personal evangelism, and no appeal is more relevant to the needs of our time. Andrew puts first things first (see *NEB*), and starts bearing his witness—as every Christian should—in his own home. (*c*) Peter was destined to become the outstanding figure among the apostles of Christ, and yet he might never have come to the Master at all had it not been for his far less prominent brother Andrew. The obscure Christian, faithfully witnessing in his own limited sphere, has often been the means of bringing to Christ someone whose influence and leadership prove mighty and far-extending. (*d*) The picture of Nathanael devoutly studying the scriptures in the peace of his own home is one that Christian families should be urged to ponder. (*e*) Philip does not seek to answer Nathanael's sceptical question, but simply invites him to come and see for himself. When we meet a sceptical attitude toward our claims concerning the Person and significance of Jesus Christ, it is not so much the cogency of our reasoning (though that should never be neglected) as the strength of our conviction and the directness of our personal testimony that will ultimately prove most effective. (*f*) Jesus had His eyes on Nathanael before ever Philip found him. How many Christians, looking back to the time of their conversion and the experiences that led up to it, have realized that, long before they became aware of Him and His call, Christ was aware of them and preparing to lay His hand upon them? It is never we who choose Him, but always He who chooses us (cf. **15^{16}**). (*g*) Faith based merely on the wondering realization of Jesus' miraculous knowledge or power is immature, and must be superseded by a faith more firmly based on a fuller appreciation of the significance of Christ. (*h*) As a result of the Incarnation, Ministry, Death and Resurrection of Jesus, 'Jacob's ladder' is now 'pitched between heaven and Charing Cross' (see Francis Thompson's poem, 'O world invisible')—and every other corner of the earth as well.

Chapter 2

2¹⁻¹¹: The Sign at Cana

'*Sign*' is one of the most important words in the vocabulary of the Fourth Gospel. It is regularly used (as in *v.* 11) of the miracles of Jesus, but the miraculous element is not essential to the idea of a sign. Essentially, a sign is something that points beyond itself to some greater and more important reality. In the OT the word usually stands for a symbolical action—an action the true meaning of which lies not in itself, but in that which it signifies (e.g. Ezek 4¹⁻³). To John, the works of Jesus selected for inclusion in his Gospel are '*signs*' in this sense (see 20³⁰⁻¹); each one symbolizes a spiritual truth, and is recorded, not for its own sake but for the sake of the truth it signifies. In each case the spiritual truth symbolized is a manifestation of the glory of Jesus Christ and has the effect of awakening faith in Him (*v.* 11, cf. 20³¹). John sees a specially deep significance in the incident at Cana, as defining the meaning of Jesus' mission, which is to replace the Old Dispensation of the law (symbolized by the '*waterpots*' of *v.* 6) by the New Order of the gospel (symbolized by '*the good wine*' of *v.* 10). Cf. the teaching of Mk 2¹⁹⁻²², where Jesus also uses the metaphors of wedding-feast and wine with similar effect (see *CLM* thereon).

Some regard the story as an allegory rather than an account of a historical event, and point to more or less parallel stories in Greek mythology. There is, however, no good reason for doubting the historicity of the wedding as such; the restraint with which the miracle is related, and the wealth of vivid details it contains, suggest that the narrative is based on the reminiscences of an eye-witness. On the other hand, the miraculous element in the story may have been added to the tradition in the course of its transmission in the early Church. Many who are convinced of the historicity of Jesus' miracles in general find the difficulties of believing that He performed this particular miracle insuperable. The motive, they feel, is too trivial, and hardly consistent with the attitude taken by

Jesus towards His supernatural powers on the occasion of His temptation (cf. Mt 4^{1-11}, Lk 4^{1-13}). This historical question is one that every reader must answer for himself. But the real truth and value of the story is the same, however that question may be answered. Here, as everywhere in *Jn*, the evangelist's chief interest is not in the incident as a mere historical event, but in the spiritual truth which he finds symbolized in it (see Introduction, p. 3).

2^{1-3}. '*the third day*'. This detail may have symbolical significance, since the expression inevitably reminds the Christian of the Resurrection of Christ. The partial and preliminary manifestation of Christ's glory at Cana (see *v.* 11) points forward to the perfect manifestation at the Resurrection.

'*Cana of Galilee*'. See comment on 1^{45}.

'*the mother of Jesus*' is mentioned again at 2^{12}, 6^{42} and 19^{25-7}, but her name is nowhere given in *Jn*. Apparently she has some part to play in the wedding festivities, and when the wine fails she turns to the Son upon whom no doubt she has long since learned to rely for help and support.

2^{4-5}. '*Woman*'. The mode of address is not (as it sounds in English) harsh and abrupt, but tender and respectful, as its use in 19^{26} indicates. A more suitable English rendering is therefore 'Mother' (*NEB*).

'*what have I to do with thee?*' This expression sometimes implies rebuke (e.g. at Mk 1^{24}), but it need not mean more than misunderstanding. Jesus is simply telling His mother not to worry, but to let Him deal with the situation in His own way and His own time.

'*mine hour is not yet come*'. On the surface this refers to the time when Jesus intends to deal with the immediate situation. But for John the words have a deeper meaning: the '*hour*' of Jesus is a prominent idea in the Gospel (cf. 7^{30}, 8^{20}, $12^{23, 27}$, 13^1, 17^1), and refers to the hour of His glorification through death and resurrection. The use of the phrase in the present context implies that this manifestation of Jesus' glory (*v.* 11) is only an anticipation of the fuller manifestation to come (see above).

2^6. '*after the Jews' manner of purifying*'. The waterpots were for use in connection with the 'Jewish rites of purification'

c

(*NEB*), i.e. the ceremonial washing of hands and vessels before eating (see *CLM* on Mk 7³⁻⁴).

'*two or three firkins*'—'from twenty to thirty gallons' (*NEB*). The Greek word used denotes a measure equivalent to nearly nine gallons.

2⁷⁻⁹. '*the ruler of the feast*' would be a prominent guest who was presiding over the festivities, or acting as 'steward' (*RSV*, *NEB*).

'*the water now become wine*'. This need not mean that the whole contents of the six jars (a total of some 120 gallons or more!) were turned into wine. Probably only the water actually drawn and taken to the steward is meant.

'*knew not whence it was*'. The miracle is presented as having been performed privately and unobtrusively; there is no suggestion that anyone present, save the servants and the disciples (*v.* 11), was aware of it at the time.

2¹⁰. The steward praises the quality of this '*good wine*', which he thinks the bridegroom, contrary to the customary practice, has deliberately kept to the last.

2¹¹. See introductory comment on this section.

(*a*) Jesus' presence at a wedding-feast is itself suggestive for the preacher. Not only does it mean that He (in the familiar words of the marriage service) 'sanctioned and adorned with His presence' the 'holy estate of matrimony', but also that, by entering actively into the festivities of the occasion, He showed that there is a legitimate place in the Christian life for healthy and happy social intercourse. Christianity never involves a kill-joy attitude towards life. Our Lord was not above enjoying Himself in the company of His friends, and helping them to enjoy themselves too. He is able, and anxious, to enter into our joys as well as our sorrows. The wine that He supplied was better than any of that previously tasted; thus the joyous experiences of life are enhanced and made infinitely more precious when He is allowed to take control of them. (*b*) The story illustrates perfectly the tremendous difference that Jesus makes to life, whenever and wherever He is received into it. It is like the difference between colourless, tasteless, stagnant water and colourful, tasteful, sparkling and stimulating wine. The life to which Christ calls us, and which He makes possible for us, is no dull, monotonous, negative round of existence; it is a gloriously positive, purposeful, exciting and adventurous way of living. Christians should bear witness to the transformation of the ordinary and humdrum that Christ is able to effect for all who respond to His call and accept His offer.

2^{12-22}: The Cleansing of the Temple

Most scholars accept the Synoptic rather than the Johannine dating of this incident (see *CLM* on Mk 11^{15-19}). John has probably brought it forward to the beginning of his account of the ministry for theological reasons. It forms, with the Sign at Cana, a pair of what R. H. Strachan calls 'title-page vignettes to the story of the ministry that follows'. As the Cana incident symbolizes the truth that Jesus transforms the 'water' of Judaism into the 'wine' of the Christian gospel, so the Cleansing of the Temple symbolizes the complementary truth that the Jewish Temple is to give way to the Church which is the Body of Christ. That this is, for John, the significance of Jesus' act is clear from *vv*. 19-22. Thus, though not involving a miracle, the incident is a *'sign'* in the Johannine sense (see introductory comment on 2^{1-11}).

2^{12}. '*Capernaum*' was the chief centre of Jesus' Galilean ministry (cf. 4^{46}, $6^{17, 24, 59}$). See *CLM* on Mk 1^{21} and *AMW* on Mt 4^{13}.

'*his mother*'. See comment on 2^{1-3}.

'*his brethren*' appear in *Jn* only here and in 7^{1-10}. See *CLM* on Mk 6^3.

2^{13}. '*the passover of the Jews*'. This is the first of three Passovers mentioned in *Jn*; for the others, see 6^4 and 11^{55}. This implies a ministry of over two years' duration. There is little doubt that John is right on the question of the length of the ministry, and in depicting it as alternating between Galilee and Judea. Although the Synoptics mention no Passover except the last, fatal one, and describe no earlier visit of Jesus to Jerusalem, they do not preclude the probability of a ministry lasting for two or three years; there is probably a 'gap' between Mk 1^{13} and 1^{14} (see introductory comment on 3^{22-36}), and a 'telescoping' of events in Mk 11-14 (see *CLM* on Mk 11^{15-19}); note also the suggestive 'how often' of Mt 23^{37} and Lk 13^{34}. There is accordingly no need to doubt the historicity of the

statement here that Jesus, soon after the opening of His
ministry, visited Jerusalem for the Passover festival; what is
doubtful is that it was on this occasion that He cleansed the
Temple (see introductory comment on this section).

2¹⁴. It was customary for dealers to sell oxen and sheep and
doves in the Court of the Gentiles, the outer court of the
Temple, for the convenience of pilgrims who desired to offer
sacrifices. There also the money-changers set up tables for
their business of exchanging Roman currency for the Jewish
coins in which the Temple taxes had to be paid (see *CLM* on
Mk 11¹⁵⁻¹⁹). The business of both animal-dealers and money-
changers was legitimate enough, and indeed necessary for the
sake of the worshippers; but there had probably crept into it
a strong element of unprincipled profiteering and merciless
exploitation of the public. This is what incenses Jesus, according to the Synoptic accounts (cf. 'den of robbers' in Mk 11¹⁷).
In John's account, Jesus goes beyond this moral accusation;
He condemns the very idea of trading at all in the sacred
precincts of God's house (see below on *vv.* 16-17).

2¹⁵. The description of Jesus' action, though fuller than that
given in the Synoptics (which do not mention the '*scourge of
cords*'), leaves much to the imagination. It is not clear whether
He used the whip on the men as well as on the animals. Jerome,
in a famous passage, says that the moral power of 'the fiery and
starry light that flashed in His eyes, and the glory of the
Godhead that shone in His face' was quite sufficient to drive
the guilty traders away.

2¹⁶⁻¹⁷. Jesus' action was prompted by His zeal for His Father's
house and His desire to preserve its sanctity. John adds that
the disciples understood this, recalling Ps 69⁹—a passage which
the early Church interpreted as referring to the Messiah. By
introducing the quotation at this point, John probably means
to suggest that the Cleansing confirmed the disciples' belief in
the Messiahship of Jesus.

2¹⁸. '*the Jews*'. See on 1¹⁹. The Jewish leaders also regard
Jesus' action as implying a messianic claim (for the Jew, the
right to cleanse the Temple was the prerogative of the Messiah
—see Mal 3¹⁻⁵). So they challenge Him to prove His authority

(cf. Mk 11²⁸) for such a claim by performing a miracle.
'*sign*' here means a miracle (as in Mk 8¹¹⁻¹³, 1 Cor 1²², etc.).
The Jews do not realize that the cleansing of the Temple is
itself a '*sign*' in the special Johannine sense of the word (see
p. 22), and that they are, in fact, asking for what they have
already been granted.

2¹⁹. With this saying of Jesus, cf. Mk 14⁵⁸, 15²⁹, and on the
probable original form of the saying see *CLM* on the former
passage. There is abundant evidence that Jesus foresaw the
final destruction of the Jerusalem Temple (cf. Mk 13², Lk
19⁴¹⁻⁴). In the saying now under consideration, He promises
to raise in its place another Temple, 'made without hands'
(Mk 14⁵⁸)—i.e. a spiritual Temple.

2²⁰. By taking Jesus' words literally, the Jews completely miss
the point.
'*Forty and six years was this temple in building.*' Herod's
Temple was begun by Herod the Great in 20-19 BC, and
completed by Herod Agrippa II in AD 63-4. Thus the work
was still in progress during the ministry of Jesus.

2²¹. John explains in a parenthesis that the new, spiritual
Temple (see on *v.* 19) of which Jesus speaks is '*the temple of
his body*'. This explains the '*in three days*' of *v.* 19. The new
Temple is none other than the Resurrection Body of Jesus
Himself. Paul's conceptions of the Church as the Body of
Christ (1 Cor 12¹²⁻²⁷, etc.) and as the Temple of God
(1 Cor 3¹⁶, etc.) represent a natural development of this idea.
The Christian Church has replaced the Jewish Temple as the
centre of true worship.

2²². The true significance of Jesus' words, however, was not
grasped even by His disciples until after His Resurrection
(cf. **12¹⁶**).
'*the scripture*'. No indication is given as to what scripture
is meant. Probably it is a general reference to such OT passages
as were understood by the early Church as referring to the
Resurrection (cf. Acts 2²⁵⁻³⁵). On the disciples' belief, see
comment on *vv.* 16-17 above.

(a) The main interest of this passage for the preacher is the replacement of the Jewish Temple by the Christian Church as the centre of true worship. This means that the worship of God has ceased to be localized in a particular place, and has become more spiritual in character (cf. 4^{21-4}). Moreover, this true worship has been universalized, so that Gentiles as well as Jews may participate in it. It is significant that the part of the Temple which Jesus cleansed was the Court of the Gentiles. The trading was confined to that part, and so did not interfere with the Jews' worship (they were free to enter other parts of the Temple), but only with the prayers of God-fearing Gentiles. Jesus is concerned with *their* rights (see *CLM* on Mk 11^{17}), in anticipation of the new order in which Gentiles will participate on equal terms with Jews in the worship of the Temple which is His Body. (b) The fact that the Temple was to be superseded did not make Jesus any less zealous for its proper use while it remained standing. Note the loyalty and devotion with which He observed the religious practices and duties of the Jew, regularly visiting Jerusalem for the festivals and worshipping in the synagogue on the sabbath (see Lk 4^{16}), and being full of zeal for the sanctity of His Father's house. We may feel that many religious institutions need changing, but until the change is effected we have no right to disregard the existing institutions. (c) The motives which led Jesus to cleanse the Temple have two clear implications: (i) dishonesty and exploitation are always despicable, but never more so than when practised under the cloak of religion; (ii) everything that is not consonant with true devotion and worship must be cast out of the sanctuary. (d) The action of Jesus reveals that there is room in the divine character of the Lord for anger—not indeed a capricious and undisciplined rage, but the righteous indignation that arises out of zeal for the holy, the just and the good. True zeal for righteousness is inevitably accompanied by wrath against all forms of unrighteousness (cf. comment on 3^{36}).

2^{23-5}: Jesus in Jerusalem

This short paragraph describes further activity of Jesus at Jerusalem during the first Passover of His public ministry. Its main point is to bring out His infallible knowledge and understanding of human nature. The paragraph thus provides a fitting introduction to the two following chapters, in which we see Jesus coming into contact with three very different persons and knowing exactly how to deal with each. These are, respectively, a Jew (Nicodemus), a Samaritan (the woman at the well), and a Gentile (the officer). By describing the three contacts in this order, John seems to be emphasizing the universality of the interest, and of the appeal, of Jesus.

2²³. '*signs*'. The word here has the same meaning as at **2¹⁸**.

2²⁴. '*did not trust himself*'. The verb here is the same as that translated '*believed*' in the previous verse. This may be a deliberate play on words: the people have faith of a kind in Jesus, but Jesus has not much faith in their faith! Faith based merely on miracles (as theirs was) is immature and inadequate (cf. **1⁵⁰, 4⁴⁸**).

2²⁵. Jesus can read all minds and hearts, as He read Nathanael's (see **1⁴⁷⁻⁵⁰**).

There is both comfort and challenge in the thought of Jesus' infallible knowledge of men. Whatever human experience we may be passing through, we may take heart from the knowledge that He understands, for He Himself was Man, and 'He hath felt the same' (*MHB* 236). On the other hand, we must never forget that we can never deceive Him. Everything in us, including our faith, is subject to His all-seeing scrutiny. Every Christian needs at times to examine the basis of his faith in Christ, and to ask, honestly and sincerely, whether it is the kind of faith in which Jesus can trust and on which He can depend.

Chapter 3

3¹⁻²¹: Jesus and Nicodemus

NICODEMUS is not mentioned in the Synoptic Gospels, but appears on three occasions in *Jn* (here, in 7⁵⁰⁻¹ and in 19³⁹). From these passages we gather that he was a man of some wealth (see on 19³⁹⁻⁴⁰), a Pharisee and member of the Sanhedrin (see on 3¹), and a well-known Rabbi (see on 3¹⁰). He thus exemplifies the religion of the Old Dispensation at its best, and it is in this representative capacity of his, rather than in Nicodemus as an individual, that John's interest lies. His interview with Jesus further illustrates that conflict between the old order and the new which was so prominent in chapter 2.

3¹. '*the Pharisees*'. See comment on 1¹⁹.
'*a ruler of the Jews*', i.e. a member of the Sanhedrin, the ruling council of the Jews.

3². '*by night*'. This does not necessarily indicate cowardice on Nicodemus' part (his words at 7⁵¹ are hardly the words of a coward who wishes to hide his sympathy for Jesus). It was customary for Rabbis to study and discuss the Law at night-time; and in any case that would be the most convenient time to seek a quiet interview with Jesus. The fact that elsewhere in the Gospel (9⁴, 11¹⁰, 13³⁰) the word 'night' has a double meaning (literal and symbolical) suggests that the same may be the case here. John may mean to suggest that it was out of spiritual darkness that Nicodemus came into the presence of Him who is 'the true light' (cf. 1⁹). The symbolism of light and darkness reappears in *vv*. 19-21.
'*Rabbi*'. See on 1³⁸. In addressing Jesus thus Nicodemus acknowledges Him as a fellow-Rabbi, despite His obscure origin and lack of official status (cf. 7¹⁵). This reveals Nicodemus as a man of humble and magnanimous spirit (cf. 7⁵¹), so full of zeal for the law that he is anxious to discuss it even with this unorthodox and unauthorized teacher.

'these signs'. See **2²³**. Nicodemus' respect for Jesus is due to the impression made upon him by His miracles, which he regards as convincing proof of divine commissioning and inspiration.

3³. Instead of discussing the law with Nicodemus, Jesus presents him suddenly with a statement of the fundamental principle of the new religion of the Spirit—namely, the necessity for a man to be reborn.

'Verily, verily, I say unto thee'. See on **1⁵¹**.

'born anew'. The literal meaning of the adverb is 'from above' (*RVm*), but it can also mean 'again'. Probably John uses the ambiguous word intentionally to suggest the idea of a *rebirth from above*. It is not a natural, but a supernatural process (cf. **1¹²⁻¹³**), and its agent is the Holy Spirit (see *v.* 5). On the subject of this rebirth, which is prominent also in *1 John*, see *GPL, Note 15*, p. 77. Paul teaches essentially the same truth, though in different terms, in such passages as Rom 6¹⁻¹¹ and 2 Cor 5¹⁷.

'kingdom of God'. This term, so common in the Synoptics (see *CLM* on Mk 1¹⁵), occurs in *Jn* only at **3³, ⁵**. John usually uses the term 'eternal life' (see below on **3¹⁶**) to express the same idea. The two terms are in fact already synonymous in Mk 9⁴³⁻⁷ (see *CLM* thereon). To see, or enter into, the kingdom of God (the different expressions in *vv.* 3 and 5 mean essentially the same thing); to inherit eternal life; and to become a child of God (**1¹²⁻¹³**)—these are three equivalent ways of describing the true end of religion.

3⁴. Nicodemus misunderstands Jesus' meaning, taking His words in a crudely literal sense (cf. **2²⁰**). This leads to further elucidation of the teaching in *vv.* 5-8.

3⁵. *'born of water and the Spirit'* describes more precisely what is meant by the rebirth already mentioned in *v.* 3; *'water'* is a reference to the sacrament of Baptism which, in the early Church, always accompanied regeneration, which was effected by the Holy Spirit. The great difference between the baptism of John the Baptist and that of Jesus is that the Holy Spirit is associated with the latter (see **1²⁶, ³³**, and Acts 19¹⁻⁷). The former was a baptism 'with water', the latter a baptism 'with water and the Spirit'.

3⁶. '*born of the flesh*' refers to physical birth (cf. **1¹³**). For '*flesh*' see comment on **1¹⁴**.

'*born of the Spirit*' refers to the spiritual rebirth described in the previous verses, which gives rise to eternal life, here characterized as '*spirit*', which means man's condition when possessed by the Holy Spirit.

3⁷ re-emphasizes the absolute necessity of regeneration. Before a man can enter the kingdom of God (see on **3³**), his nature must be radically changed; he must be raised by a supernatural, creative act of God to an entirely new level of life.

3⁸. '*The wind*'. The Greek word *pneuma* means both 'wind' and 'Spirit' (hence *RVm*), and this heightens the point of the comparison made here. There is an element of mystery about the wind, and we only know its reality because we experience its effects. Likewise the regenerating activity of the Spirit is mysterious and cannot be adequately understood or explained, but its reality is known by its effects in '*every one that is born of the Spirit*'. See *GPL*, p. 78.

3⁹⁻¹⁰. Nicodemus' question is that of a sceptic; he doubts the possibility of such a radical change in a man's life as Jesus has described. In reply, Jesus expresses surprise that such a 'famous teacher of Israel' should be 'ignorant of such things' (*NEB*); the definite article attached to '*teacher*' suggests that Nicodemus was a teacher of some eminence.

3¹¹. '*Verily, verily . . .*'. The solemn formula (see on **1⁵¹**) introduces a discourse of Jesus which continues to *v.* 21; it begins as a reply to Nicodemus ('*unto thee*'), but almost immediately there is a change to the second person plural ('*ye receive not*'). Nicodemus as such is forgotten; as we have seen, John is not primarily interested in him as an individual. The story of his conversation with Jesus simply serves as a vehicle for the exposition of a theological truth. This pattern of an incident serving to introduce a discourse of Jesus is characteristic of *Jn*. In one sense, the present section contains not so much a conversation between Jesus and Nicodemus as a conversation between the Christian Church and the Jewish Synagogue. This is especially true from *v.* 11 onwards; not only does the second person plural replace the singular, but the first person plural also comes into use—'*We speak . . . our witness*' (cf. 1$^{14, 16}$). The point of *v.* 11 is that what has been said about the regenerating activity of the Spirit, mysterious though it may be, is based upon actual experience of indubitable facts (attested by the whole Apostolic Church); the Jews, however, still stubbornly reject this testimony.

3^{12}. '*earthly things*' refers to the testimony mentioned in *v.* 11, which concerns happenings in the sphere of human experience, such as the change which occurs in a man when he is born of the Spirit. If the Jews cannot believe this testimony, there is little hope of their believing the '*heavenly things*' which Jesus has to teach them—i.e. the deeper spiritual truths that concern the life of heaven. The following verses show that these can only be known by revelation from above.

3^{13}. '*the Son of man*'. In 1^{51}, as here, Jesus as Son of man is the true Mediator between heaven and earth. He it is who '*descended out of heaven*' to reveal the secrets of heaven to man (cf. 1^{18}); and He alone it is who '*hath ascended into heaven*'. The use of the past tense in the latter phrase reflects the standpoint of the Church in whose name John is writing, rather than that of Jesus Himself during His ministry.

'*which is in heaven*'. These words, omitted in some manuscripts and versions, add nothing material to the sense of the passage.

3$^{14-15}$. The thought of the ascension of the Son of Man in the previous verse leads on to that of His exaltation. The word here translated '*lifted up*' is one of great significance in *Jn* (cf. 8^{28} and 12$^{32-4}$). Literally it means to lift up off the ground, and so it describes the physical act of crucifixion; but the word also has a metaphorical use, to exalt or glorify, and in Acts 2^{33}, 5^{31} and Phil 2^{9} it describes the ascension of Christ to heaven. John always uses the word of the crucifixion of Jesus, which he regards as His glorification (cf. 12^{23}). Here the lifting up of the Son of Man on the Cross is compared with the lifting up by Moses of the brazen serpent in the wilderness (see Num 21$^{4-9}$). As the children of Israel looked up at the serpent on the standard, their minds were directed towards God, and they were saved by Him from the bites of the fiery serpents that plagued them. Likewise, salvation and eternal

life come to believers as they look at Him who was lifted up
on the Cross, and put their trust in Him (*RVm* is preferable to
RV in *v*. 15). The word '*must*' in this passage is full of significance: the Cross is an essential element in the plan of
salvation as it was conceived in the eternal counsels of God
(cf. Mk 8³¹, Lk 24²⁶, Acts 2²³, etc.).

3¹⁶. The allusion in *vv.* 14-15 to the Cross and the redemptive
purpose fulfilled therein prepares the way for this majestic
verse in which the whole rich content of the Christian gospel
is compressed (as far as that is possible) into a single sentence.

'*For God so loved*'. The Cross was the outcome of the
amazing and boundless love of God. The purpose of the
sacrifice on Calvary was not the appeasement of an angry
God, for it was God Himself who provided it ('*that he gave*');
and to do so involved for Him the greatest possible cost, for
it meant giving His beloved and only Son.

'*the world*'. See on **1¹⁰**. The world, for all its sinfulness, is still
the object of God's love, which is all-embracing in its scope.

'*only begotten Son*'. See on **1¹⁴**.

'*that whosoever believeth on him*'. The purpose of God's
redeeming love for sinful men is expressed in the same words
as in *v.* 15, with the addition of the negative counterpart
('*not perish*') of '*have eternal life*'.

'*eternal life*' is one of John's key-phrases. For its equivalence
to the term 'kingdom of God', see above on *v.* 3. The term
literally means 'life of the Age' (i.e. the Age to come), but for
John it is not something to be inherited only after death, but a
life entered upon here and now by everyone who is born of the
Spirit (see *vv.* 3-6). The sole condition of entry into this new
life is to believe in Christ, i.e. to believe that He is the Son of
God and to trust implicitly in His redemptive act upon the
Cross. See further *GPL, Note 2*, p. 17.

3¹⁷⁻¹⁸. Following upon the classic treatment of the saving
love of God in *v.* 16, the related theme of the judgement of
God is briefly treated. Salvation and judgement are in fact the
opposite sides of one and the same process. The Son of God
did not come in order to judge the world but to save it (salvation here means the same thing as eternal life in the previous
verses); nevertheless, His coming inevitably results in judgement for some, namely those who refuse to believe in Him and

so reject the salvation which He offers. Whether the coming of Christ means salvation or judgement for a man depends entirely upon the response he makes to Christ (cf. 5²⁴).

'*hath been judged already*'. Judgement is here regarded, as was salvation in *v.* 16, not as something reserved for the future but as something already happening. The ideas of a future judgement and resurrection to life are not, however, absent from the thought of John (cf. 5²⁸⁻⁹, 6⁴⁰, etc.).

3¹⁹⁻²¹. The theme of judgement and salvation is now worked out in terms of the imagery of darkness and light (cf. 1⁴⁻⁵, ⁹⁻¹¹). Men's rejection of the light of Christ is traced to their love of their own sinful practices and their unwillingness to have them '*reproved*' ('shown up', *NEB*). Such evil men are contrasted with him '*that doeth the truth*'. This significant phrase (standing in parallelism with '*doeth ill*' in the previous verse) reveals that for John there is an ethical element in the truth; it is not merely something to be *believed*, but something to be *done*. A man must live out in practice the implications of the truth which he believes (cf. *GPL, Note 4*, p. 25). When he does so, he rejoices in the light of Christ, which shows clearly that his actions have been '*wrought in God*', i.e. in communion with God and in accordance with His will.

(*a*) Of primary importance for the preacher is the doctrine of the New Birth (see John Wesley's sermons on 3⁷ and 3⁸). This asserts that the new life of the Kingdom of God (i.e. Eternal Life) is not to be attained through any natural process. It is not just the highest *degree* of human life; it is a different *kind* of life, life on a different level. Just as an animal can never *grow* by any natural process into a human being, so a human being can never *grow* into a child of God (cf. 1¹²⁻¹³), but must be remade by a supernatural act of God that can only be adequately described as a new *birth*. (*b*) Nicodemus' sceptical question in *v.* 9 typifies the popular illusion that 'human nature cannot be changed'. The reply of the Church must always be that, though we cannot fully explain the mystery of it (*v.* 8), we *know* it is possible because we have seen it happen (*v.* 11). The ultimate proof of the power of the gospel is the transformed lives of those who have believed in it. (*c*) The One who became incarnate (with all that that means in revelation and salvation) is the One who has ascended to heaven (with all that that means in victory over evil, vindication and Lordship). (*d*) Several aspects of the significance of the Cross appear in *vv.* 14-15: its divine necessity;

its saving efficacy; the fact that for Jesus it was His path to glory. (*e*) 3^{16} is the 'golden text' of preachers. Almost every word has the deepest significance. The verse is the supreme expression of the all-embracing scope of God's love, the limitless extent to which it goes on behalf of its objects, and the glorious purpose it has in mind for them. (*f*) The relation between salvation and judgement is one that can be brought out with great effect on the basis of *vv*. 17-21. No man can ignore the fact of Christ as something that does not concern him. Confrontation with Christ, for every man, must mean *either* salvation *or* judgement. To reject the offer of salvation is to bring judgement on oneself, just as a man who fails to appreciate a great work of art judges not the work of art but himself. (*g*) The tragedy of the world's rejection of Christ is nowhere more poignantly expressed than in *v*. 19. For a man to perish in darkness when all he has to do is to throw open the shutters to let in the light that is waiting to shine upon him and give him life—this is the height of tragedy, and a terrible judgement on the man himself. (*h*) Men still reject Christ and resolutely shut Him out of their lives because they are not prepared to face the consequences of accepting Him. They need to be reminded that, if they will but take the plunge of faith, they will not only receive something infinitely more precious than anything they have had to give up, but their values will be so changed that they will not even miss what they have forfeited. (*i*) The practical implications of accepting the truth is something that needs always to be stressed in preaching, and we need to remember that it is only when 'God is in all he does' (*v*. 21, *NEB*) that a man's actions can measure up to the demands of truth.

3^{22-36}: Further Testimony of John the Baptist

This section reveals that for a period, prior to the arrest of the Baptist, Jesus exercised a ministry parallel to his in the Jordan valley. The Synoptics do not mention such a ministry, but there is no reason why it could not have taken place before Jesus came to Galilee (Mk 1^{14}). John's peculiar and genuine historical tradition supplements the Synoptic record at this point. The direct testimony of the Baptist ends at *v*. 30, and the final paragraph (*vv*. 31-6) is best regarded as the evangelist's own inspired meditation upon the themes which have been treated in the chapter.

3^{22}. '*the land of Judæa*', i.e. the country outside Jerusalem itself (where the events of 2^{13}–3^{21} have been located).

'*baptized*'. This, along with *v*. 26 and 4^1, suggests that Jesus Himself administered baptism—a fact not hinted at in the other Gospels. In spite of the parenthetic comment in 4², there seems to be no good reason for doubting the fact, which would certainly help to explain why the Church came to practise baptism after the Resurrection.

3²³. '*Aenon near to Salim*'. The sites of these places are uncertain, though clearly they were in the Jordan valley.

3²⁴. Cf. Mk 1¹⁴, and see p. 36.

3²⁵. '*with a Jew*'. Some manuscripts here read the plural 'Jews' (so *NEB*). Who this Jew, or Jews, were is not indicated and is of no great moment.

'*purifying*'. Cf. 2⁶. No doubt the chief point at issue here was the significance of the rite of baptism as administered by John and Jesus respectively. The dispute seems to have convinced John's disciples that Jesus' ministry is meeting with increasing success and popularity at the expense of their master's, so that they become jealous for his reputation.

3²⁶. '*Rabbi*'. See on 1³⁸. This is the only ascription of the title to the Baptist.

'*beyond Jordan*'. Comparison with 1²⁸ suggests that the Baptist is now baptizing on the Western bank.

'*thou hast borne witness*'. See 1¹⁵, ²⁶⁻³⁴.

'*the same baptizeth*'. See on 3²².

'*all men*', i.e. 'crowds' (*NEB*).

3²⁷⁻⁸. The Baptist's answer reveals that, as so often, the master is more tolerant than his disciples. He acknowledges that the success which attends every mission is given '*from heaven*'. If Jesus' mission is succeeding more than his own, that is the will of God. He reminds his disciples of his own consistent testimony about himself and his relationship to the Messiah (see 1¹⁵, ¹⁹⁻³⁴).

3²⁹. The Baptist develops the comparison of himself with Jesus by means of the imagery of marriage. He is 'the best man', so to speak, to Jesus as Bridegroom, and so cannot compare with Him in importance. The illustration, no doubt, is deliberately chosen because of the association in Jewish thought of the figure of the Bridegroom with the Messiah (cf. Mk 2^{19-20}, where Jesus, in comparing His disciples with the Baptist's, speaks of Himself as 'the bridegroom'; cf. also Mt 22^{1-14}, 25^{1-13}, 2 Cor 11^2, Eph 5^{25-33}, Rev 19^7).

'*this my joy* . . .'. The Baptist not only acknowledges Jesus' superiority, but rejoices in it, as the best man rejoices in the bridegroom's happiness.

3^{30}. This verse epitomizes the Baptist's attitude towards Jesus, as it is depicted in *Jn*. With these memorable words he takes his last exit from the evangelist's stage. He has fulfilled his purpose of ushering in his Greater Successor to the centre of the stage, and is well content to disappear from view.

3^{31}. Here the evangelist's meditation begins (see introductory comment on the present section). The contrast drawn here would naturally be suggested by that between the Baptist and Jesus in the previous paragraph. It is the contrast between a mere man and the Son of God who came down from heaven. The idea of two realms of being, the heavenly ('above') and the earthly ('beneath'), is a prominent one in *Jn* (see especially 8^{23}). The Son of Man descended from the former to the latter realm (see 3^{13}), and man, by being 'born from above' (see 3^3), comes to partake of the life that belongs to the heavenly realm.

'*from above*' represents the same adverb as is found in 3^3; the literal meaning is clearly correct here, as the parallel '*from heaven*', later in the verse, shows.

'*is above all*'. The second occurrence of this phrase is omitted in some manuscripts (see *RVm* and *NEB*), and may be a later insertion into the text.

3^{32} echoes 3^{11}; '*no man*' is clearly not to be taken too literally, as the following verse shows.

3^{33-4}. As a man by setting his seal to a legal document attests that the contents of the document are true, so the man who believes the words of Jesus attests that 'God speaks true' (*NEB*), for Jesus speaks as the Messenger of God (note the negative counterpart of this in 1 Jn 5^{10}). Jesus' words are the words of God because God has endowed Him with the Spirit in His fulness (cf. 1^{32-3}).

3³⁵. Here the relationship between the Father and the Son is defined as one of perfect love and trust. This theme is worked out fully in 5¹⁹⁻⁴⁷.

'*hath given all things into his hand*'. Cf. 5²², ²⁶, 17², ¹¹, etc., and the great Synoptic passage in Mt 11²⁷, Lk 10²².

3³⁶ forms a fitting conclusion to the chapter by re-emphasizing the great truth of 3¹⁶. As in 3¹⁷⁻²¹, so here, men are divided into two classes according to their attitude towards Christ. Here the contrast is stated as being between believing and disobeying, thus revealing that belief in Christ is ultimately a matter of obedience. The opposite of eternal life, which in 3¹⁷⁻²¹ was characterized as 'judgement', is here described by the stronger term '*the wrath of God*'. This is the only occurrence of that phrase in *Jn*. '*Wrath*' means the righteous condemnation of God. Every sinner lies under this condemnation. For the holy and righteous God not to condemn sin would be to deny His own nature. To believe in the wrath of God is not inconsistent with belief in His love, provided we remember that His love is *holy* love, and that His wrath is not a capricious and undisciplined rage (cf. comment (*d*) on p. 28).

(*a*) The Baptist's attitude in verses 27-9 provides an admirable example for all Christians in their attitude towards the success which attends the ministry of other Christians. It is possible to acknowledge that success given to someone else is God-given (though we are sometimes too prone to doubt this), but to do so grudgingly and with bad grace, when we ought rather to *rejoice* in the fact. The only consideration that should count is whether Christ's cause is being furthered or not; if it is, our joy should be fulfilled, whether or not we personally have had any part in the success. (*b*) 3³⁰ perfectly sums up the self-effacing attitude which should be characteristic of every witness for Christ. We must always be prepared to keep ourselves out of the picture, in order that He may take His rightful place in the centre of the picture. (*c*) By believing in Christ we have the wonderful privilege of signing our name, so to speak, to the revelation of God's truth given in Him. To refuse to believe, on the other hand, is tantamount to calling God a liar (cf. 1 Jn 5¹⁰). (*d*) The idea of faith as obedience is a suggestive one; cf. Rom 1⁵, where 'obedience of faith' can mean 'obedience which is faith'. (*e*) The critical choice with which every man is faced when he is confronted by the challenge of the gospel is nowhere more pointedly put than in *v*. 36.

D

Chapter 4

4¹⁻⁴²: Jesus in Samaria

JESUS now leaves Judea (see on 3²²) to return to Galilee, following the most direct and usual route through Samaria. The Jews regarded the religion of the Samaritans as a degenerate and heretical form of Judaism (see on *vv.* 9, 20). By introducing this episode at this point in his Gospel, John indicates that the ministry of Christ extends to this despised race (see introductory comment on 2²³⁻⁵). This short ministry in Samaria is nowhere mentioned in the Synoptics, though Jesus' interest in and sympathy for the Samaritans appears in such passages as Lk 10²⁹⁻³⁷, 17¹¹⁻¹⁹.

4¹. '*the Pharisees*'. See on 1¹⁹. They had opposed the Baptist, and now their opposition to Jesus has been aroused because of His similar activity.

4². This parenthetical comment may be due to John's desire to emphasize the difference between Jesus and the Baptist. On the question whether Jesus Himself administered baptism, see on 3²².

4⁵. '*Sychar*' is probably to be identified with the modern town Askar, which is near the traditional site of Jacob's well.
'*the parcel of ground . . . Joseph*' refers to Shechem (see Josh 24³², cf. Gen 33¹⁹, 48²²).

4⁶. '*being wearied*'. This detail underlines John's characteristic emphasis on the full humanity of Jesus (see on 1¹⁴).
'*the sixth hour*', i.e. noon by our reckoning. This helps to explain Jesus' weariness and thirst.

4⁷. '*a woman of Samaria*'. That she should come to draw water at such an unusual hour (when the well would normally be deserted) may suggest that she was something of a social outcast because of her immoral life (see *v*. 18). If so, Jesus' attitude towards her (see on *v*. 9) is all the more significant.

'*Give me to drink*'. Jesus opens the conversation (which is a private one—see *v*. 8) by asking a favour of the woman (cf. His attitude to Zacchaeus in Lk 19⁵).

4⁹. Jesus' request surprises the woman for two reasons. (*i*) Because He is a Jew (His dress or His accent may have betrayed the fact to her) and she a Samaritan. This point is explained in the parenthesis at the end of the verse. The rendering of *RV* here is misleading; the very fact that the disciples had gone to buy food in a Samaritan town is evidence that Jews and Samaritans had some dealings with one another. Recent study has shown that the correct meaning of the verb used in the parenthesis is that adopted in *NEB*: 'Jews and Samaritans . . . do not use vessels in common.' Jews regarded Samaritans (and particularly their women) as ceremonially unclean, and so shrank with horror from the thought of using anything like an eating or drinking utensil in common with them. (*ii*) She is not merely a Samaritan, but a woman also. It was considered unseemly for a man to converse with a woman in public, and this was especially so in the case of a Jewish Rabbi. Thus Jesus, by entering into conversation with the Samaritan woman, rises above two deep-seated prejudices that were common in His day—namely, those of religion and of sex.

4¹⁰. Jesus now carries the conversation a stage further by suggesting that the woman has not appreciated the significance of their encounter. As a thirsty traveller, He has asked her for a drink of water; but as Son of God He has a gift to offer her from God, the gift of a different kind of water. Had the woman realized who He was and what He had to offer, she would have answered His request not by expressing surprise but by requesting in turn His gift.

'*living water*' is an ambiguous phrase. It can mean literally 'running water' such as is found in a natural spring; or, metaphorically, it can mean 'the water that gives and sustains life'. The woman clearly understands the phrase in the former sense (see *vv*. 11-12), but Jesus is using it in the latter (see *vv*. 13-14).

4[11-12]. The woman again expresses surprise. Jesus cannot be referring to the water of Jacob's well, which He has no means of drawing. On the other hand, if He is claiming to be able to provide water from some other source, that would be tantamount to a claim to be greater than the patriarch Jacob— which, in her view, is impossible. Jacob provided the well, and it was good enough for his own use and that of his family and flocks; there can be no superior water to this.

4[13-14]. After the woman has misunderstood Him by taking His words in a too literal sense, Jesus proceeds to explain Himself more fully (cf. the case of Nicodemus in 3[4]). The '*living water*' of which He has been speaking is not natural water of the kind Jacob's well provides, which can only for a while satisfy man's physical thirst. It is supernatural and spiritual water which satisfies permanently the needs of the soul that drinks it. Jesus is here using the metaphor of water (suggested by the occasion of His conversation with the woman) to describe His gift of eternal life (see on 3[16]). In a hot, dry climate such as that of Palestine, it is perfectly natural that the deepest cravings of the human spirit should be likened to the physical thirst for water, and this comparison is common in the OT (cf. Ps 42[1-2], Jer 2[13], etc.). In *Jn* it appears here and at 7[37-9] (where the 'water' represents the Holy Spirit). The man who accepts the gift of Jesus will have within himself a never-failing supply of living water, '*springing up unto eternal life*'.

4[15]. The woman takes a step in the right direction by requesting the gift of Jesus, though in a somewhat jocular and sceptical manner that betrays a complete misunderstanding of the meaning of His offer.

4[16-18]. The conversation takes a fresh turn when Jesus reveals that He is fully aware of the woman's immoral life (for such supernatural knowledge, cf. 1[48], 2[24-5]). It is possible that the reference to the five husbands and the present illicit partner reflects an allegorical interpretation of the incident by the evangelist, the woman representing the Samaritan people, the husbands the false gods formerly worshipped by them (see 2 Kings 17[24-41]), and the illicit relationship their present improper worship of the true God. This is not to say, however, that the whole story of the woman at the well is a mere allegory composed by the evangelist on this theme.

4¹⁹. Jesus' insight into her life and character convinces the woman that He is a prophet. Thus she advances a further step in her understanding of His significance (cf. *v.* 15), and takes the opportunity of questioning Him on a burning religious issue—at the same time adroitly changing the subject from the painful question of her own moral lapses.

4²⁰. The woman's question is one that was the subject of continuous dispute between Jews and Samaritans.

'*this mountain*' is Mount Gerizim, which was near Jacob's well. The Samaritans had built a temple there, and still continued to worship on the site, though the temple itself was destroyed in 129 B C. They interpreted Deut 12⁵ ('the place' of centralized worship) as referring, not to Jerusalem (as the Jews understood it), but to Mount Gerizim.

4²¹. The burden of Jesus' reply is that the question raised by the woman is one that is no longer relevant. What matters henceforth is not the *place* at which worship is offered, but the *spirit* in which it is offered.

'*the hour cometh*'. See on *v.* 23.

'*shall ye worship the Father*'. This, Jesus' favourite designation for God, is especially common in *Jn* (cf. 3³⁵). The use of the second person plural is significant; Samaritans, though their worship hitherto has been irregular and imperfect, will join in the true worship of the future.

4²². '*Ye worship . . . ye know not*'. The Samaritans worship the true God, but in an imperfect way because of their ignorance. The Samaritan Bible consisted only of the Pentateuch. Their rejection of the prophetic teaching inevitably meant that their knowledge of God was deficient.

'*we worship . . . we know*'. Jesus reckons Himself among the orthodox Jews, and claims that their worship is based on a true knowledge of God derived from the full biblical revelation.

'*salvation is from the Jews*'—because they are the people chosen by God to be the recipients of His self-revelation and the instruments of His mighty saving purposes (cf. Paul's claim in Rom 9⁴⁻⁵).

4²³. '*the hour cometh, and now is*'. This characteristically Johannine phrase occurs again at **5²⁵**, and a very similar phrase is found in **16³²**. It expresses a paradox that runs through the teaching of Jesus and the thought of the NT generally. Eschatological events (the Kingdom of God, Judgement, etc.) are still expected to occur in the future, but at the same time they are regarded as already happening. In the present context the thought is probably that true worship will be offered in the Christian Church in the period following the Resurrection ('*the hour cometh*', cf. *v.* 21), but that, at the same time, this true worship is already being offered in and through Jesus by those who already believe in Him.

'*in spirit and truth*'. This is the positive counterpart to *v.* 21. True worship does not depend upon the location of the sanctuary in which it is offered. What matters is the inward disposition of the worshipper, and the consistency of his offering with the truth (see further on *v.* 24).

'*for such doth the Father seek*'. This suggests that God desires and rejoices in the true worship of His people.

4²⁴. '*God is a Spirit*'. This rendering of *RV* is misleading, and *RVm* should be followed (cf. *RSV* and *NEB*). In form the statement may be compared with 'God is light' (1 Jn 1⁵) and 'God is love' (1 Jn 4¹⁶). In content, it means not only that God is non-material, and therefore not confined to any time or place, but also that He is the living God, the Almighty and ever-active Creator and Sustainer of all life (i.e. the statement must be understood in the light of the whole biblical teaching about the Spirit of God). To worship '*in spirit and truth*' means not only to be genuinely sincere in one's worship, but to have a clear and true conception of the nature of God as Spirit, and to be in harmony with, and under the inspiration of, the Holy Spirit Himself. The phrase inevitably reminds one of the term 'Spirit of truth', used of the Holy Spirit in **14¹⁷**, **15²⁶** and **16¹³**.

4²⁵. The woman, realizing that Jesus is speaking of things usually associated with the coming of the Messiah, expresses her belief that when he comes the Messiah will explain everything. Like the Jews, the Samaritans also expected a Messiah, whom they called *Taheb* ('he who returns' or 'he who restores'). As in **1⁴¹**, the Greek equivalent of '*Messiah*' is given.

4²⁶. Jesus now discloses to her that He is the Messiah of whom she speaks. Here again, as in the case of the Baptist and that of the first disciples, it is doubtful whether, as a fact of history, Jesus declared His Messiahship at this early stage in His ministry. Thus John may be adapting his account of Jesus' conversation with the woman, to make it the vehicle of his teaching about the significance of Christ (cf. comments on 1³²⁻⁴ and 1⁴⁹).

'*I . . . am he*'. This phrase often has in *Jn* a deep theological significance (see on 6³⁵, 8²⁴), which may be, to some extent, present here.

4²⁷. The disciples return from the town (see *v.* 8), and are surprised to find Jesus talking with a woman (see comment on *v.* 9). Yet they refrain from questioning either the woman or Jesus.

4²⁸⁻⁹. The woman departs, obviously intending to return again, for she leaves her waterpot. Like the disciples in 1⁴¹, ⁴⁵, she immediately turns missionary after hearing that Jesus is the Messiah, and urges her fellow-citizens to come and see (cf. 1⁴⁶). Her faith, however, is as yet imperfect, being based (like that of Nathanael in 1⁴⁹⁻⁵⁰) on Jesus' miraculous knowledge of her past life. Her hesitant question, '*Can this be the Christ?*' confirms this.

4³⁰. The Samaritans of Sychar immediately respond to her urgent message. Meanwhile, Jesus converses with His disciples (*vv.* 31-8).

4³¹⁻³. When they invite Him to partake of the food they have brought from the town, Jesus takes up the figure of food (just as He took up that of water in *vv.* 10-14), and uses it in a spiritual sense. The question which the disciples ask of one another reveals that they too, like the woman (see *vv.* 11-12) and Nicodemus (see 3⁴), have taken His words too literally and so failed to understand His meaning. This leads to the further elucidation in *v.* 34.

4³⁴. This saying of Jesus is reminiscent of His reply to the Tempter in Mt 4⁴ (cf. Deut 8³). There is no suggestion that material food is not necessary, but rather a salutary reminder that man needs feed other than the physical kind (cf. **6**[27] and the whole discourse on the Bread of life in Chapter 6). Jesus is referring to the deep spiritual satisfaction that He receives in the fulfilment of His mission in obedience to His Father's will. His words suggest that, in receiving this satisfaction through His conversation with the woman, He has lost the sense of weariness and hunger which He felt earlier.

'*him that sent me*'. Jesus continually in this Gospel refers to God in this way (cf. **3**[34] and especially **5**[30]), thus emphasizing His complete submission to His Father.

'*to accomplish his work*'. The verb means to finish, completely and perfectly. This emphasis on the perfect completion by the Son of the mission entrusted to Him by the Father is also characteristic of *Jn* (cf. **17**[4], **19**[28, 30]).

4[35-8] describe the results of this work, the fulfilment of which brings Jesus such satisfaction. The description is given in terms of seed-time and harvest.

'*Say not ye*' implies that the words that follow represent a familiar statement, possibly a proverb.

'*There are yet four months . . . harvest*'. This does not imply that the incident in Samaria is to be dated at a time four months prior to the harvest season; it is more likely that the harvest time itself is approaching, and that the sight of the cornfields which are '*white already unto harvest*' is what actually suggests the illustration to Jesus' mind. The point of the illustration, as He uses it, is that what is true in the natural world (four months is roughly the period between sowing and reaping in Palestine) is not necessarily true in the spiritual realm. The farmer has to wait four months for *his* harvest, but the fruit of Jesus' sowing of His word in the heart of the woman at the well is already appearing, in the persons of the Samaritans whom she has urged to come to Him, and who can already be seen approaching. They are the '*fields . . . white already unto harvest*' at which Jesus bids His disciples look. The work of reaping this spiritual harvest is already beginning (the reading of *RVm* may well be correct). The sowing was done by Jesus alone, but the disciples are to share in the work of reaping (*vv*. 36-8).

'*He that reapeth receiveth wages*', i.e. the reward that belongs to all faithful servants of God.

'*gathereth fruit unto life eternal*'. Eternal life (see on **3**[16]) is the inheritance of all believers whom the Christian mission gathers into the Kingdom of God.

'may rejoice together'. Every harvest successfully gathered leads to rejoicing, and in the case of this spiritual harvest to which Jesus has referred, the sower and the reaper can rejoice together since the interval between sowing and reaping has been removed. Amos 9[13] suggests that this overtaking of the sower by the reaper was to be a feature of the Messianic Age as envisaged by the Jews; thus there may be a hint in *v.* 36 that the age of fulfilment has dawned.

'One soweth, and another reapeth'. Here Jesus quotes another proverbial saying, which He proceeds to apply to the situation of the disciples (see above). From the evangelist's standpoint, however, these words of Jesus are equally applicable to the situation of the Church of his own day, which has entered into the labours of both Jesus and the apostles. The same principle, of course, is applicable to the mission of the Church in every age.

4[39-42]. Here the fruit of Jesus' ministry in Samaria is more directly described. The woman had testified concerning Jesus, with the result that many Samaritans *'believed on him'*. This idea of testimony to Jesus leading to faith in Him is prominent in *Jn* (cf. 1[7-8] and the whole treatment of John the Baptist). The main point of the present paragraph, however, is that to believe on the basis of others' testimony is only the beginning of faith. Full and mature faith is that which is based on personal experience of Jesus and *'his word'*. The Samaritans are able to attain to this faith because Jesus, in response to their request, remains in their neighbourhood for two days.

'the Saviour of the world'. The Samaritans confess their faith by acclaiming Jesus in these terms. The title occurs only here in *Jn*, but is found in 1 Jn 4[14] (see *GPL, Note 23*, p. 104). The truth enshrined in the title, however, is common in *Jn* (see especially 3[16-17]). It is significant that the title occurs on the lips of Samaritans; the clear implication is that Jesus is not only the Messiah of the Jews but also the Saviour of the whole world. Thus the confession forms an effective and dramatic conclusion to the whole of the present section.

(*a*) Jesus' attitude to such prejudices as those of sex and religion is strikingly illustrated in this section. Conventions and human distinctions mean nothing to Him when confronted by men and women in need. (*b*) Jesus' manner of approach to the woman is suggestive. He asks for, rather than offers, a favour; this is often the best way to help a person in need. Moreover, He adapts His teaching to the actual situation of the hearer, speaking here of His offer of eternal life in terms of 'living water' (cf. *vv*. 31-4). (*c*) The woman's gradual progress towards an apprehension of Jesus' significance is revealing. There are still those who, beginning in complete scepticism as to whether Christ has anything to offer them, later begin to look to Him for certain benefits (material things that will spare them trouble and worry in this world), without realizing what the great and precious spiritual gift is that He is offering them. But the fact that they are prepared to look to Christ at all, even in this inadequate way, provides an opportunity for the Church to lead them on to a fuller understanding of what He can do for them. (*d*) 4¹⁴ is a golden text. In every man's soul there is a thirst for life— a life that can really satisfy, and set his heart at rest. Men seek to slake this thirst by various means—pleasure, culture, philosophy, religion, etc. These things may *seem* to satisfy for a while, but they are really man-hewn cisterns (cf. Jer 2¹³). By contrast, Jesus offers to implant in man's soul a well of living water, a perennial spring that will never run dry. His gift of eternal life alone can satisfy, completely and permanently, the soul's deepest needs and longings. 'Our hearts are restless till they find their rest in Thee' (St Augustine). See *MHB* 109, *v*. 1 ('Jesu, Thou Joy of loving hearts') and 110 ('Jesu, Lover of my soul'), *v*. 4. (*e*) 4²¹⁻⁴ is the classic expression of Christian teaching about the essential nature of true worship (see commentary). (*f*) The deep satisfaction that comes from fulfilling the will of God and accomplishing His work is food for the soul, and to lose oneself in the devoted fulfilment of a spiritual task can even lead to the renewal of physical strength (see *v*. 34). (*g*) 4³⁵⁻⁶ suggests the abundant opportunities of evangelism which ever confront the Church (cf. Mt 9³⁷⁻⁸), and the ample reward that belongs to those who respond to the challenge—a reward that consists in the joy of performing the service itself, the reward of 'knowing that we do Thy will'. (*h*) 4³⁷⁻⁸ readily suggests the truth that every generation reaps the benefit of the labour and service of former generations. It is our privilege to reap what our forefathers have sown. It is equally our privilege, and our responsibility, to sow what those who come after us may reap. In God's universe no good seed is ever sown in vain (cf. Gal 6⁷, which applies to good seed as well as bad—as the succeeding verses show). It matters little whether the Lord calls us to the work of sowing or that of reaping, or a little of each; all is the work of the one Lord, and our highest privilege is to be allowed a part in the work at all. And in the end it will be true in the case of all His labourers that sower and reaper will rejoice together. (*i*) We must never be content until we have entered into a personal relationship with Christ, not relying solely on the testimony of others, valuable as that may be in leading us to Him. And the preacher must never be content that his hearers should take his word for the truth of the gospel; he must always seek to lead them to this personal encounter with Christ Himself. (*j*) Jesus Christ as 'the Saviour of the world' is the fundamental theme of Christian preaching (see on *v.* 42).

4⁴³⁻⁵⁴: The Officer's Son

This section describes a second '*sign*' performed by Jesus at Cana in Galilee. John seems anxious to point to a connection between the two signs located there (see *vv.* 46 and 54). The truth symbolized by this '*sign*' represents a development of that of 2¹⁻¹¹. There we saw that Jesus transforms and enriches life; here we see Him rescuing a life that is on the point of extinction (*v.* 47). Later, in 11¹⁻⁴⁴, this development reaches its climax in the greatest of all Jesus' 'signs', the raising of Lazarus, where He even revives a life already extinguished.

4⁴³. The journey begun in 4³ is completed.

4⁴⁴ is parenthetical, referring to a comment of Jesus which is also reported in the Synoptics (Mk 6⁴, Mt 13⁵⁷, Lk 4²⁴). The saying may be a familiar proverb which Jesus applied to Himself—possibly on more than one occasion. In the Synoptics, '*his own country*' refers to Nazareth. Here in *Jn*, however, it is evident that the phrase refers to Jerusalem, for *v.* 45 describes the welcome given to Jesus in Galilee. For John, Jerusalem is the chief centre of Jesus' ministry, and so is essentially His 'home'. Thus he applies the saying to the rejection of Jesus in Jerusalem, which led Him to leave for Galilee (see on 4¹).

4⁴⁵. The Galileans receive Jesus enthusiastically because of what they have seen Him do in Jerusalem. Their faith is like that of the 'many' in 2²³.

4⁴⁶. '*Cana of Galilee*'. See on 1⁴⁵ and 2¹.
'*a certain nobleman*'. The word is one that was used of military officials in the service of Herod Antipas, the ruler of Galilee at the time; hence the translation, 'officer in the royal service' (*NEB*). This makes it probable that he is to be

identified with the centurion of Mt 8$^{5\ 13}$, Lk 7$^{1-10}$, and that the
Johannine narrative is an independent version of that Synoptic
incident. Thus the officer is probably a Roman centurion
seconded to Herod's service. The identification is strengthened
by the fact that the word translated 'servant' in Mt 8^6 could
equally well mean 'boy' (see *RVm* and *NEB*), so that the sick
person there, as here in *Jn*, could have been the centurion's *son*.

'*at Capernaum*'. A further point of contact with the Synoptic
story. There, however, Jesus is actually in Capernaum when
approached by the centurion, whereas here He is approached
at Cana. It is likely that John has located the incident at Cana
partly out of a desire to point the connection with 2$^{1-11}$ (see
p. 49), and partly out of a desire to heighten the miracle by
increasing the distance between Jesus and the sick boy.

4^{47}. '*at the point of death*'. On the significance of this detail, see
p. 49. Cf. Lk 7^2.

4^{48}. Jesus' rebuke is scarcely merited by the officer, and is
probably meant rather for the bystanders (note the plural '*ye*').
No doubt John includes the words to remind his readers of the
Jews' tendency to 'ask for signs' (see 1 Cor 1^{22}) as a ground for
faith, and of Jesus' deprecation of such faith (cf. 1^{50}, 2^{24}).

'*signs and wonders*'. These two words occur together only
here in *Jn*, but frequently elsewhere, especially in Acts (2^{22}, etc.).

4^{49}. The urgency of the repeated request, heedless of the
rebuke, shows that the officer is in deadly earnest.

'*my child*'. The diminutive form is used here, revealing the
father's tender affection for his 'little boy'.

4^{50}. Jesus, satisfied that the father's faith is genuine, speaks the
word (cf. Mt 8$^{8-10}$), and the officer immediately takes Him at
His word and obeys His command to return home. His
attitude clearly reveals a higher level of faith than that described
in *v*. 48.

4$^{51-2}$. '*Yesterday*' suggests that the journey from Cana to
Capernaum—a distance of about twenty miles—took the party
the best part of a day.

'*at the seventh hour*', i.e. 'at one in the afternoon' (*NEB*).

4⁵³. The father, realizing that Jesus' word, spoken at a distance, had immediately effected the cure of his son, '*believed*'. This verb indicates a still higher level of faith than that of *v.* 50. The verb is used here in the full sense in which it is used in *Jn*, implying that the officer believed that Jesus was the Christ and surrendered himself to Him in full trust and commitment. In saying that the officer and his household believed in this sense, John is probably going beyond the actual historical facts (cf. comments on 1³²⁻⁴, ⁴⁹, 4²⁶); his interest in this narrative again is not primarily historical but theological. The story illustrates the different levels of faith, culminating in the true Christian faith which is the proper response to the signs of Jesus (see 2¹¹, 20³¹). It also illustrates very vividly the central truth of the Gospel—namely, that Christ, the Word of God, gives life (true life, eternal life) to men.

'*his whole house*'. This reflects what was a common practice in the earliest period of the Church—namely, for a whole household to become Christians together (cf. Acts 10², 16³¹⁻⁴). Thus we have a further indication that here John is thinking more in terms of the Early Church than of the historical incident of the healing of the officer's son.

4⁵⁴. '*the second sign*'. Cf. 2¹¹, and see introductory comment on this section.

(*a*) The main point of interest for the preacher in this section is the development in the conception of faith through *vv.* 48, 50, and 53. Verse 48 reveals an inadequate basis for faith. Christian faith usually begins, however, as a simple, unquestioning willingness to take Jesus at His word and accept what He says as true (*v.* 50). He who so believes, and acts on the basis of such an acceptance, finds that experience confirms the reality of Jesus' promises, and so is led on to that fuller understanding, commitment and trust that is mature Christian faith. (*b*) The connection suggested between 2¹⁻¹¹, 4⁴⁶⁻⁵³, and 11¹⁻⁴⁴ reveals the completeness of the victory of life (i.e. the life that Christ imparts) over death. (*c*) While it is no longer usual for whole families to become Christians together (though such occurrences are not unknown among some of the younger Churches), it is often the case that the conversion of the head of a family leads naturally to the conversion of the family as a whole.

Chapter 5

5¹⁻¹⁸: The Cripple at the Pool

FOR the second time in this Gospel, Jesus leaves Galilee to attend a festival at Jerusalem (cf. 2¹³). While there He performs a 'sign' on a sabbath, which involves Him in a controversy with the Jewish leaders, which in turn prepares the way for the long discourse of 5¹⁹⁻⁴⁷. The 'sign' itself is an incident not mentioned in any other Gospel, though some features of the narrative recall the story of the paralytic in Mk 2¹⁻¹² (see *vv.* 8-9). It is possible that familiarity with *Mk* has influenced John's language here; on the other hand, if he wrote in complete independence of the Synoptic Gospels as such (see Introduction, p. 2), it may be that John was familiar with the tradition underlying Mk 2¹⁻¹² and that this accounts for the verbal similarities. In any case the differences between the two narratives preclude the view that they refer to the same incident, and there is no good reason for doubting the historicity of the Johannine narrative.

5¹. '*a feast*'. Some manuscripts read 'the feast' (*RVm*), but the definite article is probably a later addition to the text. John does not specify, as he usually does (see 2¹³, 6⁴, 7², etc.), which feast is meant; had the question been of any significance no doubt he would have been more explicit. He mentions the festival simply in order to explain Jesus' presence in Jerusalem; it is interesting to note that each visit of Jesus to the capital mentioned in *Jn* is in connection with the observance of one of the Jewish festivals.

5². '*by the sheep gate a pool*'. The Greek contains no noun corresponding to '*gate*' (note the italics in *RV*), but simply an adjective meaning 'to do with sheep'. *AV* understands the noun 'market', *RV* and *RSV* (influenced no doubt by Neh 3¹, 12³⁹) the noun 'gate'. But the most natural solution is that adopted by *NEB*, which connects the adjective with the noun '*pool*'.

'*Hebrew*' here means Aramaic, the spoken language in Palestine in Jesus' time.

'*Bethesda*'. Some manuscripts read 'Bethzatha' (so *RSV*), and others 'Bethsaida' (*RVm*). The original text was probably 'Bethzatha', which seems to have been the name of a region in the northern part of Jerusalem, where excavations have revealed the ruins of a building, beside the double pool of St Anna, which may well be the site of the incident.

'*five porches*'. It is unlikely that this detail has any allegorical significance—as some commentators have claimed, suggesting that the five porches symbolize the five books of the law, in the shadow of which Israel lay, without receiving salvation thereby.

5³ᵇ⁻⁴. These words, omitted in all modern versions, were added to the text to provide an explanation of the sick man's words in *v.* 7. It seems that the healing properties of the pool depended on an intermittent spring which fed it periodically, and that popular belief attributed this periodic disturbance of the water to the agency of an angel.

5⁵. '*thirty and eight years*'. Those who interpret the narrative allegorically (see on *v.* 2) see here a reference to the period of Israel's wanderings in the wilderness according to Deut 2¹⁴, but this interpretation is unconvincing.

5⁶. '*and knew*'. A further example of Jesus' supernatural knowledge of men (cf. 1⁴⁷, 2²⁵, etc.).

'*Wouldest thou be made whole?*' The question reveals that Jesus not only was aware of the man's physical condition, but also understood his mental attitude. He has probably become accustomed to his infirmity and resigned to the impossibility of availing himself of the cure that lies so near. Consequently, he may have lost all hope, and possibly also all desire, of healing. The excuse he offers in reply to Jesus' question confirms this impression that he lacks any real resolve to be healed.

5⁷. The man's words imply that only one person could be cured at each disturbance of the water, so that it was a case of 'first come, first served'. This may have been due to the size of the pool and the brief efficacy of the curative property of the water (see note on *vv.* 3b–4).

5⁸⁻⁹. The manner of the question in *v*. 6 was no doubt designed to reawaken the man's desire to be healed. Jesus now tests his desire, and his faith, by issuing a clear and authoritative command. As in **4⁵⁰⁻³**, Jesus' word is sufficient to effect the cure; the sick man is healed immediately and completely. On the similarity to Mk 2¹¹⁻¹², see p. 52.

'*Now it was the sabbath*'. This note, with which the story of the miracle as such closes, is of great significance, as the following verses show. The controversy to which Jesus' act gives rise turns entirely on the fact that it was performed on the sabbath (contrast Mk 2¹⁻¹², where the subject of controversey is Jesus' claim to forgive sins). Jesus' attitude to the sabbath law was one of the chief causes of conflict between Him and the Jewish leaders (see *CLM* on Mk 2²³⁻⁸, 3¹⁻⁶, and *AMW* on Mt 12¹⁻¹⁴; cf. also Lk 6¹⁻¹¹, 13¹⁰⁻¹⁷, 14 ¹⁻⁶). In *Jn*, the question arises again at 7²¹⁻³ and 9¹⁴⁻¹⁶.

5¹⁰. '*the Jews*'. See on 1¹⁹.

'*it is not lawful*'. The authorities first accuse the cured invalid. The accusation is strictly legitimate, for the Jewish law, though permitting the carrying of a man upon a bed on the sabbath, forbade the carrying of an empty bed.

5¹¹⁻¹². The man justifies his action on the grounds that he is obeying the command of Him who cured him. In the circumstances he could hardly be blamed, and his accusers immediately enquire about the identity of the healer.

5¹³. The man is unaware of the identity of his benefactor, 'for the place was crowded and Jesus had slipped away' (*NEB*). He had not stayed to be questioned by the man He had healed or by any of the eye-witnesses. Jesus was unwilling to foster excitement amongst the crowds who were so prone to misunderstand the nature of His mission (cf. 6¹⁵).

5¹⁴. Jesus, however, has not lost sight of the man He has healed. He has something more to say to him, and so follows him to the Temple, whither the man has very fittingly gone to offer thanks to God for his cure.

'*sin no more*' seems to imply that the man's past sins have been forgiven and that this is in some way connected with his cure (cf. *CLM* on Mk 2¹⁻¹²). Jesus, however, did not share the

Jewish belief that sin was always the cause of physical disease (see on 9¹⁻³). In the present case there seems to be a recognition that the sinfulness of the man's mental attitude (see on *v.* 6) is a contributory factor to his physical condition. The warning about '*a worse thing*' may mean that if he relapses into the same mental attitude as before his condition may become worse than ever. On the other hand, it may simply be a reference to the judgement of God upon sin—a subject that is to be dealt with in the discourse that follows in 5¹⁹⁻⁴⁷. Jesus may be warning the man that the consequences of moral and spiritual disease (sin) are far more serious even than those of physical disease.

5¹⁵⁻¹⁶. The man, having discovered the identity of his benefactor, passes the information on—no doubt in all innocence—to the Jews (see on *vv.* 11–13), and they immediately turn their attention to Jesus and persecute Him for breaking the sabbath.

5¹⁷. Jesus' reply to the charge of sabbath-breaking is here developed on rather different lines from those He adopts in the Synoptic narratives (see comment on *v.* 9). His argument is that God works on the sabbath, and therefore He too, as the Son of God, has the right to work. Jews of the time of Jesus believed that God was continuously active, and interpreted Gen 2²⁻³ as meaning that God rested on the seventh day from all His *creative* work. This did not mean that He ceased from His activity in the moral government of the universe; He was continuously at work in His capacity as Judge and Life-giver. It is of the very nature of God to express Himself in works of mercy and judgement, and God does not cease to be Himself on the sabbath or at any other time. Jesus claims that the works of compassion and healing which He performs on the sabbath are a part of this ceaseless divine activity, since His work is essentially that of the Father who sent Him (see on 5¹⁹).

5¹⁸. The Jews are quick to realize the implication of this claim of Jesus. The way in which He has referred to God as '*My Father*', and justified His own act by reference to God's ceaseless activity, implies a claim to be in a unique filial relationship with God ('*his own Father*')—and this the Jews regard as '*making himself equal with God*'. In their eyes this

E

amounts to blasphemy, punishable by death; thus their determination to kill Jesus is intensified. In the discourse that follows, Jesus explains more fully the nature of the special and unique relationship in which He stands to God His Father.

(*a*) Jesus' question in *v.* 6 reminds us of the important fact that the first requisite in a sick person, if he is to be healed, is the *will* for health; to that extent the patient must co-operate with the physician. People in need of psychiatry, for instance, cannot be helped unless they are willing to be helped. Similarly, before a sinner can be saved by Christ, he must be aware of his need of salvation and earnestly desire it. The first task of the evangelist is often to awaken this sense of need and desire. (*b*) 5¹⁴ raises the important question of the relationship between sin and physical disease, and the effect of the experience of forgiveness on a person's physical health (see the discussion of 5¹⁻¹⁶ in Leslie D. Weatherhead's *Psychology, Religion and Healing*, pp. 56-8). (*c*) 5¹⁷ reveals an important truth about the nature of God as ceaselessly active. (*d*) The same verse has important implications for Christians concerned with problems of Sunday observance; it means that any work which is an expression of God's compassion for human need is legitimate.

5¹⁹⁻⁴⁷: Discourse on the Father and the Son

This long and very important discourse arises naturally out of the preceding sign, and particularly out of the claim whereby Jesus justified His act of healing the cripple on the sabbath (5¹⁷). The idea of Jesus' unique Sonship has already occurred in 1¹⁴, ¹⁸, ⁴⁹, 2¹⁶, 3¹⁶⁻²¹, ³⁴⁻⁶, 4³⁴. It has reached its climax in the unambiguous claim of 5¹⁷, and the time has now come for John to develop the theme fully. The discourse falls into three parts: (*i*) 5¹⁹⁻³⁰, The unity and co-operation of the Father and the Son in life-giving and judgement; (*ii*) 5³¹⁻⁴⁰, Witness to Christ; (*iii*) 5⁴¹⁻⁷, The unbelief of the Jews.

5¹⁹. '*Verily, verily, I say unto you*'. See on 1⁵¹.

'*The Son . . . doeth in like manner*'. The Jews have rightly understood Jesus' words in *v.* 17 as implying a claim to equality with God (*v.* 18), but the claim does not mean what they think it means—namely, setting oneself up as an independent rival to God, after the manner of Lucifer in Isa 14¹²⁻¹⁴. Jesus' claim, as He now proceeds to show, means the exact opposite; far from asserting His independence of God, His relationship with the Father is one of absolute submission and dependence. The proper word to define the relationship of Father and Son is not 'equality' but rather 'unity' or 'co-operation'. Jesus is claiming that His communion with the Father is so constant and perfect that He is able to see all that the Father does and to imitate Him in all things.

5²⁰. '*the Father loveth the Son*'. If the relationship, on the Son's part, is one of perfect obedience and submission, on the Father's part it is one of perfect love and trust (cf. 3³⁵), which allows the Son to share all the secrets of the Godhead.

'*greater works than these*', i.e. than those already accomplished by Jesus. These are exemplified by the activities of life-giving and judgement described in *vv.* 21-2.

5²¹⁻². The twin functions of life-giving and judgement are the prerogative of God, but Jesus claims that the Father has given the Son authority to exercise them. It is here that the unity and co-operation of the Son with the Father is seen at its clearest.

5²³. From the point of view of man, this relationship between the Father and the Son can only mean that Jesus' status is that of God Himself, so that He is worthy of the same honour as is accorded to the Father.

5²⁴. For the idea of eternal life and judgement as opposite sides of the same process, cf. 3¹⁶⁻²¹. To give heed to what Jesus says and to trust in God is already to possess eternal life, and so to escape judgement (cf. 3¹⁸ and 1 Jn 3¹⁴, on which see *GPL*). The thought is similar to that of Paul in Rom 8¹.

5²⁵⁻⁹. The Son's work as Life-giver and Judge is further described in terms of the resurrection of the dead.

'*The hour cometh, and now is*'. For this paradoxical expression, see on 4²³. The resurrection of the dead is represented here as something which is both present and future, whereas in *v.* 28 ('*the hour cometh*', cf. 4²¹) we have the future reference only. Verses 28-9 reflect the traditional apocalyptic idea of a general resurrection and judgement at the last day; '*all that are in the tombs*' clearly refers to those who have died in the

literal sense. The truth expressed in these verses is to be
symbolized very powerfully in the sign of the raising of
Lazarus in 11[1-44]. Christ as '*the Son of man*' (*v.* 27) is to be the
Judge of these dead, and the criterion of their judgement will be
the quality of their behaviour on earth (cf. 3[20-1]). Verse 25, however, represents the process of resurrection as already happening in the earthly ministry of Jesus. By contrast with those '*in
the tombs*' (*v.* 28), '*the dead*' here is to be understood in a
metaphorical rather than a literal sense; *v.* 24 has implied that
unbelievers are in a state of spiritual death, out of which they
may pass into life by faith in Christ. The same idea is expressed
in *v.* 25 in terms of hearing '*the voice of the Son of God*' and
living thereby. Verses 26-7 re-emphasize the fact (cf. *vv.* 21-2)
that the Son's authority to impart life and to execute judgement
is derived from the Father; '*life*' in *v.* 26 appears to mean 'life-
giving power' (*NEB*).

'*Son of man*'. Cf. 1[51], 3[13-14]. This title is used here possibly
because the figure of the Son of Man was traditionally associated in Jewish thought with the function of judgement (cf.
Mt 25[31-46]), but possibly also because the title, in *Jn*, always
suggests the truth of Jesus' full and real humanity, which is an
important part of His qualification to act as Judge of men.

5[30] serves as a transition from the first to the second part of the
discourse (see p. 56). Jesus repeats, in the first person and in
terms of judgement, what He has already said in the third
person and in more general terms in *v.* 19. His judgement is
righteous because it is the judgement of God Himself, since
He fulfils it in perfect obedience to the Father's will.

5[31]. In the first part of the discourse Jesus has been witnessing
to Himself, i.e. explaining the true nature of His unique
relationship with God and making stupendous claims for
Himself as Son of God. The Jews' natural reaction is that
such self-testimony is invalid, since Jewish law forbade anyone
to bear witness in his own case and required the agreement of
at least two witnesses to prove any point (see Deut 19[15], cf.
Mt 18[16]). In the second part of the discourse Jesus deals with
this objection. He begins by allowing, for the present, the force
of the argument (later, however, in 8[13-14], He shows that the
objection can be overcome); then He proceeds to claim that
His testimony to Himself is corroborated by other witnesses.

5³². '*another that beareth witness of me*'. First Jesus claims God the Father as His witness, whose testimony He knows to be true. This idea of the Father's witness is developed in *vv.* 37-8; meanwhile, Jesus refers to other witnesses.

5³³⁻⁵. The Jews are reminded that they themselves sent to John the Baptist and received his witness about the Messiah (see **1¹⁹⁻²⁸**). The Baptist's testimony is corroborative evidence for the claims of Jesus. He Himself does not rely on any such human testimony (*v.* 34, *NEB*), but if the Jews are prepared to believe in Him on the basis of such testimony He is happy to avail Himself of it, for the sake of their salvation. Jesus then adds (*v.* 35) His own evaluation of the ministry of the Baptist: he was 'a lamp, burning brightly' (*NEB*). The lamp's is a borrowed light; it has to be kindled, and it burns itself out by shining. Just as the lamp fades and becomes unnecessary after the sun has risen, so the Baptist faded into insignificance (cf. **3³⁰**) after the arrival of 'the true light' (cf. **1⁹**). Thus Jesus' words are in harmony with the presentation of John the Baptist which is characteristic of *Jn* (see on **1⁶⁻⁸, ¹⁹⁻³⁴, 3²²⁻³⁰**).

'*ye were willing to rejoice for a season*'. Like moths drawn to a lighted lamp at night, the Jews took a lively interest in the Baptist during the brief period of his ministry, but they have not taken seriously the testimony to Jesus which it was his purpose to declare. They are thus like men still living by the light of a candle, when outside the full light of a new day is shining.

5³⁶. Here Jesus refers to another witness, which is greater than the Baptist's, and on which He is willing to rely (cf. *NEB*)— namely, the witness of His own works. These, of course, are not really His own but His Father's (cf. *vv.* 19⁻30). The fact that Jesus performs such works is sufficient proof that the Father has sent Him, and so that His claims for Himself are true.

'*to accomplish*'. See comment on **4³⁴**, where the same word was used.

5³⁷⁻⁸. Jesus now returns to the original point of *v.* 32—namely, that the Father Himself witnesses directly to Him. There is a sense, of course, in which all the various testimonies mentioned in this part of the discourse derive ultimately from God, who

witnesses to His Son through these different media. But He
also witnesses more directly and immediately. This direct
witness can only be apprehended inwardly, by faith in Christ.
It is not a witness given to unbelievers to serve as a basis for
faith, but one that is given to believers to confirm the faith
they already possess; by means of it the believer may have
perfect assurance—independent of all rational arguments and
proofs—that Jesus Christ is the Son of God. This inward
witness does not belong to the Jews because of their unbelief.
The Father is not a witness whose voice can be heard or whose
form can be seen (cf. 1¹⁸). His witness is given in His '*word*',
which finds a home in the heart of the believer (*v.* 38, *NEB*).
With these verses, cf. 1 Jn 5⁹ and *GPL* thereon.

5³⁹⁻⁴⁰. Finally, Jesus appeals to the testimony of the scriptures.

'*Ye search*'. The verb is indicative, not imperative as in *AV*
and *RVm* (the Greek could mean either). Jesus' Jewish
contemporaries (unlike most modern Christians!) did not
need to be urged to search the scriptures. They did that, but
they did it in the wrong way and for the wrong purpose. This
is Jesus' complaint here. They fail to apprehend the true
significance of the OT.

'*these are they which bear witness of me*'. The OT points
forward to Christ, and the diligent study thereof should have
prepared the Jews to be able to recognize Jesus as the Messiah
and to believe in Him. The Jews, however, misunderstand and
misuse the scriptures by treating them as an end in themselves,
rather than as a witness to a Person. They suppose that the
possession of the scriptures in itself confers eternal life (cf.
NEB), and consequently they refuse to come to Jesus, who
alone can give them life (cf. 3¹⁶, 5²⁴). As in the case of the
Baptist (see on *vv.* 33-5), the Jews here again mistake the
witness for the One witnessed to.

5⁴¹⁻⁷. Throughout the previous verses, the Jews' failure to
accept the witness borne to Jesus, and so to believe in Him, has
been emphasized. In this final part of the discourse, the reasons
for this unbelief are examined. They appear in the two questions, each introduced by '*How?*' in *vv.* 44 and 47. First, the
Jews cannot believe because they think more of the honour
they receive from one another than of the honour which comes
'from Him who alone is God' (*v.* 44, *NEB*); cf. 12⁴³. With this

human honour Jesus is not concerned (v. 41). The Jews, however, seek it because they have no love for God (v. 42, *NEB*). Thus they reject Jesus, who comes with the authority of the Father (cf. vv. 19-30), whereas they are ready enough to welcome anyone who comes to them with no authority but his own; the readiness with which the Jews listened to false Messiahs and false prophets is proof of this fact (cf. Mk 13[6, 21-2], Acts 5[36-7]). Such a pretender would be of the same nature as themselves, and so they would understand and welcome him (v. 43). The second reason for the Jews' unbelief appears in vv. 45-7: it is their complete failure to believe truly their own great prophet, Moses, through whom was given the law upon which their religion was founded (cf. 1[17]). The Jews regarded Moses and the law as a mediator between themselves and God, and believed that, so long as they took their stand upon the law (as they did, for instance, in condemning Jesus' attitude to the sabbath), Moses would defend and support them. Jesus points out, however, that far from defending them, Moses will in fact be their 'accuser at God's tribunal' (v. 45, *NEB*), thus making it unnecessary for Jesus Himself to accuse them. Their attitude to Jesus proves that they have completely misunderstood the purpose and message of Moses, which, like that of the OT generally (v. 39), was to point forward to Christ (v. 46). If they will not believe the written testimony of Moses, which they regard as so sacred and authoritative, there is little likelihood of their believing the spoken testimony of Jesus (v. 47).

(*a*) The perfect unity of will and purpose between the Father and the Son has important theological and practical implications which the preacher may bring out. (*i*) Any theory, e.g. of the nature of the Atonement, which sets the Father and the Son in any kind of opposition to one another is mistaken and dangerous. (*ii*) The unity of Father and Son is the pattern which is to be repeated in the unity which should mark the Church (cf. 17[21-2]); the latter should therefore be a unity of will and purpose, based on mutual trust, love, and understanding, and a perfect obedience and submission to the will of God. (*iii*) To dishonour Jesus Christ is to dishonour God (v. 23); it is only in Christ that we can really see and know God (cf. 14[6-9]), and our attitude to Him is in the long run our attitude to God. And it is upon the attitude that we take to Him, who is both Judge and Life-giver (vv. 21-2), that our eternal destiny depends. (*b*) Verses 24-5 imply that the difference between the ordinary life of this world and the life which Christ imparts to the believer is such that the former, by comparison, can only be regarded as death. The way of deliverance from this 'living death' is even now open to men, by the word and power of the Son of God who is the Life-giver (cf. Eph 2^{1-10}). (c) Christ's qualification to act as Judge of the living and the dead is primarily based upon His divine authorization as Messiah, but also (see on v. 27) on the fact that, as fully human, He is 'touched with the feeling of our infirmities' (Heb 4^{15}). To be assured of His sympathy, and of the righteousness of His judgement (v. 30), is a great consolation to anyone who may be troubled at the thought of standing before the judgement seat of Christ. (d) Christ does not *rely* on human witness, and yet it often happens that such witness is the means whereby men are led to faith in Him; He does not depend on us, but He is graciously pleased to *use* us. (e) There is always a danger for men to mistake the lamp for the light (v. 35). How often the crowd will make an idol of a colourful and forceful prophetic figure without ever paying serious heed to his true message? (f) Actions speak louder than words, and greater than the testimony of human witnesses to the truth of Jesus is the evidence of the wonderful works done by Him and in His name (cf. 14^{12}). There is great scope here for the modern preacher, with nineteen centuries of Christian history behind him. (g) Valuable as are all external witnesses in leading men to faith in Christ, in the last analysis the only absolutely convincing proof of His claims is that which comes from the inward witness borne directly in a man's heart by God Himself. The truth about the Person of Christ is self-authenticating for those who are willing to give God's word a home in their hearts by accepting the message of Jesus as true (vv. 37-8). (h) Verses 39-40 contain an important message about the right and the wrong way to regard Holy Scripture. The Bible's value and authority rest not on itself as such, but on Him to whom it bears witness. A man may possess an expert knowledge of the contents of the Bible without really coming to know Christ; but rightly used and interpreted the scriptures lead us, as nothing else can, to Christ, and enable us to believe in Him and so inherit eternal life. (i) It often happens that the false prophet receives a readier welcome and hearing from men than does the true prophet of God (v. 43). This is because he corresponds to men's expectations and shares their outlook and values. The popularity of such prophets, however, is short-lived, whereas the true prophet, though unheeded and rejected at first, leaves his mark permanently on the world's life. (j) Verse 45 contains the solemn warning that we may so delude ourselves as to look for support from that which in fact will prove to be our condemnation. The very privileges granted to us (like the law for the Jews) may be so misunderstood and misused as to become a veritable stumbling-block (cf. Paul's teaching in Rom 9^{31-2}).

Chapter 6

6^{1-15}: The Feeding of the Five Thousand

THE miracle of feeding is described in all four Gospels; indeed if, as is likely, the narrative of the Four Thousand is a doublet of that of the Five Thousand, the miracle is described twice in Mk (6^{32-44}, 8^{1-9}) and Mt (14^{13-21}, 15^{32-9}). It is thus one of the best attested of all the Gospel incidents. There can be no doubt that Jesus and His disciples shared a meal in the wilderness with a multitude. The size of the multitude and the miraculous multiplication of the food supply, however, are questions upon which different opinions are held (see CLM on Mk 6^{32-44} and AMW on Mt 14^{13-21}). The difficulties are similar to those felt about the miracle at Cana (see on 2^{1-11}), though it is true that the motive here is less trivial than on that occasion, since it is an act of compassion performed to meet human need. As in the case of the Cana miracle, however, John's primary interest is in the incident as a 'sign' which symbolizes a spiritual truth. This is obvious from the way in which the narrative serves to introduce the discourse on the Bread of Life (6^{22-59}).

6^1. *'which is the sea of Tiberias'*. John adds this explanation since by his day Lake Galilee was generally known by this name (cf. 21^1). Tiberias was a town on the shore of the lake, founded by Herod Antipas in AD 26 and named in honour of the Emperor Tiberius.

6^{2-3}. Jesus' departure with His disciples across the lake, in search of solitude, and the multitude's pursuit, are described in less detail than in Mk 6^{31-4}, but the general impression is the same.

6^4. *'the passover . . . was at hand'*. This confirms the detail in Mk 6^{39}, where 'green grass' suggests springtime (cf. *v.* 10); but the reference to the Passover is no doubt primarily intended to underline the symbolical interpretation of the incident in terms of the Eucharist. This is the second of the three Passovers of Jesus' ministry (see on 2^{13}).

6^{5-6}. Whereas in Mark's account the disciples first express concern about the hungry crowd, John characteristically represents Jesus as taking the initiative. This He does by questioning Philip (see on 1^{43-4}). John explains that Jesus' question does not imply ignorance on His part, but is intended to test the disciple's reaction.

6^7. '*Two hundred pennyworth*' corresponds exactly to Mk 6^{37} (see *CLM*) and represents about 'twenty pounds' (*NEB*) in our currency.

6^{8-9} introduces the distinctive feature of the Johannine narrative, as compared with that of the Synoptics: the food is provided, not by the disciples, but by a lad brought to Jesus by Andrew (see on 1^{40-1}). This is probably a genuinely historical detail unknown to Mark, though some regard it as an expansion of the narrative, due to the influence of 2 Kings 4^{42-4}, where Elisha feeds a hundred men with twenty barley loaves and has some left over.

'*five barley loaves*'. Only *Jn* refers to '*barley*', but this need not be due to the influence of the Elisha story (see above), since the cheap bread eaten by the poor was in fact made from barley.

6^{10-13}. The account of the meal corresponds in substance to Mark's narrative, except for the significant detail that in *Jn* Jesus distributes the food Himself, and not through the agency of the disciples; it is characteristic of this Gospel to present Jesus as acting independently and on His own initiative (cf. *vv.* 5-6). Jesus' actions recall those at the Last Supper (see *CLM* on Mk 6^{41})—a fact which again underlines the eucharistic significance of the incident (see on *v.* 4).

6^{14-15} describes the effect of the '*sign*' upon the people, and contains tradition independent of that of the Synoptics.

'*the prophet that cometh into the world*'. See on 1^{21}. Here the title seems to be a messianic designation. In describing this upsurge of messianic excitement as a result of the wilderness meal, John is probably preserving a genuine historical reminiscence; this fact may well have been the reason why Jesus was so anxious to send His disciples away, lest they should be influenced by the dangerous enthusiasm of the crowd (see *CLM* on Mk 6⁴⁵). The passage reveals how far-removed Jesus' conception of Messiahship was from the popular expectation of an earthly ruler who would free Israel from the Roman yoke.

(*a*) The story strikingly illustrates Jesus' compassion for people and His concern for their physical as well as their spiritual needs. (*b*) It also symbolizes the fact that Jesus is able to take the woefully inadequate resources of His followers, when they are willingly surrendered to Him, and to use them so that, under His blessing, they prove more than sufficient for the fulfilment of His purposes. (*c*) At a deeper level, we have what was no doubt the original significance of the meal as an anticipation of the perfect fellowship of the messianic community of the Kingdom of God, and of the fellowship meal in which Christians are fed upon the true Bread from heaven which is Jesus Himself (see the discourse in 6²²⁻⁵⁹). (*d*) The misunderstanding of Jesus' true mission by His contemporaries is nowhere more dramatically illustrated than in *v*. 15. Such misunderstanding abounds in every age; there are always those who wish to take Jesus and fit Him into the scheme of their own aims and ambitions, to use Him for their own ends. But He never consents to be 'used' in such a way. It is we who must be willing to be used by Him for the fulfilment of His purposes.

6¹⁶⁻²¹: Jesus walking on the water

As in *Mk*, this story is the immediate sequel of the Feeding. This raises the question of the relationship between the Gospels of John and Mark. The agreements, both in the contents and the sequence of these two narratives, seem to suggest John's dependence on *Mk*, but the facts can be adequately accounted for by the view that he was familiar with a tradition similar to, or identical with, that underlying Mk 6³⁰⁻⁵³ (see Introduction, p. 2).

6¹⁷. '*unto Capernaum*'. In Mk 6⁴⁵ Jesus sends the disciples to Bethsaida, but because of the contrary wind they eventually land at Gennesaret (see *CLM* on Mk 6⁵³). This may account for John's representing them as making for Capernaum, which like Gennesaret was on the western shore. In any case, he wishes to locate the discourse that follows in Capernaum (see 6[24, 59]).

6[19]. '*about five and twenty or thirty furlongs*', i.e. 'about three or four miles' (*NEB*). This is consistent with Mk 6[47], 'the boat was in the midst of the sea', since the lake at its widest point is about seven miles across.

'*walking on the sea*'. Cf. Mk 6[48], on which see *CLM*. The phrase translated '*on the sea*' occurs also at 21[1], where it clearly means 'by the sea'. Thus the statement *could* mean that Jesus was walking through the shallow water near the shore. It is almost certain, however, that John, like Mark, intends to record a miraculous walking on the surface of the sea. As a nature-miracle, this raises for many people difficulties similar to those we have found in such stories as the Wedding at Cana and the Feeding of the multitude. Here again, whatever answer may be given to the *historical* question, the spiritual truth conveyed by the 'sign' is the same; and this was John's main concern, as it was that of the early Christians generally (see *CLM*, p. 52). This spiritual truth is brought out in *vv.* 20-1.

6[20]. '*It is I*'. Cf. Mk 6[50], on which see *CLM*. The phrase in the Greek is identical with that often translated 'I am' or 'I am he', which in *Jn* has deep theological significance (see on 6[35]). This significance may be in John's mind here (as in 4[26]), though the words actually used by Jesus probably meant no more than '*It is I*'.

'*be not afraid*'. See *CLM* on Mk 6[50].

6[21]. No sooner is Jesus willingly received into the boat than the voyage which was proving so difficult is successfully completed (cf. Ps 107[30], which may have been in John's mind here).

This story's significance for the preacher lies in its vivid illustration of the truth that Jesus appears to His own in the midst of their difficulties and distresses, assuring them of His presence and thereby banishing their fears, and bringing them to their destination in safety and peace.

6²²⁻⁵⁹: Discourse on the Bread of Life

As in 5¹⁹⁻⁴⁷ the discourse arises naturally out of the 'sign' with which the chapter opens. Here, however, two 'signs' have been related—the Feeding and the Walking on the water; but the latter plays no part in the ensuing discourse, and was probably included by John simply because of its traditional connection with the story of the Feeding. Unlike 5¹⁹⁻⁴⁷, this discourse is not a long monologue by Jesus, but a dialogue; the Jews' contribution, however, becomes progressively less as the discourse proceeds. After a brief narrative introduction (*vv.* 22-5), the discourse proper falls into three parts: (*i*) 6²⁶⁻⁴⁰, The Bread of Life; (*ii*) 6⁴¹⁻⁵¹, The Origins of Jesus; (*iii*) 6⁵²⁻⁹, Eucharistic teaching.

6²²⁻⁵ explains how the crowd is rejoined with Jesus and His disciples at Capernaum (cf. 6¹⁷). The passage contains some obscurities, but its general meaning is clear (see *NEB*, which provides a much smoother reading than *RV*). Being puzzled as to how Jesus crossed the lake, the crowd ask the question of *v.* 25.

6²⁶⁻⁷. Instead of answering their question, Jesus makes a solemn pronouncement.

'*Verily, verily*'. See on 1⁵¹.

'*not because ye saw signs*' must mean 'not because you appreciated the significance on the events', the word 'sign' being used in its distinctively Johannine sense (see on 2¹⁻¹¹) and not as a mere synonym for miracle (as in 2¹⁸, etc.). The point is that the feeding meant no more to them than a much-needed, cheap and satisfying meal: '*ye ate of the loaves, and were filled*'.

'*Work not for the meat which perisheth*' does not imply that they need make no effort to earn their material food. Jesus' point is that they must be prepared to make just as strenuous efforts to avail themselves of '*the meat which abideth unto eternal life*'. The implication is that the obtaining of the latter requires effort; but the verse also indicates that the food in question is not earned as wages, but is the gift of the Son of Man.

'*eternal life*'. See on 3¹⁶. Jesus here describes His gift of eternal life in terms of 'food that lasts' (*NEB*), just as He described it in 4^{13-14} in terms of a perennial spring of water.

'*the Son of man*'. See on 1^{51}.

'*him the Father . . . hath sealed*' means that He is the divinely authorized Life-giver (cf. 5^{26-7}).

6^{28-9}. The Jews take up the verb '*work*' from Jesus' words, and carry the discussion a stage further by their question.

'*work the works of God*' means 'work as God would have us work' (*NEB*). The question reflects the character of Judaism as a religion of works in an attempt to please God and win His favour.

'*that ye believe*'. Jesus' reply is in terms of salvation by faith. What God requires is simply faith in Jesus as God's accredited Messenger. This faith is a permanent attitude of obedient trust; there is no suggestion that it is a 'work' comparable to the works on which the Jews placed their reliance.

6^{30-1}. Jesus' call for faith immediately arouses the characteristic Jewish demand for a sign, i.e. a miracle (cf. 2^{18}). They instance the miracle of the manna provided for the Israelites of old in the wilderness, and quote Ps 78^{24}.

6^{32}. In reply, Jesus makes two points, which are somewhat compressed together: (*a*) Moses was not the actual donor of the manna, but God (cf. 1^{17}). (*b*) The manna was not the true (i.e. 'real', as in 1^9) bread from heaven, which is also given by God.

'*my Father giveth*'. The present tense indicates that the gift is now being given.

6^{33}. '*that which cometh down out of heaven*'. This could be equally correctly translated 'he who comes down from heaven' (*NEBm*). Whether or not the latter is the intended meaning, the words clearly suggest (in view of 3^{13}) the identification with Jesus which becomes explicit in *v.* 35.

6^{34}. The Jews, however, misunderstand because of their preoccupation with material bread (cf. the request of the Samaritan woman in 4^{15}). The misunderstanding as usual leads to further elucidation in the great utterance of *v.* 35, which sums up the theme of the first part of the discourse.

6[35]. *'I am the bread of life'* is the first of the seven great similitudes of this Gospel, in which the phrase *'I am'* is used by Jesus with a predicate (the others occur at **8**[12], **10**[7], **10**[11], **11**[25], **14**[6] and **15**[1]). The phrase is also found in **8**[24, 28, 58] and **13**[19] without a predicate, in which case it may be translated 'I am he'. The significance of this phrase for John can only be understood against the background of such OT passages as Ex **3**[14], Deut **32**[39], Isa **41**[4], **43**[10], etc., where 'I am' or 'I am he' is used in a sense which is appropriate only to God Himself. It is the style of Deity, so that when Jesus uses the phrase it is usually tantamount to a claim to divine status. The same Greek phrase, however, can also mean no more than 'It is I' (see on **6**[20]). It is doubtful whether Jesus Himself used the phrase in the profound theological sense we have just noted, since it does not occur in that sense in the Synoptics (except possibly at Mk **14**[62], but see *CLM* thereon). It is more likely that these great Johannine sayings represent a reinterpretation in the evangelist's own idiom of what was implicit in the actual teaching of Jesus (see Introduction, p. 3). Most of the 'I am' sayings, in fact, do reflect elements in Jesus' teaching as found in the Synoptics. Thus the present similitude of the Bread of life expresses essentially the same truth as is contained in the words of Jesus as He distributes the bread at the Last Supper, 'This is my body' (Mk **14**[22], on which see *CLM*). The actual institution of the Eucharist is nowhere related in *Jn* (see on **13**[1-20]), but this does not mean that John is uninterested in the sacrament; the whole of the present discourse is in fact an exposition of His teaching on the meaning and significance of the Lord's Supper (see especially on *vv.* 52-9).

'he that cometh . . . he that believeth'. The two phrases are parallel and more or less synonymous. Having made it clear that He Himself is the 'true bread out of heaven' of *v.* 32, Jesus claims that it is only by coming to Him and believing in Him that men can find lasting satisfaction for their deepest yearnings. The thought here is essentially the same as that of **4**[13-14], and the reference to thirst as well as hunger recalls that passage, though the reason for its inclusion here is probably to prepare the way for *vv.* 53-6.

6[36]. Jesus again laments the Jews' unbelief, in spite of all that they have seen of Him, especially the sign of the Feeding, which pointed to Him as the Bread of life.

6³⁷ reveals that coming to Jesus (i.e. believing in Him—see on *v.* 35) is dependent upon the will of God (cf. *v.* 44). Those who come in this way will never be rejected, for it is God's will to give them eternal life, and the will of Christ is that of the Father (*v.* 38, cf. 5^{19–30}).

6^{38–40}. Here we find the same tension between realized and futurist eschatology as appeared in 5^{24–9}. Eternal life is both something to be enjoyed here and now (cf. 3¹⁶, 5²⁴), and something to which the believer will be raised by Christ '*at the last day*' (cf. 5^{28–9}).

6^{41–2}. The beginning of the second section of the discourse is marked by the Jews registering their objection to Jesus' claim in *v.* 35. To them He is '*Jesus, the son of Joseph*' (cf. 1⁴⁵); knowing His human origin, they cannot accept His claim to have descended from heaven.

6^{43–4}. Jesus silences the objection and proceeds to develop the point already made in *v.* 37. Only those can come to Him who are drawn by the Father. This means that the initiative in man's salvation is always with God, the very faith by which a man avails himself of salvation in Christ being the gift of God. Jesus repeats the promise to all who so come to Him that He will raise them at the last day (cf. *vv.* 39-40).

6⁴⁵. The quotation from Isa 54¹³ reinforces the point just made. Everyone who pays attention to and learns the lesson taught him by God responds to the divine 'drawing' and comes to Christ in faith.

6⁴⁶. '*he which is from God*', i.e. the Son (cf. 1¹⁸).

6⁴⁷. '*hath eternal life*', i.e. in the present (see on *vv.* 38-40).

6⁴⁸ repeats the similitude of *v.* 35.

6^{49–50}. As in *vv.* 32-3, the contrast is drawn between the bread of life upon which the believer feeds and the manna eaten by the Israelites in the wilderness, which sustained them only for the brief period of their earthly life.

6[51]. '*I am the living bread . . . out of heaven*'. Jesus again repeats the claim of *v*. 35, this time in a slightly different form (cf. *vv*. 33, 50) which expresses more clearly the fact of the Incarnation.

'*he shall live for ever*' expresses more positively the truth of the previous verse. The believer who feeds on the bread of life has eternal life both here and hereafter (cf. *vv*. 38-40).

'*my flesh, for the life of the world*'. Here, for the first time in the discourse, we have an allusion to the vicarious death which Jesus is to die. This view of His death is prominent in *Jn* (cf. 10[11, 15], 11[50-2], 15[13]). His giving of Himself as the Bread of life will be complete only as the result of His sacrifice on the Cross; only then will men be able to feed on Him. This explicitly introduces the idea of the Christian Eucharist, which is developed in the third and last part of the discourse.

6[52]. As in *vv*. 41-2, the new section is marked by an objection from the Jews, who engage in 'a fierce dispute' (*NEB*) among themselves. As always, they interpret Jesus' words in a too crudely literal sense, and the misunderstanding leads to further elucidation (cf. *v*. 34).

6[53-6]. Jesus now adds to the idea of eating His flesh (see *v*. 51) that of drinking His blood—an idea most offensive to the Jewish mind, since the law forbade the drinking of the blood of any sacrificed animal (see Lev 17[14], Deut 12[23]). Such language can only be understood in the light of the Christian sacrament of the Eucharist, which is the divinely appointed means of grace whereby the believer is enabled to feed on the 'real food' and 'real drink' (*v*. 55, *NEB*) made available by the outpouring of Christ's life in sacrifice upon the Cross. So to feed on Him is the only way to obtain eternal life, both here and hereafter (this truth is expressed negatively in *v*. 53 and positively in *v*. 54). This eternal life consists of mutual indwelling of Christ and the believer (*v*. 56)—a theme which is worked out fully in 15[1-10]. The language of *vv*. 53-6 is a translation into Johannine idiom of the words of Jesus over the bread and the cup at the Last Supper (Mk 14[22-4]; see comment on *v*. 35). It is significant, however, that John substitutes the word '*flesh*' for 'body'. This is in line with his emphasis on the full humanity of Christ (see on 1[14]). The same desire to emphasize His humanity may account for the use

F

of the title '*Son of man*' in *v.* 53 (cf. 5^{27}); the emphasis is further heightened by the repeated occurrence, side by side, of the terms '*flesh*' and '*blood*', for in the Bible 'flesh and blood' is a common way of referring to humanity (cf. Mt 16^{17}, Gal 1^{16}, etc.).

6^{57}. '*the living Father*', i.e. the Father who has life in Himself (cf. 5^{26}). Jesus receives His life from the Father (again cf. 5^{26}), and in the same way believers, by feeding on Him, will receive life from Him. We have here the first occurrence of an idea that is prominent in *Jn*—namely, that the relationship between believers and Christ corresponds to that between the Son and the Father (cf. 13^{20}, 14^{20}, 15^{9-10}, 17^{18}, 20^{21}).

6^{58} effectively summarizes the whole discourse, repeating the language of *vv.* 49-51.

6^{59}. '*in the synagogue*'. For Jesus' teaching in synagogues, cf. 18^{20}, and see *CLM* on Mk 1^{21-8}.
'*in Capernaum*'. See on *vv.* 17, 24.

(*a*) There is always the danger for men to adhere to Christ and His Church merely for the sake of the material and worldly benefits it may provide for them (*v.* 26); and this danger is not confined to the poor and destitute who benefit from the welfare work of the Church. There are other benefits, such as social position and business success, which membership of the Church may help one to obtain. (*b*) The interrelation between man's efforts and God's grace (*v.* 27) is a fruitful theme for preaching. There is a sense in which 'God helps those who help themselves', i.e. those who show a serious desire for His gifts and are prepared to go all out to secure them. (*c*) Any danger there may be for the previous point to be misunderstood as implying salvation by works is offset by *vv.* 28-9, which contain a clear statement of the doctrine of salvation by faith. All that God requires of us is to believe in His Son—and to accept the consequences which, if our faith is genuine, will follow in a new life full of works well-pleasing to God. (*d*) The theme of Jesus as the Bread of Life is essentially the same as that of 4^{13-14}, but there is something very suggestive in His choice of the term 'bread', since it is the 'staff of life', the food which is man's basic necessity, and of which he never tires. (*e*) There is a message of great comfort in *vv.* 37-40. God's purposes of good for His own will never be defeated; provided they look to Christ and trust in Him, they are assured of 'present grace and joys above' (*MHB* 702). (*f*) God's initiative in man's salvation is nowhere more pointedly stated than in *v*. 44 (cf. *v*. 37). When a person first believes in Christ, it appears to be his own free decision; but when the mature Christian looks back on his initial act of faith, he realizes more and more that it was not he who chose Christ but Christ him (cf. 1^{48}, 15^{16}). He was only able to come because of the divine 'pull' upon him. This is what we call prevenient grace, and without it we could never be saved. Note, however, that nothing is said about any whom God does not draw; indeed the quotation in *v*. 45 suggests that all men are subject to His drawing. There is no reason to suppose that God limits His prevenient grace to an elect minority; but it is only those who heed His voice and respond to His appeal who come to Christ (cf. Mt 22^{14}: 'many are called, but few chosen'). (*g*) Verse 51 contains the very important truth that the provision of the bread of life for the hungering souls of men involved for Jesus the sacrifice of His own life. This bread, like the manna in the wilderness, is God's free gift; it costs nothing to those who partake of it, but it cost the ultimate price to Him who provides it. (*h*) The idea of eating Christ's flesh and drinking His blood (*vv*. 53-6) may seem at first to be offensively crude, but that is because we understand it, as did the Jews, in too literal a fashion. Viewed in the light of the Eucharist, which is clearly how John intended the words to be understood, they are full of spiritual significance. The Incarnation and Atonement were necessary in order that the outpoured life of Christ might become available for us, and the Eucharist is the divinely appointed means whereby we can avail ourselves of this life, by 'feeding on Him in our hearts by faith with thanksgiving', so that 'we may evermore dwell in Him and He in us' (cf. *v*. 56).

6^{60-71}: The Conclusion of the Galilean Ministry

Jesus' words about eating His flesh and drinking His blood could not but sound most offensive in Jewish ears (see on 6^{53-6}). They prove to be too much even for some of Jesus' own disciples, who accordingly give up following Him. This leads to a declaration of loyalty on the part of the Twelve, expressed in Peter's confession. This is clearly the Johannine version of the confession at Caesarea Philippi which forms the great turning-point of the ministry of Jesus in the Synoptics (see *CLM* on Mk 8^{27-30}). Although Caesarea Philippi is not mentioned in *Jn*, the confession here, as in the Synoptics, is made by Peter; is Messianic in character; follows not long after the Feeding and at a time when the crowds of the earlier Galilean ministry have been separated from Jesus and the

Twelve; and constitutes the climax of Jesus' activity in Galilee. In *Mk*, after the confession of Peter the public ministry in Galilee is not resumed, and similarly in *Jn*, Jesus goes up to Jerusalem at the beginning of Chapter 7, and never returns to Galilee.

6⁶⁰. '*his disciples*' here indicates a larger group than the Twelve (cf. *vv.* 66-7).

'*a hard saying*' means not 'hard to understand' but 'hard to accept'; cf. *NEB*, 'more than we can stomach'.

6⁶¹. '*his disciples murmured*'. Thus they aligned themselves with the Jews (cf. 6⁴¹, ⁵²).

6⁶². Jesus' question here is in the Greek an incomplete sentence, and so is ambiguous. It could mean that '*to behold the Son of man ascending where he was before*' will be a greater cause of offence to them even than what they have just heard; or it could mean that the vision referred to will remove the offence which they now feel. It may be that the ambiguity is deliberate, in order to suggest both ideas. The ascension of the Son of Man to heaven, whence He came (cf. 3¹³⁻¹⁴), is understood in this Gospel as being by way of the Cross, and the Cross constitutes the chief 'stumbling-block' or 'offence' of the Christian gospel for the Jews (cf. 1 Cor 1²³). The point at which the offence is greatest, however, is the very point at which the offence can be removed, for the understanding of the true meaning of the Cross and Resurrection of Jesus is what makes sense of the whole gospel. The Jews, and the disciples of *v.* 60, have been offended by Jesus' references to eating His flesh and drinking His blood because they have completely misunderstood His meaning. Jesus may now be suggesting that His words can only be properly understood in the light of the Cross and Exaltation of the Son of Man. However that may be, in the following verse He warns them against the danger of taking His words in a crudely literal and material sense.

6⁶³. '*It is the spirit that quickeneth*', i.e. that 'gives life' (*NEB*). This is best understood as a reference to the Holy Spirit, who will be given to believers after the death and exaltation of Jesus (see 7³⁹). It is then, by the illumination and guidance of the Spirit, that men will really understand what eating the flesh and drinking the blood of Christ means, and will be able to do so. It seems probable that John was concerned about a crudely materialistic interpretation of the Eucharist prevalent in his own day, and that the teaching of the discourse in 6²²⁻⁵⁹ was intended to correct such tendencies. If this is so, the point is effectively summarized in the present verse.

'*the flesh profiteth nothing*'. Human resources are of no avail for the understanding of Jesus' words or for the obtaining of life.

'*the words that I have spoken unto you*', i.e. the words 'flesh' and 'blood' in 6⁵³⁻⁶.

'*are spirit, and are life*'. They are to be understood in a spiritual, not a material, sense; and so understood they can mean life for the believer.

6⁶⁴. '*there are some of you that believe not*', i.e. the disciples mentioned in *vv.* 60-1.

'*For Jesus knew . . .*'. A further indication of Jesus' super-natural knowledge of men (cf. 2²⁴⁻⁵, etc.). His knowledge extended even to the identity of His betrayer (see on *vv.* 70-1).

6⁶⁵. Cf. 6³⁷, ⁴⁴. The defecting disciples have revealed that their supposed faith in Jesus was not real faith, and this can only mean that they are not among those to whom the Father has given faith.

6⁶⁶⁻⁷. '*many of his disciples went back*', i.e. those of *vv.* 60-1. The sequel implies that these included everyone except the Twelve, whom Jesus proceeds to challenge with the question, '*Would ye also go away?*'

6⁶⁸⁻⁹. See p. 73. Having recognized Jesus as Messiah, and believed in Him, and heard His '*words of eternal life*' (cf. *v.* 63), the Twelve cannot think of abandoning Him; whatever the difficulties and dangers involved in following Him, they know that they can never now be satisfied apart from Him.

'*thou art the Holy One of God*'. There are variants to this title in some manuscripts, but all these represent attempts to harmonize the words of confession with those found in the Synoptic accounts. The title '*Holy One*' is equivalent in meaning to 'the Messiah' (cf. *CLM* on Mk 1²⁴).

6⁷⁰⁻¹. The Twelve have *chosen*, in response to Jesus' challenge, to follow Him, come what may. But Jesus now reminds them that the choice is not really theirs; it is He who has chosen them (see note (*f*) on p. 73). This fact, however, raises the perplexing problem of the presence, among the Twelve so chosen, of one who is to betray Him.

'*one of you is a devil*'. This term is used, no doubt, because Judas is to become the instrument of Satan (see 13[2, 27]). This verse, taken with *v.* 64, implies that Jesus knew from the beginning that Judas would betray Him. If this was so, we cannot hope ever to understand why He chose him, and kept him, as a member of the Twelve. But we may be sure that the fact that He did so does not make Judas' sin any the less heinous; indeed it is all the greater in view of his position of privilege and trust. This point is strikingly emphasized in the phrase '*being one of the twelve*'.

'*Judas the son of Simon Iscariot*'. Only John refers to Judas' father (cf. 13[2, 26]). 'Iscariot' means 'man of Kerioth', a place in the south of Judea.

(*a*) There are always those who are happy to go so far with Christ and His Church, but for whom the full gospel, with all its implications, is 'more than they can stomach' (*v.* 60). This passage has much to teach us about the nature of the 'offence' of the gospel, and about the way it can be overcome (see on *vv.* 62-3). (*b*) Verse 63 provides an effective warning against a too materialistic and mechanical view of the sacraments. (*c*) Jesus' question to the Twelve in *v.* 67 reminds us that the disciples He looks for are those who, having counted the cost, are aware of the consequences of following Him, and are determined to go through with it (or rather, with *Him*). And Peter's reply reminds us that the only disciples who will fulfil these requirements are those who have come to know who Jesus is and to realize that His words are the words of eternal life. Those who possess such an experience know that life without Christ would be unthinkable; really to have known the company of Jesus means that one can never be satisfied in any other company. (*d*) The terrible defection of Judas (and to a lesser degree that of the 'fair-weather disciples' of *v.* 66) contains a solemn warning. No member of the Church can take it for granted that because he is a member he cannot fall. The greatest danger to the Church may indeed come from the treachery of those within, rather than from the attacks of those outside; the anvil that has worn out the hammers may be corroded by rust from within. The greater the privileges we enjoy, the greater the fall that is possible for us, and the greater the harm that we can do.

Chapter 7

7^{1-13}: Jesus' Departure to Jerusalem

JESUS finally leaves Galilee for Jerusalem, and the whole of the rest of *Jn* (to the end of Chapter **20**) is located in Judea and the South (see p. 74 for comparison with *Mk*).

7^1. *'because the Jews sought to kill him'*. Cf. 5^{18}. This does not mean that Jesus is afraid of the Jews, but simply that the time is not ripe for Him to come into open conflict with His enemies (see *v.* 6).

7^2. When eventually Jesus does go up to the capital, it is on the occasion of one of the great annual festivals (see on 5^1).

'the feast of tabernacles' was celebrated in the autumn and lasted for seven days, with a further closing ceremony, in post-exilic times, on the eighth day (see on *v.* 37). In its origins it was the Feast of Ingathering or 'Harvest Festival' (see Ex 23^{16}), but later it came to be associated with the commemoration of the settlement of Israel in the promised land (see Lev 23^{33-43}, Deut 16^{13-15}). Jews from all districts crowded to Jerusalem to celebrate the festival, and dwelt in tents within the city throughout the period (see Lev 23^{43}). Tabernacles was the most popular of Jewish festivals and was often called simply 'the Feast' (hence the emphatic way in which it is referred to in this verse).

7^3. *'His brethren'*. See on 2^{12}. They advise Him to take advantage of the vast congregation assembled in Jerusalem for the festival by performing miracles there and so recovering His lost popularity.

'thy disciples' here may well refer to those who have forsaken Jesus (see 6^{66}).

7^4. The brothers offer what, from the standpoint of worldly wisdom, is good advice: there can be no success without publicity cf. *NEB*).

7⁵. The brothers' advice to Jesus merely reveals their unbelief. This attitude on their part appears also in the Synoptics, but there it is expressed rather differently (see *CLM* on Mk 3²¹, ³¹⁻⁵). It may be that *Mk* and *Jn* contain different elements of the truth about the attitude of Jesus' family to His mission, and that it was on these lines: 'We think it is nothing short of madness and that it would be better for you to give it up. But if you are determined to carry on with it, don't waste your time in a backwater like Galilee; go to Jerusalem and show yourself to the multitudes assembled there at festival-time'.

7⁶⁻⁸. '*My time is not yet come*'. This is the same idea as appeared in 2⁴. Jesus' '*time*' or 'hour' is, for John, the time of His glorifying through death and resurrection. In this connection it is significant that the word translated '*go up*' in *v.* 8 is the same verb as is used in 3¹³ and 6⁶² to describe the exaltation of the Son of Man. Thus, underlying the superficial literal meaning of Jesus' words here is a deeper theological meaning—namely, that the present festival is not to be the occasion of His exaltation. Jesus bids His brothers go up to this festival, since they, unlike Him, are not tied to any preordained programme: 'any time is right for you' (*v.* 6, *NEB*).

'*The world*'. See on 1⁹⁻¹³. The brothers are not exposed to the world's hatred, since they accept its standards (cf. *v.* 4). It hates Jesus, however, 'for exposing the wickedness of its ways' (*NEB*, *v.* 7; cf. 3¹⁹⁻²¹). He could never win the world by the method suggested by His brothers in *vv.* 3-4, because His message is one that can only antagonize the world. The only way He can really show Himself to the world (*v.* 4) is by being lifted up on the Cross—and that can only happen when His appointed '*time*' arrives.

'*I go not up yet*'. The original reading is undoubtedly that of *RVm*, omitting '*yet*' (cf. *NEB*). The reading of *RV* arose in an attempt to remove the apparent contradiction with *v.* 10. The contradiction, however, is only superficial; what Jesus refused to do was to go up to the festival in the manner, and for the purpose, suggested by His brothers.

7¹⁰. '*not publicly, but as it were in secret*'. This is reminiscent of Mk 9³⁰.

7¹¹⁻¹³. Meanwhile the Jews at Jerusalem were looking out for Jesus—no doubt with evil intent (cf. *v.* 1). There was much speculation about Him among the festival crowds; not unnaturally, opinions about Him differed, but none dared to voice their opinions too publicly, *'for fear of the Jews'*.

(*a*) The 'worldly' advice offered by Jesus' brothers has its counterpart in the ever-present temptation with which the Church is faced—to seek to win the world by the use of the world's methods. The irreconcilable attitudes of 'the world' (in the Johannine sense) and Christ are well summed up in *v.* 7. (*b*) Verse 12 illustrates the controversy that has always raged among men about the Person of Jesus Christ. The two opinions expressed in this verse still have their supporters: on the one hand there is the all too prevalent and lamentably inadequate estimate of Jesus as '*a good man*'; and on the other hand the view that Christianity leads people astray from the realities of life—e.g. the claim that Christianity is the opiate of the people.

7¹⁴⁻⁵²: Conflict during the Feast of Tabernacles

About half-way through the festival week (see on *v.* 2) Jesus begins to teach in the Temple. His teaching involves Him in controversy with the Jews, the record of which continues to the end of Chapter **8.** In these two chapters John seems to have gathered together the bulk of the tradition he possessed concerning the debates between Jesus and the ecclesiastical authorities in Jerusalem, and to have set the whole loosely in the context of the Feast of Tabernacles. There is a natural break at **7⁵²,** and the record of the debates is resumed at **8¹²** (the paragraph **7⁵³–8¹¹,** as we shall see, is not part of the original text). The present section may be divided into four parts: (*i*) **7¹⁴⁻²⁴,** Moses and Christ; (*ii*) **7²⁵⁻³⁶,** The Origin and Destination of Jesus; (*iii*) **7³⁷⁻⁴⁴,** Conflicting Opinions about Christ; (*iv*) **7⁴⁵⁻⁵²,** Failure of the attempt to arrest Jesus. Many commentators regard *vv.* 15-24 as the conclusion of the discourse in 5¹⁹⁻⁴⁷; cf. the arrangement in Moffatt's translation and in W. Temple's *Readings in St John's Gospel*. This theory has much plausibility (cf. the references to Moses with 5⁴⁵⁻⁷, and 7²³ with 5¹⁻⁹), but the paragraph is not out of place in its present position, and in the absence of any proof that the original order of the Gospel was disturbed (see Introduction, p. 4) it is wiser to follow the traditional arrangement.

7[15]. '*The Jews therefore marvelled*'. They cannot understand how anyone not trained in the Rabbinical schools could reveal such learning (cf. *NEB*).

7[16-18]. Jesus replies, in effect, that He has been trained in a better school than that of any Rabbi; He has been to school with His Father, and the teaching He imparts is not His own but the Father's. We see here the same sense of complete dependence on the Father as characterizes the discourse in **5**[19-47]. The Rabbis shrank from teaching on their own authority, taking care always to quote the opinions of eminent teachers whom they regarded as their 'authorities' (see *CLM* on Mk 1[22] and *AMW* on Mt 7[29]). Jesus implies here that He too has His authority, namely God, so that He does not speak 'on my own authority' (*RSV*). In the face of such a claim, the question would inevitably arise in Jewish minds: How can we know that his teaching has such divine authority? The answer given in *v.* 17 is that the only way to prove the truth of Jesus' teaching is by obedience to God's will—and that means believing in Him whom God sent (cf. **6**[29]). It is only by taking the venture of faith in Christ, and facing life with Him, that we can attain to intellectual certainty of the truth of His claims. In St Augustine's words, one must 'believe in order to understand'. Just as Jesus does not teach on His own authority, so neither does He seek honour for Himself, but rather for His Father, and this is a guarantee of His sincerity (*v.* 18, see *NEB*).

7[19]. '*Did not Moses give you the law*'. For the Jew, to do God's will meant to obey the law of Moses, so it is natural for Jesus, after His statement in *v.* 17, to refer to the law. He accuses the Jews of breaking it; their desire to kill Him is sufficient proof of their guilt in this respect. Their opposition to Jesus proves how little the Jews really understand of the law of Moses, for He is the fulfilment of all that Moses wrote (cf. **5**[46]).

7[20]. '*Thou hast a devil*' here means madness. The crowd, presumably unaware of the intentions of the Jewish leaders (cf. *v.* 1), think Jesus is suffering from some kind of persecution-mania.

7[21-4]. Jesus ignores the crowd's opinion and proceeds to refer to the '*one work*' of His which has caused such general astonishment and which has led the Jews to seek His life—His healing of the cripple on the sabbath (5^{1-18}). He further justifies that action (cf. 5^{17}) by the argument that the Jews themselves, in certain circumstances, perform the rite of circumcision on the sabbath. Circumcision concerns only one of the two hundred and forty-eight members which, according to Jewish ideas, constituted the human body. If then it is right to perform this act on the sabbath, how can it be wrong to restore health to the whole of a man's body? Some Jewish Rabbis had in fact used this argument to justify healings on the sabbath in cases where life was in danger, but Jesus carries it further by applying it to cases (like that of 5^{1-18}) where life is not in danger. By giving the law of circumcision preference over that of the sabbath the Jews recognized the principle that God's purpose to restore and redeem men is of greater importance than sabbath-observance as such. But circumcision merely points forward to the full salvation which Jesus has now brought to men. By failing to recognize this, the Jews reveal how superficial their judgement is. Regarded superficially, the healing at Bethesda was merely a matter of sabbath-breaking, but Jesus in *v.* 24 appeals to His hearers to look beneath the surface and to perceive its real significance.

7^{25-7}. Some of the people of Jerusalem (as distinct from the festival crowd from far and wide, to whom *v.* 20 referred) are mystified because Jesus, whom they know the authorities are wanting to put to death, is being allowed to teach, unmolested, in the Temple. Perhaps the authorities have changed their minds and decided that Jesus, after all, is the Messiah! But that is impossible, for even they themselves, the common people, know that He cannot be the Messiah, for the simple reason that His place of origin is well-known (cf. 6^{42}). Many Jews believed that the Messiah would appear suddenly, without anyone knowing where he came from. Others held a different view (see on *vv.* 40-4).

7^{28-9}. Jesus perceives how they are reasoning, and replies. No doubt they are able to trace His earthly origin, but that does not mean that they can explain His real origin. One must go further back than the home at Nazareth, and further back than the manger at Bethlehem, to discover the origin of Jesus. Behind Him stands the One who sent Him, the Father (cf.

5^{19-47}). The Father, though unseen, is a Real Person (cf. *NEB*, 'the One who truly is'), but the Jews do not know Him, and that is why they fail to recognize Jesus' true origin as being in Him. If they had really known the Father they would not have rejected the Son. Jesus, on the other hand, does know the Father, and knows that He has come from Him.

7^{30}. To suggest to Jews that they did not know God could not but provoke resentment and hostility. The Jerusalemites (of *v.* 25) now attempt to do what the authorities have sought to do—to arrest Jesus. But their attempt fails because His '*hour*' (see on 2^4 and 7^{6-8}) has not yet arrived. The time for Jesus' glorifying through death and resurrection has been appointed in the divine counsels, and no attempt to arrest Him can succeed until the appointed time arrives.

7^{31}. '*many believed on him*'—as Messiah. The question that follows shows that their faith is based on His performance of so many miracles. On the inadequacy of such faith, cf. 1^{50}, 2^{23-4}, 4^{48}.

7^{32}. '*The Pharisees*' were the popular religious leaders, associated with the synagogues and in close touch with the people. It is they, no doubt, who take the initiative in this move to arrest Jesus, acting in consort with '*the chief priests*', i.e. members of the leading priestly families, most of whom would be Sadducees (see *CLM* on Mk 12^{18}). The Pharisees and Sadducees together represent virtually the whole Sanhedrin (see on 3^1). Normally in opposition to one another, these two parties agree and co-operate in their antagonism to Jesus. '*officers*', i.e. 'temple police' (*NEB*).

7^{33-4}. '*Yet a little while am I with you*'. Jesus is undeterred by the decision to arrest Him, knowing that His 'hour' (*v.*30) has not yet come.

'*I go unto him that sent me*'. When the 'hour' does come, it will mean His return to the Father. Then they will look for Him in vain, unable to follow Him.

7^{35-6}. The Jews can no more understand Jesus' reference to His impending departure than they could the reference to His origin in *vv.* 28-9. Interpreting His words over-literally, they wonder whether He intends to leave Palestine and go to '*the Dispersion among the Greeks*' (i.e. those parts of the Hellenistic world where Jews of the Dispersion lived), to teach not only the dispersed Jews but '*the Greeks*' (i.e. Gentiles) also. Perhaps this (they may have argued) would be a way of escaping the clutches of the Jews in Palestine who wished to kill Him. They are hardly satisfied, however, with this interpretation, and the meaning of Jesus' words remains a puzzle to them (*v.* 36). We have here an outstanding example of the irony which is a characteristic feature of the Fourth Gospel. Beneath the surface meaning of the Jews' words, John sees a deeper meaning than that intended. Unconsciously they have made a true prophecy; Jesus will indeed go out to the Gentile world and teach the Gentiles. He will do so in and through the Church which is His Body. But far from going there to escape the clutches of the enemies who seek to kill Him, He will go rather as a direct and inevitable result of His having willingly submitted, in obedience to His Father, to being put to death by those enemies.

7[37-8]. '*the last day, the great day of the feast*' refers either to the seventh or the eighth day (see on **7**[2]); it hardly matters which.

'*Jesus stood and cried*'. This suggests a more public utterance than the teaching which He has been imparting in the Temple (for which He would probably *sit*, in the manner of the Rabbis). Thus the invitation contained in His pronouncement is a general one to all who wish to hear.

'*If any man thirst . . .*'. Part of the Tabernacles ceremonial consisted of the drawing by a priest of water in a golden vessel from the pool of Siloam (see on **9**[7]), and the carrying of it up to the Temple, where it was poured upon the altar as a libation to God. The rite was accompanied by the joyous singing or recitation of words like those of Isa 12[3]. The form of Jesus' invitation is prompted, no doubt, by this ceremony.

The punctuation of *vv.* 37-8 is uncertain, so that Jesus' words can be understood in two different ways. If the *RV* reading is followed, the words '*his belly*' must refer to the believer, and the meaning is that the living water which he has received from Christ (cf. **4**[14]) flows out of him so as to reach others also. The alternative punctuation is adopted by *NEB*: ' "If anyone is thirsty let him come to me; whoever believes in me, let him drink." As Scripture says, "Streams of living water shall flow out from within him".' Here the words 'from within him' could refer either to the believer or to Christ Himself, but the latter would be the more likely interpretation; i.e. the living water flows constantly out of Christ and so becomes available for those who are willing to receive it. The reference to scripture does not introduce any strict quotation from the OT, and may merely indicate generally that the idea expressed is thoroughly rooted in the OT. Perhaps, however, Zech 14[8] is most particularly in view, for this chapter is the prophetic lesson for the Feast of Tabernacles, and Jerusalem (from which living waters go out in Zech 14[8]) is often described in rabbinic thought as 'the navel of the earth'—which might explain the somewhat crude expression *'out of his belly'*.

7[39]. John explains in a parenthesis that the *'living water'* of which Jesus has spoken means the Holy Spirit, who *'was not yet given'* (i.e. during the period of Jesus' incarnate ministry). The Holy Spirit, it is true, was active before Pentecost (cf. 1[32]), but He was not given as a source of new, divine life to Christian believers until after Jesus had been glorified through death and resurrection. This teaching about the Spirit is characteristic of *Jn* (cf. 14[16], 16[7], 20[22]).

7[40-4]. Different groups of hearers react differently to Jesus' great pronouncement. Some conclude that He is *'the prophet'*, which here seems to mean a forerunner of the Messiah rather than the Messiah himself (see on 1[21] and 6[14]). Others go further and acclaim Jesus as the Messiah. Others again insist that this cannot be so, since Jesus is a Galilean, whereas scripture (the reference is to Mic 5[2]) teaches plainly that the Messiah must be of Davidic descent and be born at Bethlehem (these critics could hardly be expected to know the traditions which later came to be embodied in Mt 1-2 and Lk 1-2). It is obvious that there was no unanimity among the Jews concerning the origin of the Messiah; some believed that his origin would be wrapped in mystery (see on *v.* 27), while others held that he would come from Bethlehem. Thus Jesus causes a 'split among the people' (*v.* 43, *NEB*). Some were intent on arresting Him, but were unable to do so (see on *v.* 30).

7[45-6]. Accordingly, the temple police return to the authorities without having fulfilled their commission (see 7[32]), and being called to account they can only reply, '*Never man so spake*'. This suggests that they had felt, in listening to Jesus' teaching, that they were listening to One who was more than a mere man, and that they were so overcome with awe as to be unable to lay hands upon Him (cf. **18⁶**).

7⁴⁷⁻⁹. The Pharisees mock the officers for allowing themselves to be misled by Jesus, just as the common mob have been misled into believing in Him (cf. *vv.* 31, 41). They themselves, and the rulers generally, know better! The Pharisees despised the common 'people of the land' who were not expert in all the complicated precepts of the law, and regarded them as under a curse. The implication is that the officers should have followed the example of their masters (the Sanhedrin) rather than that of the ignorant and accursed rabble.

7⁵⁰⁻². '*Nicodemus*'. See on **3¹⁻²¹**. His words here reveal that his attitude is more open-minded than that of the Sanhedrin generally. He does not seek to defend Jesus' standpoint, but he does defend His right, like that of every other man under Jewish law (cf. Deut 1¹⁶), to a fair hearing before being condemned by the Sanhedrin. Nicodemus attracts the scorn of his fellow-councillors, whose words reveal that they tended to despise Galileans and to regard it as unthinkable that any prophet should come from Galilee.

'*Search*'. The word is the same as that used in **5³⁹**, and is probably to be understood in the semi-technical sense of 'study the scriptures' (*NEB*). Thus the Sanhedrin claims that the scriptures prove that no prophet could arise from Galilee. The claim is not entirely justified, since 2 Kings 14²⁵ speaks of the prophet Jonah as coming from Gath-hepher, a village in Galilee. The rulers themselves were apparently not so sure of their facts as they ought to be!

(*a*) The formal education of school and college is never to be despised—and not least in the case of Christian teachers and preachers. Nevertheless, in the long run, the question 'What school and college did he go to?' is less important than the question 'Has he learned his message by direct contact with God?' (cf. Acts 4¹³, where Peter and John, though lacking official education, had been to school with Jesus). (*b*) Verse 17 underlines a truth of the utmost significance for preaching. It is vain and foolish to postpone faith in Christ until all our intellectual problems are solved, for it is only by taking the venture of faith, by committing ourselves to Him in trust and obedience, that we shall attain certainty as to the truth of His teaching. (*c*) The danger of making superficial judgements in such matters as Sunday observance is illustrated by *vv.* 21-4. (*d*) There is always a tendency for men to pay more attention to a teacher who appears suddenly, out of obscure or mysterious origins, than to one who is familiar and whose earthly origins are known (cf. 4[44]). Witness the attraction of new and unorthodox sects. What matters is not the familiarity or otherwise of a teacher's earthly origins, but whether he is truly sent from God; and those who truly know God will recognize those who are genuinely sent from Him. (*e*) It is often true that rival groups are prepared to forget their differences temporarily, as do the Pharisees and Sadducees in *v.* 32 (cf. Lk 23[12]), in order to achieve an end desired by each. The sad thing is that they are usually readier to do this in pursuit of selfish and unworthy ends than in seeking good ends; witness the reluctance of ecclesiastical groupings to co-operate in pursuit of the supreme end which they all profess to seek. (*f*) The 'unconscious prophecy' of *v.* 35 is suggestive. Jesus often fulfils men's expectations in ways very different from those envisaged by them. (*g*) If the *RV* reading is adopted in *vv.* 37-38, the words suggest that he who really drinks of the water of life in Christ becomes a channel through which that water may reach others in turn. If the alternative reading is followed, the passage points to Christ as the never-failing source of eternal life (cf. 4[14]). (*h*) Verse 39 sums up the truth that there can be no Pentecost without Calvary; this leads us to the very heart of the gospel . (*i*) Men cannot escape, in the presence of Jesus and in hearing His words, the sense of awe which comes from a recognition of His unique authority (*v.* 46; cf. comment on *vv.* 16-18). (*j*) Verses 48-9 warn us of the ease with which religious leaders can adopt a 'superior' and contemptuous attitude towards the ordinary people who look to them for guidance.

Chapter 8

7⁵³–8¹¹: The Woman Taken in Adultery

THIS paragraph is no part of the original text of *Jn* (see *RVm*). Modern English versions quite properly relegate it to the margin (*RSV*) or to the end of the Gospel (*NEB*); for the sake of convenience, however, we deal with it in this commentary in its traditional and familiar position. The story is probably a fragment of genuinely historical tradition about Jesus which failed to be included in any of the canonical Gospels as originally written, but which nevertheless was preserved in the Church until, eventually, the conviction grew that it was a story too valuable to lose. This led to its insertion between 7⁵² and 8¹² (though some manuscripts place it elsewhere, see *NEBm*)—probably because it was felt to illustrate Jesus' words in 8¹⁵.

7⁵³–8². The historical setting of the incident is probably the period of Jesus' ministry in Jerusalem as described in Mk 11 and Lk 21 (cf. 8² with Lk 21³⁸; some witnesses place the paragraph after the latter verse).

8³⁻⁴. '*taken in adultery, in the very act*'. This is emphasized because the fact of adultery had to be proved by eye-witnesses before punishment could be inflicted (cf. Deut 19¹⁵).

8⁵. '*in the law Moses commanded*'. See Deut 22²²⁻⁴.

8⁶. '*tempting him . . . to accuse him*'. Their chief reason for bringing the woman to Jesus was not the desire to see her punished in accordance with the law (it is unlikely that the death-penalty for adultery was frequently enforced), but rather to put Jesus to the test (cf. Mk 10², 12¹³), 'hoping to frame a charge against him' (*NEB*). With callous cruelty they were prepared to 'use' the unfortunate woman to further their own

G

purpose. Knowing Jesus' compassionate attitude towards sinners, they hoped that their challenge would provoke Him to contradict the Mosaic law in public.

'*Jesus . . . wrote on the ground*'. There has been much speculation as to why Jesus acted in this way, and what He wrote. Some interpret it as a refusal to give judgement, others as a way of hiding His confusion, others as an ironical pretending to give judgement. The traditional theory is that He wrote a list of the accusers' names and of the particular sins of each. More satisfactory than any of these is the suggestion recently made that Jesus wrote in the dust the words of Ex 23[1b]. This presupposes that the case is one in which the accused woman's husband has conspired with witnesses who have spied upon her in the act of adultery; by allowing her to proceed in her sinful act without giving her a warning the witnesses have condoned the adultery and incurred guilt themselves. There are thus doubts as to the competence of the witnesses, and to convict and execute the woman on the evidence of such witnesses would be to pervert justice. By writing Ex 23[1b], Jesus points the accusers to a section of the law which warns them of this danger.

8[7]. The accusers press for a more explicit judgement from Jesus, and He replies in words which imply that if the witnesses are indeed '*without sin*' (see previous note) and so competent, the stoning may commence (Deut 17[7] lays down that the witnesses must take the initiative in the stoning).

8[8-9]. According to the theory just outlined, when Jesus stooped to write a second time on the ground, He wrote the words of Ex 23[7a], thus rounding off His 'opinion'. This has the effect of causing the accusers to retire one by one, in order of seniority, leaving the woman alone with Jesus.

8[10]. '*Woman*'. He uses the same tender mode of address as in 2[4] and 19[26].

8[11]. '*Neither do I condemn thee*'. This does not mean that Jesus in any way condones her sin, but that His desire is not to condemn but to save her from her sin (cf. 3[17], 8[15]). By dismissing her with the injunction to '*sin no more*' (cf. 5[14]), He gives her the admonition which should have been provided by her husband and the witnesses who had maliciously conspired to secure her condemnation (see on *v.* 6).

(*a*) The chief interest of this story for the preacher lies in the light it throws upon Jesus' attitude towards sin and its punishment. His concern is not so much the exacting of punishment for past sins, but the restoration of the sinner so as to ensure that he does not fall a victim to future temptations. Such too must be the constant concern of the Church. (*b*) The danger of such an attitude of compassion for the sinner is that it may encourage him to persist in his sin (it was probably the fear lest Jesus' words in *v.* 11 might be misunderstood as condoning adultery that kept the story out of the Gospels as originally written). This danger, however, is avoided by the injunction to '*sin no more*'. It is possible to hate the sin while loving the sinner. (*c*) The story is a classic rebuke of Pharisaic self-righteous censoriousness—an attitude into which religious people are all too prone to fall. We need to be reminded constantly that not we, but God is the Judge of our fellows—and our Judge too.

8¹²⁻⁵⁹: Further Conflict during the Feast of Tabernacles

We return now to the record of Jesus' controversy with the Jews in Jerusalem during the Festival. This section falls into three parts: (*i*) 8¹²⁻²⁰, The Validity of Jesus' Self-testimony; (*ii*) 8²¹⁻³⁰, The Identity of Jesus; (*iii*) 8³¹⁻⁵⁹, The Son who makes men free.

8¹². '*I am the light of the world*'. This is the second of the seven great '*I am*' sayings, the form of which implies a claim to divine attributes (see on 6³⁵). The idea of light as a divine attribute is commonplace in Greek religion. In the OT also light is a prominent theme; light was the first thing God created (Gen 1³), the law is described as light (Ps 119¹⁰⁵, Prov 6²³), and the Psalmist speaks of God as his light and salvation (Ps 27¹). In Isa 42⁶, 49⁶, the Servant of the Lord is described as 'a light to the Gentiles', and this prophecy is regarded in Lk 2³² as being fulfilled in Christ (cf. Mt 4¹⁶ which speaks of Jesus as fulfilling the prophecy of Isa 9¹⁻²). The idea of Christ as Light—shining amidst the darkness of the world and conquering it—is central in *Jn*; we have already met it in 1⁴⁻⁵, ⁹ and 3¹⁹⁻²¹, and it will be further developed in Chapters 9 and 12. Here the idea is not developed, except for the point that he who follows Jesus (i.e. believes in and obeys Him) '*shall not walk in the darkness, but shall have the light of life*' (for the connection between light and life cf. 1⁴). By faith in Christ a man is delivered out of darkness into light (cf. Eph 5⁸, 1 Pet 2⁹) and the light gives him new life. The idea of light, like that of water (see on 7³⁷⁻⁸), was specially associated with Tabernacles. On the first day the great golden candlesticks that stood in the Court of the Women in the Temple were lit, and they remained alight throughout the festival. The light was so bright, according to tradition, that it lit up every courtyard in Jerusalem. This symbolism of light, no doubt, was what prompted Jesus at this time to declare Himself to be '*the light of the world*'.

8¹³⁻¹⁴. The Pharisees object that Jesus' words, being self-testimony, cannot be accepted as true. At 5³¹ Jesus admitted, for the moment, the force of this objection. Here, however, He claims that His self-testimony *is* true—because He knows, as they do not, where He comes from and where He is going. A mere man cannot bear witness to himself in such a way as to compel belief, because he does not know enough about himself, his origin and his destiny. Jesus, however, is not open to this criticism. The Jews were completely mistaken in their views about Him (cf. 7²⁸⁻⁹, ³⁴⁻⁵), and in their ignorance they could not possibly form a true judgement about His Person and significance.

8¹⁵⁻¹⁶. '*after the flesh*', i.e. 'by worldly standards' (*NEB*).
'*I judge no man*', i.e. in the way the Pharisees do (see on 7⁵³–8¹¹). The sense in which Jesus does judge is that of 3¹⁷⁻²¹ (cf. 9³⁹), but this judgement of His is true, because it is not His alone but the Father's also.

8¹⁷⁻¹⁸. '*in your law*'. The reference is to Deut 19¹⁵. This requirement of Jewish law is fulfilled in that the Father's witness substantiates Jesus' own (cf. 5³¹⁻⁴⁰).

8¹⁹. The Pharisees' question reveals how completely they misunderstand Jesus' reference to His Father. They do not realize that only Jesus Himself can make the Father known to men (see 1¹⁸), so that the Father can only be known by those who first know Jesus. This is the point of Jesus' reply.

8²⁰. '*in the treasury*', i.e. part of the Court of the Women,
where chests were placed for the reception of offerings (see
CLM on Mk 12⁴¹⁻⁴). It was in this Court that the candlesticks
were lit (see on *v.* 12). Near the treasury too was the meeting-
place of the Sanhedrin; it was not in a secret corner that Jesus
declared Himself as the light of the world, but in the public
eye. Yet He was not arrested, for the reason noted at 7³⁰.

8²¹. Here begins another debate between Jesus and His
opponents on the subject of His Person and destiny. Jesus
begins by referring again (as in 7³³⁻⁴) to His approaching death.
They will not be able to find Him because they cannot follow
Him where He is going. On the contrary they will die in their
sin (cf. *v.* 24).

8²². As in 7³⁵⁻⁶ the Jews misunderstand Jesus' words. They
think He is contemplating suicide. There may be here a touch
of the same irony as appeared at 7³⁵⁻⁶; John may regard the
words of the Jews as having been fulfilled (in a very different
sense from that intended by them) in that Jesus voluntarily
laid down His life (cf. 10¹⁸).

8²³⁻⁴. Jesus explains why the Jews cannot follow Him, and
why they will die in their sins (cf. *v.* 21). It is because He and
they belong to two completely different worlds, the heavenly
and the earthly. He has come '*from above*' (cf. 3¹³, 6³³, 7²⁸⁻⁹)
and is to return there (cf. 6⁶²). Men belong to this world, and
can only rise from it to the heavenly world by believing in
Christ so as to be 'born from above' (cf. 3³) and to inherit
eternal life (cf. 3¹⁶). To refuse to believe in Christ is to be
condemned to die in one's sins (cf. 'to perish' in 3¹⁶). This
unbelief is the basic and all-inclusive sin of the Jews, from
which all individual sins stem (this distinction between 'sin'
and 'sins' is suggested by the use of the singular noun in *v.* 21
and the plural in *v.* 24). The unbelief is defined by Jesus as
refusal to believe '*that I am he*'. This is the absolute use of the
phrase which plays so important a part in the Johannine
teaching on the Person of Christ (see on 6³⁵). As in 6³⁵ and
8¹² the phrase, on Jesus' lips, implies a claim to divinity.

8²⁵. '*Who art thou?*' The Jews are clearly puzzled by Jesus'
words. Jesus' reply to their question is ambiguous. According

to one possible interpretation, He does not reply directly, but expresses His disappointment with them in a further question (see *RVm, NEB*). One can readily understand such a feeling on Jesus' part (cf. Mk 9¹⁹), but on the whole the alternative interpretation is to be preferred. According to this, Jesus answers the question directly by explaining that He is 'What I have told you all along' (*NEBm, RV, RSV*). Yet even this interpretation is not entirely satisfactory, and it would seem better (with C. K. Barrett and R. H. Lightfoot) to connect the words *'from the beginning'*, not with the verb *'I have spoken'* but with the implied 'I am': '(I am) from the beginning what I tell you' (namely 'I am', the divine name). This fits the context of 8²⁴⁻⁶ more satisfactorily than any other interpretation, and is consistent with the teaching of 1¹⁻². Jesus is claiming to share the eternal existence of God.

8²⁶. He adds that He has much to say about His opponents— and that by way of judgement. What He will say, however, will be what He has learned from His Father (cf. 5³⁰, 8¹⁶), and will be true, because 'he who sent me speaks the truth' (*NEB*).

8²⁷. A parenthetic comment by John. For their lack of perception, cf. *v.* 19.

8²⁸. *'lifted up the Son of man'*. Cf. 3¹⁴. Jesus tells them that later, after they have crucified Him, they will come to understand the truth about His Person ('*I am he*', cf. *v.* 24), and about His relation to the Father (a relation of obedient submission, cf. 5¹⁹⁻³⁰).

8²⁹. Jesus adds that His constant obedience to His Father means that the Father is constantly with Him. The Word is 'with God' (1¹⁻²) during His incarnate life no less than before and after.

8³⁰. *'many believed on him'*. The next paragraph, however, will reveal how imperfect and inadequate their faith is.

8³¹. *'those Jews which had believed him'*. This probably means those mentioned in *v.* 30. The rest of the chapter is concerned with a discussion between Jesus and these 'believers'.
     'abide in my word'. This means not just to accept His

message (which they have done) but to make it the foundation and governing principle of their whole life.

8³². '*ye shall know the truth*'. On '*truth*' in *Jn* see on **1¹⁴**. Here the truth about the Person of Christ seems to be particularly in mind (cf. *v*. 28), but the knowledge of this truth is more than an intellectual grasp of facts—it is a direct knowledge of Christ in a personal relationship with Him. To know the truth for the Christian is to know Christ, for He is 'the truth' (cf. **14⁶**).

'*the truth shall make you free*'. The freedom envisaged here is freedom from the bondage of sin (cf. *v*. 34). In this section the salvation offered by Christ to men is represented in terms of release from captivity.

8³³. The Jews misunderstand the reference to freedom and protest that they need no release from any captivity; they have never been in slavery. Clearly they are not thinking in terms of political freedom, for the nation had often been deprived of that. It is simply that they know themselves to be God's chosen People, heirs of the promise made to Abraham (Gen 12²⁻³)—his heirs through Isaac, 'the son of the freewoman' (see Gal 4²²⁻³¹). As such they claim never to have lost their inner freedom of soul.

8³⁴. Jesus explains that what He has in mind is release from the spiritual bondage of sin. The fact that a man commits sin proves that he is subject to sin's tyrannical power; and by every sin that he does commit he falls more deeply under that power.

8³⁵⁻⁶. This condition of slavery to sin is underlined by comparison with the privilege of sonship. The difference in status between Ishmael and Isaac (cf. Gen 21⁹⁻¹⁰) is no doubt in mind. The '*bondservant*' (Ishmael, son of the slave-woman) was not allowed to stay '*in the house for ever*', as was the son (Isaac, the true 'seed of Abraham', cf. Gen 21¹²). So also the Jews, being slaves by nature (i.e. slaves to sin) will not be reckoned amongst God's true family. That privilege belongs by right only to '*the son*' (note that in *Jn* the word 'son' in relation to God is used only of Jesus, cf. **1¹²**). Christ Himself is thus the true 'seed of Abraham' (cf. Gal 3¹⁶), and He alone posessess by right the freedom which belongs to God's family. But the

Son is able to set free the slaves and so give them a share in His own freedom. The Jews supposed that they were free by reason of their physical descent from Abraham (*v.* 33), and Jesus had to show them that such freedom was illusory (*v.* 34). The only real freedom is that which the Son possesses and which He is able to impart to all who become His true disciples by believing in Him and abiding in His word (*vv.* 31-2). This way of describing salvation in Christ in terms of freedom is reminiscent of Paul's treatment of the same theme in Rom 8$^{15-23}$ and Gal 4^{21}-5^1 (in the latter passage he refers explicitly to the story of Isaac and Ishmael).

8^{37}. Jesus takes up the Jews' claim to be '*Abraham's seed*'. He admits that as far as physical lineage goes this is true enough, but points out that their actions reveal that they are not true children of Abraham, for true sonship consists not in physical descent but in moral and spiritual resemblance (cf. *v.* 39). In seeking to kill Jesus, who has brought them an authentic revelation from God (*vv.* 38a, 40), they are showing an attitude towards divine truth exactly opposite to that shown by Abraham (*v.* 40b). And the reason why they show such an attitude is that the word of Jesus '*hath not free course*' in them. The verb here is ambiguous and can mean either 'finds no place' (*RSV*, cf. *RVm*) or 'makes no headway' (*NEB*). In any case, what is meant is that the Jews refuse to allow Jesus' message to take control of their lives (cf. *v.* 31).

8^{38}. '*from your father*', i.e. the devil (cf. *v.* 44).

8$^{39-40}$. See above on *v.* 37. The text of *v.* 39 is uncertain, but the *RV* reading is probably correct (see, however, *RVm* and *NEBm*).

8^{41}. '*We were not born of fornication*'. Having failed to substantiate their claim to be Abraham's children, the Jews try to turn the argument against Jesus in a new and personal way. Their words seem to imply a sneering suggestion that Jesus' birth was illegitimate; this kind of unpleasant aspersion was certainly cast against the Church in later days by Jews as a counterblast to the Christian claim regarding the Virgin Birth. The Jews now claim to be children, not of Abraham, but of 'God alone' (*NEB*).

8⁴². Jesus denies this claim too (cf. *v.* 39), still on the grounds that true children are those who reproduce in themselves their father's character. It would be impossible for true children of God to take such an attitude as the Jews have taken towards the Son who has come from God (for the stress on Jesus' divine origin, cf. 7²⁸).

8⁴³. '*my speech . . . my word*'. There is a deliberate contrast between the two terms. They cannot make sense of Jesus' 'language' because they have failed to accept and obey (which is what '*hear*' means in this context) the 'revelation' which He has brought (see *NEB*, and cf. *vv.* 31, 37).

8⁴⁴. '*your father the devil*' makes explicit what was implicit in *vv.* 38 and 41. They are the devil's children because they emulate his character and works. The devil's '*lusts*', or desires, are the destruction of the life created by God and the denial of the truth revealed by God; his murderous character finds expression in the Jews' desire to kill Jesus, and his falsehood in their rejection of His word. This teaching on the devil and his children is echoed in 1 Jn 3⁸⁻¹⁵ (see *GPL* thereon, and especially his *Note 12* on 'The Evil One', p. 56).

8⁴⁵⁻⁷ reiterates the theme of the Jews' unbelief. None of them can prove Jesus guilty of sin, yet they still refuse to believe Him and to listen to the words of God which He speaks—and the only possible reason for this is that they are not God's children but the devil's.

8⁴⁸. '*thou art a Samaritan*'. By denying their claim to be the elect children of God and accusing them of being the devil's progeny, Jesus has—in the Jews' eyes—placed Himself on the same level as the despised Samaritans (see on 4¹⁻⁴²). To call a Jew a Samaritan was regarded as the height of insult. To this insult, the Jews add the charge that Jesus is mad (cf. 7²⁰).

8⁴⁹. Jesus characteristically ignores the suggestion that He is a Samaritan; the differences between Jew and Samaritan mean nothing to Him (cf. 4¹⁻⁴²). The charge of madness, however, He denies; it was not madness, but the obedience with which He honours the Father which made Him speak as He did. The Jews, however, dishonour Him by their unbelief, and to dishonour Him is to dishonour the Father also (cf. 5²³).

8⁵⁰. '*there is one*'. The reference is clearly to God. The Father seeks the glory of the Son, and judges men according to the attitude they adopt towards the Son.

8⁵¹. Jesus adds the promise—which follows naturally upon the reference to judgement—that anyone who obeys His word (cf. *vv.* 31, 37, 43) will escape death (cf. **5²⁴**). In *vv.* 31-6 believers were promised freedom from sin; here they are given the further promise of freedom from death.

8⁵²⁻³. The promise just made refers, of course, to the death of the soul, not that of the body. The Jews, however, characteristically misunderstand Jesus' words by taking them over-literally, and regard them as conclusive proof of His madness (cf. *v.* 48). By claiming that His followers will escape death, Jesus has made Himself out to be greater than Abraham or the prophets—for they all died.

'*whom makest thou thyself?*' They fail to realize that Jesus makes Himself no one, since He seeks no glory for Himself (*v.* 50).

8⁵⁴⁻⁵. '*it is my Father that glorifieth me*'. His Father makes Him what He claims to be. And this is the One whom the Jews claim as their God; but they have no right to claim such a relationship with Him, for they '*have not known him*'. Jesus, on the other hand, knows God, and would be a liar if He denied it—as they are liars in claiming to know Him. Moreover, He obeys God's word; as always in *Jn*, the Son's perfect submission to the Father is emphasized (cf. especially **5¹⁹⁻³⁰**).

8⁵⁶⁻⁸. In the final paragraph of the long series of debates recorded in this chapter, Jesus explains the relationship between Himself and Abraham, the father to whom the Jews have so constantly referred (*vv.* 33, 39, 52-3). He answers the question of *v.* 53 by claiming, not only that He is greater than Abraham, but that Abraham himself acknowledged His superiority. There was a Rabbinic tradition to the effect that Abraham had been granted a vision of the days of the Messiah; Jesus no doubt is thinking of this tradition and identifying Himself with the Messiah. Another possible interpretation of *v.* 56 is represented by the translation: 'Abraham rejoiced that he was to see my day' (*RSV*). This would mean that Abraham rejoiced in the hope of seeing the Messiah, and that now, in Jesus, his hope is fulfilled, and Abraham himself sees it so from heaven. Whichever interpretation of the verse is adopted, the clear implication is that Abraham is inferior to Jesus. Once again the Jews take Jesus' words over-literally (cf. *v.* 52) and protest that a comparatively young man such as He is cannot possibly have seen Abraham. In reply, Jesus makes the solemn pronouncement which is the climax of the whole discourse.

'*Before Abraham was, I am*'. The verb translated '*was*' means 'came into being' or 'was born' (*NEB*); cf. the use of the same verb in **1⁶**. Unlike Abraham, Jesus did not appear at a particular time in history; His is an eternal existence (see on **1¹⁻²**), and this is best expressed by the continuous present tense '*I am*' (on the significance of this see on **6³⁵**). By speaking in this way Jesus claims equality with God, and by virtue of such status He is older than Abraham and incomparably greater.

8⁵⁹. Such a claim is blasphemous in the eyes of the Jews, who accordingly prepare to stone Him (cf. **5¹⁸**) in accordance with the provision of Lev 24¹⁶. But such an attempt cannot succeed (see on **7³⁰**), so that Jesus inevitably escapes unhurt. John does not explain how Jesus '*hid himself*' (the longer text of *AV* is not original, being due to assimilation to Lk 4³⁰).

(*a*) The idea of Christ as the Light of the world has always proved a fruitful one for preaching. To follow Him is to know where one is going, and to understand the meaning of life. But more than that, to receive the light is to share in His life. **8¹²** is not inconsistent with the description of disciples as 'the light of the world' in Mt 5¹⁴ (cf. Phil 2¹⁵); it is the presupposition of the latter truth. By coming to Him who is the true Light of the world, believers partake of His nature and are given a share in His mission to the world. (*b*) The fundamental question at issue in *vv.* 13-19 is one that, in some form or other, is constantly being asked. It is: What evidence have we to *prove* that Jesus' claims are true and legitimate? The answer given is that the only evidence is that of Jesus' own testimony, which is also the testimony of His Father. If we reject that testimony there is no hope of our ever being convinced of the truth. One cannot prove, by any process of reasoning, to a blind man that the sun is shining: 'the evidence for light is that it shines' (W. Temple). The truth about Jesus is the kind of truth that is self-authenticating to anyone who experiences it. If we are to know Jesus for who He is, we must first take Him at His word, by faith (cf. **7¹⁷**). (*c*) Unbelief is the basic sin from which all other sins stem (see on *vv.* 23-4), just as faith is the basic requirement from which stem all good works (cf. **6²⁸⁻⁹**). (*d*) The idea of sin as bondage (*v.* 34) is one that is true to the experience of many sinners; the whole of *vv.* 31-6 is concerned with the only means of release from this bondage. (*e*) Pride such as that displayed by the Jews in *v.* 33 is always the greatest obstacle to the acceptance of the gospel. 'The first of our needs is to know what our first need is—to be set free from bondage; but then we must accept and confess the fact that we are in bondage, and the more complete the bondage, the less are we aware of it' (W. Temple). The evangelist's first task is to awaken this sense of need in sinners. (*f*) Verses 37-47 illustrate very clearly the truth that to be a true son is not so much to be physically descended from one's father, but to reproduce his character (as when we speak of a man as 'his father's son'). In one sense we may determine what family a man belongs to by consulting his birth certificate; but in another, and more important, sense we may determine it by studying his character and behaviour. This throws light on the Johannine truth that only believers have 'the right to become children of God' (**1¹²**; cf. Mt 5⁴⁵). (*g*) Those who fail, or refuse, to grasp the revelation of Jesus (i.e. His essential message, which is embodied in His own Person and life) cannot be expected to understand what He says. But once a man is convinced as to the identity of the Speaker, all His words are filled with meaning and significance, and he finds in them 'the words of eternal life' (cf. **6⁶⁸**). (*h*) The promise of *v.* 51 does not mean that the Christian will be spared the necessity of physical death, but it does assure us of that conquest of death which is guaranteed to the believer who lives in obedience to Christ; for him death has lost its sting (cf. 1 Cor 15⁵⁵) and all its terror. (*i*) In *v.* 58 the vital truth of the eternal existence of Christ is expressed more clearly than anywhere else. This verse reveals the absolute uniqueness of Christ. He is not the greatest of men, but belongs to a different order of being from all men (cf. *v.* 23).

Chapter 9

9^{1-41}: The Man born Blind

THE whole of this chapter is a development of the great pronouncement of Jesus in 8^{12}. John sees in the miracle of restoring sight to a man blind from birth a 'sign' of the spiritual truth that Jesus, as the Light of the world, brings salvation to those who receive Him and judgement to those who reject Him (cf. 3^{19-21}).

9^1. *'blind from his birth'*. This fact is emphasized, not merely to add to the wonder of the miracle (cf. *v.* 32), but because the man's condition symbolizes the condition of unregenerate mankind, which is one of spiritual darkness (cf. comment on 3^2).

9^2. The disciples' question reflects the Jewish belief that all disease and suffering is the result of sin (see on 5^{14}). On this premiss the man's blindness must be due either to sin on the part of his parents or to his own sin. If the latter, the man must have sinned before being born, but Jews believed in the possibility of such a thing; e.g. if a pregnant woman were to worship in a pagan temple, the child in her womb, as well as she herself, would be regarded as committing idolatry.

9^3. Jesus rejects both explanations suggested by the disciples' question. This is not to deny that there is often a connection between sin and suffering (cf. 5^{14}), but simply means that not *all* suffering can be explained as directly due to sin. The alternative explanation offered by Jesus is, however, not without its difficulty: 'he was born blind that God's power might be displayed in curing him' (*NEB*). This must not be understood, however, in the sense that God deliberately inflicts disease upon men in order to create opportunities for the display of His own power and glory in healing them; such an idea is completely out of harmony with the character of God as revealed in Christ. Jesus is concerned, not so much with the question, 'How can this man's condition be explained?' as with the question, 'How can this man's condition be made to redound to God's glory?' Every human situation, however tragic and inexplicable it may be, can become the occasion of glorifying God. Jesus makes this man's blindness such an occasion by curing it through an act of divine power.

9⁴. '*We must work*'. Jesus uses, not the singular 'I' (the reading of *NEBm* is inferior), but the plural '*we*', thus associating His disciples with Himself in the obligation to perform God's work while the opportunity lasts. His words suggest that for them, as for Him, the period of opportunity will not be prolonged indefinitely.

'*while it is day*' corresponds to '*when I am in the world*' (*v*. 5).

'*the night cometh . . .*' refers to the time when the powers of darkness will have brought Jesus' life on earth to a close.

9⁵. '*I am the light of the world*'. These words are not an exact repetition of the pronouncement in **8¹²**; the emphatic pronoun 'I' is missing here, so that the words do not contain the formula 'I am' with its profound theological content. In **8¹²** Jesus states a fact which is eternally true about Himself, but here He is merely explaining what His presence in the world, during the period of the Incarnation, means for the world. Thus the present verse is not to be understood as suggesting that Jesus ceased to be the Light of the world when His incarnate life was over.

9⁶⁻⁷. The method of healing used is the same as in similar cures recorded in the Synoptics (see *CLM* on Mk 7³³ and 8²³). The cure is not, however, completed at once, but only after the man has obeyed the command to go and '*wash in the pool of Siloam*'. As John explains in parenthesis, the Hebrew word '*Siloam*' means '*Sent*'. The pool was known by this name because its waters were conducted to it through the artificial tunnel built by Hezekiah (see 2 Kings 20²⁰). It was from this pool that water was drawn for the ceremonial of the Feast of Tabernacles (see on 7³⁷⁻⁸). As we have seen in 1³⁸, etc., it is John's regular practice to translate Hebrew names. In the case of Siloam, however, there is a special reason for doing so, since the word signifies the truth (so central throughout *Jn*) that Christ, as the 'One sent' from God, is the Giver of life and light. It is of great significance for John that it is the waters of '*Sent*' that give sight to the blind.

9^{8–9} reveals the bewilderment of the neighbours who had long known the man. They cannot agree amongst themselves that it is the same man, until their argument is settled by the man's own admission of his identity.

'*that he was a beggar*'. There was little that a blind man could do save beg, in biblical times; cf. Mk 10^{46–52}.

9^{10–12}. In reply to their enquiry the man tells the story of his cure, referring to his healer as '*the man that is called Jesus*'. As yet he knows but little about his benefactor (cf. **5**¹³). He has not even seen Him—for by the time he returned from Siloam with his sight restored, Jesus had disappeared—nor does he know where He has gone. Before long, however, the man will be led to a much fuller knowledge of Jesus (see on *v.* 38). He has already been granted physical sight, but more than that is in store for him; he is to have the eyes of his spiritual understanding gradually opened (cf. *v.* 17). For John, the act of restoring the man's physical sight is symbolic of the imparting to him of spiritual sight.

9^{13–17}. Meanwhile, the man is brought before '*the Pharisees*'. Probably a small local synagogue court or council is meant—a body capable of investigating the unusual circumstances of the case. The first thing that concerns this court is the fact that the act of restoring the blind man's sight was performed on the sabbath; it was illegal both to heal on the sabbath unless life was in danger (see on **7**^{21–4}), and also to make clay on the sabbath. When, therefore, the man in reply to the Pharisees' questions reports how Jesus healed him, the charge of sabbath-breaking is clearly established. Yet the Pharisees remain puzzled, and divided in their opinions. They resume their questioning by asking the man to express *his* opinion about his benefactor, and he immediately replies, '*He is a prophet*'. As in the case of the Samaritan woman (see **4**¹⁹), his understanding of Jesus' significance is gradually developing from his original estimate in *v.* 11.

9^{18–21}. The Jews now try to resolve their dilemma by denying that the man had really been blind. In an attempt to prove this theory they call in the man's parents and question them. The parents confirm that he is their son and that he was born blind, but refuse to express any opinion as to how he is now able to see; they simply point out that their son is of age and qualified to speak for himself.

9²²⁻³. John comments that the parents gave this evasive answer out of fear.

'*put out of the synagogue*'. It is probable that John's language here reflects the situation of his own day. By the time this Gospel was written many Jewish Christians had come to know what it meant to be excommunicated from the synagogue (cf. **16²**). It is unlikely that a decision in these exact terms had been taken by the Jewish authorities during the ministry of Jesus. Nevertheless the authorities' hostile attitude towards Jesus is plain for all to see, and the man's parents are clearly not prepared to risk their position in Jewish society by making any favourable reference to one whom they know to be the enemy of the nation's leaders.

9²⁴⁻⁵. Having failed to establish that the man had not in fact been blind, the Pharisees recall him, as it were, to the witness-box, and try to intimidate him into agreeing with their 'official' verdict that Jesus is a sinner.

'*Give glory to God*', i.e. 'Speak the truth before God' (*NEB*).

'*one thing I know*'. The man's reply reveals that he is not concerned with any technical verdict such as that Jesus is a sinner. He takes his stand firmly on the evidence of his own experience, which for him is an undeniable fact.

9²⁶. When he refuses to accept their verdict, the Pharisees ask the man to go over the story a second time (cf. *v*. 15). Possibly they hope to detect some inconsistency in his account.

9²⁷. The man now begins to show signs of impatience, accusing them of not listening to his former explanation, and taunting them with the suggestion that they desire to become Jesus' disciples.

9²⁸⁻⁹. At this the Jews become abusive and point out to the man that it is he who has become Jesus' disciple. They themselves remain, as they have always been, '*disciples of Moses*'.

They declare—quite rightly, of course (see Ex 33[11], etc.)—that *'God hath spoken to Moses'*, but that as for Jesus they know not *'whence he is'*. This appears to contradict 6[42] and 7[27], but probably the meaning here is that they do not know on whose authority Jesus speaks.

9[30-3]. The man replies quite bluntly that they ought to know, in view of the fact that Jesus has performed an act such as has never been known (*v.* 32), and such as can only be explained on the assumption that He is *'from God'* (*v.* 33; cf. 3[2]). Only God-given power could perform such a miracle, and God would never give such power to a sinner, but only to one 'who is devout and obeys his will' (*v.* 31, *NEB*; such must be the meaning of the verse, which certainly does not mean that God *never* listens to *any* sinner).

9[34]. In their reply the Pharisees' arrogance and self-righteousness is very evident. They are not prepared to be taught by one whom they regard as a completely sinful man. There may here be a suggestion that they now admit that he was born blind (contrast *v.* 18), and explain his blindness as the result of sin (cf. *v.* 2). Unable to tolerate him any longer they expel him from the synagogue (see *NEB*, and cf. *v.* 22).

9[35]. This means that the man is now (in Paul's words in Eph 2[12]) 'alienated from the commonwealth of Israel' and like a lost sheep. It is not long, however, before the Good Shepherd finds him and invites him to join a new and better flock (this interpretation points to a close connection, in John's mind, between Chapters **9** and **10**). Jesus does this by asking him whether he believes in the Son of Man (on the title, see on 1[51], 3[13-4], 5[27]). Both *AV* and *RV* read *'Son of God'* here, but the better reading is that of *RVm* (cf. *RSV* and *NEB*).

9[36-7]. The man does not understand who the title 'Son of Man' refers to, but seems anxious to believe, and Jesus now reveals that He Himself is meant.

'Thou hast . . . seen him'. These words have a special significance, in the case of a man so recently healed of blindness.

9[38]. The man's immediate reaction is to declare his belief and to worship Jesus. The same kind of historical problem arises

H

104   *The Gospel According to St John*

here as in the case of the Samaritan woman (see on 4²⁶). Once
again we must recognize the possibility that John, in depicting
Jesus as revealing His Messiahship to this man, is adapting the
story to make it serve his own theological purpose. The great
truth which he is seeking to convey through this 'sign' is that
Jesus is the Light of the world. The act of restoring the blind
man's physical sight symbolizes the work of Christ in giving
spiritual sight to the believer. Thus, throughout the story, we
have seen the man's spiritual eyes being gradually opened
(cf. *vv.* 11, 17 and 25), and the process becomes complete with
the confession of this verse.

9³⁹⁻⁴¹. As a conclusion to the episode, these verses emphasize
the truth that Jesus, as the Light of the world, not only brings
salvation to those who receive Him, but also judges those who
reject Him (cf. 3¹⁷⁻²¹). The effect of His judgement is to reverse
the standards of the world—'to give sight to the sightless and
to make blind those who see' (*NEB*). Those who acknowledge
their own spiritual blindness, and accept the deliverance which
Jesus offers, shall see, while those who claim to be able to see
and so reject Him will become blind. The Pharisees belong to
the latter class. They are affronted by the suggestion that they
of all people are blind, and Jesus' final words admit that they
are not, in one sense, blind—since they claim to be able to see.
They have a kind of vision, but it is a false and distorted
vision. And their condemnation lies in their clinging to this
rather than accept the true vision which Jesus offers them.

(*a*) The belief that *all* suffering is the direct consequence of sin is one
that is still found in some circles. It may give rise, in sensitive souls,
to unhealthy morbidity and unnecessary distress of mind. Jesus'
words in *v.* 3 give the lie to this mistaken belief. On the other hand,
it must be recognized that much suffering can be traced directly to
sin, and where this is the case the sufferer must be led to a recognition
of the fact and urged to a genuine repentance. (*b*) A true understanding of the closing words of *v.* 3 means that even the most tragic
circumstances, if God is allowed to take control of them, can be
made the means of glorifying Him. This has repeatedly been proved
true in Christian history, and the faith that it can be so is of great
sustaining power to sufferers. (*c*) The solemn words of *v.* 4 emphasize the urgency of God's work: 'the king's business requireth
haste'. There is so much to do, and we never know how long

opportunity will last, so that the call to work '*while it is day*' is always a pressing one for the Christian. (*d*) The method of healing (*vv*. 6-7) is suggestive: Jesus was not above adopting commonly-accepted methods such as the use of saliva; the patient's co-operation was required before the cure was completed (cf. 5^{1-9}); at the same time it must be recognized that the healing power belongs entirely to Him who was '*sent*' from God. (*e*) The neighbours find it difficult to believe that the man they now see (and who now sees them) is the same man as the blind beggar they formerly knew. Ought not the convert to Christianity be so changed as to present his neighbours with a similar perplexity? And the only way to convince them is to bear one's testimony, as this man does (*vv*. 9-12, 25). (*f*) Three strikingly different attitudes to Jesus are illustrated by *vv*. 13-25. (*i*) For the Pharisee He is simply the subject of an academic debate. (*ii*) The man's parents adopt a non-committal attitude—out of considerations of expediency. (*iii*) The man himself does not express a mere opinion about Jesus, but states a simple fact, which he knows to be true out of his own experience. He who has experienced Christ's power at work in his own life says 'One thing I *know*'—and as long as he holds on to that, nothing can shake his faith in Christ. (*g*) Verse 31 bears upon the question of the conditions on which God answers prayer. It certainly does not mean that He never answers the prayer of a sinner. The two halves of the verse must be taken together; thus the prayers which God does not answer are those offered by men who selfishly seek His blessings without giving Him the glory or seeking to do His will (cf. 14^{13-14}; see also *GPL* on 1 Jn 3^{22}, 5^{14-15}). (*h*) The gradual development in the man's understanding of Christ reaches its climax in *v*. 38. The process by which a man comes to know and believe in Christ is often such a gradual one. But when he does come to know and believe in Him (however that may come about), the inevitable result, as in this case, is worship.

Chapter 10

10¹⁻²¹: The Good Shepherd

THIS section is a continuation of the previous one. The connection of thought has already been noted in the comment on 9³⁵. The *'thieves and robbers'* of *vv.* 1, 8, and the *'hireling'* of *v.* 12 may be intended to remind the reader of the Pharisees who cast the formerly blind man out of the synagogue (9³⁴). If so, the great chapter describing the unfaithful shepherds of Israel (Ezek 34) is probably in John's mind. Jesus' words in *vv.* 1-5 are described in *v.* 6 as a *'parable'*. The word used is different from the one translated 'parable' in the Synoptics; elsewhere in *Jn* (16²⁵, ²⁹), the word means something like 'figure of speech', and the contrast is drawn between using such figures and speaking in plain language. Thus the word for John seems to suggest symbolical language which needs to be interpreted before its meaning can be fully understood (cf. *v.* 6b). Jesus accordingly interprets the parable in *vv.* 7-18. First he does so by referring to Himself as *'the door of the sheep'* (*vv.* 7-10), and secondly He applies the parable rather differently to Himself by describing Himself as *'the good shepherd'* (*vv.* 11-18). In each case He uses the significant formula *'I am'* (see on 6³⁵). Thus what Jesus does is to apply the parable to Himself in order to teach important truths about His own Person and divine mission.

10¹⁻⁵ contains the parable itself (see above). In it Jesus paints a vivid picture drawn from the life of an Eastern shepherd. The sheepfold is the courtyard in front of a house, surrounded by walls but without a roof. There the sheep are gathered for the night, and the door giving entrance to the fold is watched by a gate-keeper. Sheep from various flocks are brought into the same fold. Each genuine shepherd who brings his flock there is recognized by the gate-keeper and granted entrance through the door. If anyone is seen entering the fold otherwise than by the door (e.g. by climbing over the wall), it is certain that he is not a shepherd but a thief or robber. The sheep will not follow such a stranger but will rather flee from him, because they do not know his voice. On the contrary, they know their own shepherd's voice and follow him when he calls. Likewise the shepherd knows his sheep, each one by name, and leads them out, after the night's rest in the fold, to their pasture.

10⁶. See introductory comment above.

10⁷. *'I am the door of the sheep'.* This first application of the parable (see p. 106) is somewhat unexpected; we should expect Jesus to compare Himself to the shepherd, but hardly to the door. In the parable, the door has two distinct functions: through it the true shepherd gains access to his sheep, and through it also the sheep pass in and out of the fold. In the interpretation, the former purpose seems to be in mind in *vv.* 7-8 and the latter in *v.* 9.

10⁸. *'thieves and robbers'.* In view of *vv.* 1 and 5, this must refer to false shepherds who seek access to the sheep without entering through the door and try to get the flock to follow them. Jesus places in this category *'all that came before me'.* The reference clearly cannot be to the great figures of the OT, or to John the Baptist; they, as has been made clear in 1⁷, 5⁴⁶ and 8⁵⁶, bore their witness to Jesus, so that, far from being thieves and robbers seeking entrance by unauthorized means, they might be said to approach the flock *through* Jesus Himself. The reference is rather to the false Messiahs of whom many appeared in Israel both before and after the ministry of Jesus. From the evangelist's standpoint, the description *'thieves and robbers'* clearly fits those false teachers who in his own day are trying to lead the Church astray from the truth. The point of *vv.* 7-8 is that the only true shepherds of God's flock are those who come to the sheep through Christ, who is the Door; i.e. they must be in real communion with Him, and have received their commission from Him.

10⁹. Here, on the other hand, the idea is that Christ is the Door through which the sheep of God's flock may enter into the fold of the Kingdom of God. None can enter the Kingdom except through Christ (cf. **14⁶**, where the same truth is taught by means of the figure of 'the way'). He who enters by this Door is '*saved*', and enjoys both the freedom ('*shall go in and go out*') and the sustenance ('*shall find pasture*') that belong to the flock of God's Kingdom (for the idea of freedom cf. $8^{32, \, 36}$, and for that of sustenance cf. 4^{14} and 6^{35}). In a word, such a person comes to possess life in all its fulness (see next verse).

10^{10}. The contrast between Jesus and '*the thief*' (cf. *v.* 8) is again underlined. Jesus alone can impart to men 'life . . . in all its fulness' (*NEB*), i.e. the 'eternal life' so frequently mentioned in *Jn*, and to do this was the purpose for which He became incarnate (cf. 3^{16}).

10^{11}. '*I am the good shepherd*'. Jesus now proceeds to apply to Himself the figure of the shepherd from the parable of *vv.* 1-5. In the OT God is frequently depicted as Shepherd (cf. Ps 23^1, 80^1, Isa 40^{11}, etc.) and Israel as His flock (cf. Ps 74^1, 95^7, etc.). The Davidic Messiah is also referred to as Shepherd in such passages as Ezek 37^{24} and Ps 78^{70-2}. It was natural, therefore, for Jesus to adopt the same imagery. In the Synoptics, it is found in Mk 6^{34}, 14^{27}, Lk 12^{32}, 15^{3-7}, Mt 18^{12-14}, 25^{31-45}. Characteristically, John expresses the imagery in the form '*I am* . . .' (see on 6^{35}). The Early Church continued to apply the title 'Shepherd' to Jesus (cf. 1 Pet 2^{25}, Heb 13^{20}). In view of the OT background, it is clear that the title must be understood as Messianic, with special reference to the corporate aspect of the Messiah's work, i.e. his relationship to the new community which he constitutes. The adjective used to qualify '*shepherd*' (translated '*good*') is one that refers primarily to his perfect fitness to fulfil the function of the shepherd, but it also contains the suggestion of beauty or attractiveness.

'*layeth down his life for the sheep*'. Jesus is not here describing a characteristic that belongs to every good shepherd; it is no part of the duty of even the best of shepherds to sacrifice his own life, literally, for his sheep. He is describing rather a characteristic that belongs to Himself as the Good Shepherd of God's flock. It is an essential part of His ministry on behalf of men to die for them (cf. 6^{51} and the great synoptic saying Mk 10^{45}, on which see *CLM*). In His readiness to lay down His life for the sheep, the Good Shepherd is at the furthest remove from the thief described in *v.* 10, who comes to *kill* the sheep, not to *be killed* for them.

10$^{12-15}$. The further contrast is now drawn between the Good Shepherd and the '*hireling*', who watches the flock as a means of livelihood, and not because the sheep are his and he takes a personal interest in them. At the approach of danger he deserts them. The Good Shepherd, on the other hand, stands in a personal relationship to His sheep, knowing them and being known by them (cf. *vv.* 3-4). This relationship between Jesus and His disciples corresponds to that between His Father and Himself (see on 6^{57}).

10^{16}. Jesus proceeds to show that the flock for whom He is to lay down His life is not limited to the sheep of '*this fold*'—by which He clearly means the Jewish nation. As we have seen (on *vv.* 1-5), sheep from more than one flock could be found within the same fold. Thus there are those within the fold of the Jewish nation who do not belong to Christ's flock (i.e. the unbelieving Jews); but there are also those who do belong to His flock (the disciples and other Jews who have believed, e.g. the man born blind). There are also those among the Gentiles who will believe in Him and so become part of His flock. Jesus is referring here to the Gentile mission that will be undertaken by the Church and that, from the evangelist's point of view, is already well under way.

'*one flock, one shepherd*'. The *AV* translation 'one fold, . . .' is completely incorrect and misleading. The Good Shepherd's sheep are distributed among various folds, but they constitute one *flock* because they all look to Him as their one Shepherd.

10$^{17-18}$. To close the discourse, Jesus returns to the thought of His death for the sheep (see on *v.* 11). His self-sacrifice, like everything else that He does, is an expression of His perfect obedience to the Father's commandment, and for it the Father loves Him. The relationship between Father and Son is one of perfect love and trust on the Father's side and one of perfect dependence and obedience on the Son's (cf. 5$^{19-47}$). Yet Jesus stresses that His self-sacrifice is an entirely voluntary act. This, however, does not exonerate those who plotted to send Jesus to the Cross. The crucifixion may be looked at from two standpoints. As an event in human history, it was a dastardly crime committed by men—Judas, Caiaphas, Pilate and the rest—and there is no word for it but murder. But from the standpoint of the divine Providence that overrules and

governs all things in heaven and earth, the crucifixion constitutes a glorious divine act—and there is no word for it but
redemptive sacrifice. Throughout the NT the Cross is represented as a necessary element in God's gracious purpose of
salvation (see on 3¹⁴⁻¹⁵). Jesus' voluntary self-sacrifice is in line
with this divine purpose. He has the 'right' to lay down His
life (see *RVm*)—a right given Him by His Father, who also
gave Him the commandment as to how He was to exercise the
right. The act of Jesus is thus an act of voluntary obedience.
Not only, however, has He the right to lay down His life, but
also '*to take it again*'. This is a clear reference to the Resurrection, which, no less than the Cross, is part of the divine
purpose (cf. Mk 8³¹). It was in order to '*take it again*'
—and so obtain life not only for Himself but for all believers
—that Jesus laid down His life.

10¹⁹⁻²¹ reveals the effect of Jesus' discourse on the Jews who
heard it. As usual, opinions are divided (cf. 7⁴³, 9¹⁶). Some
regard Him as raving mad (cf. 7²⁰, 8⁴⁸), and so as not worthy of
serious attention. Others, however, are uneasily aware that
His words are not those of a madman, and that a miracle such
as that recorded in Chapter 9 can hardly be ascribed to a demon.
The Jews do not believe in Jesus, but remain perplexed about
Him (cf. 10²⁴).

(*a*) The idea of Christ as the Door, as used in *vv.* 7-8, provides the
test whereby true shepherds of the flock of God may always be
distinguished from false; it is a question whether their approach to
the flock is 'through Christ' or not. If it is not, the so-called shepherd
will turn out to be a thief, destroying the flock and depriving it of
life (cf. *v.* 10). (*b*) the same symbol of the Door also teaches the vital
truth that the only way of salvation, or means of entry into eternal
life, is through Christ, and that the life obtained through Him is one
of freedom, satisfaction and complete fulfilment (*vv.* 9-10). It is an
important part of the preacher's task to draw the contrast between
the richness and satisfaction of this life in Christ and the poverty and
unsatisfying nature of any other kind of human life (cf. 2¹⁻¹¹). (*c*)
Of the adjective translated '*good*' in *v.* 11, W. Temple writes that it
'represents, not the moral rectitude of goodness, nor its austerity,
but its attractiveness. We must not forget that our vocation is so to
practise virtue that men are won to it; it is possible to be morally
upright repulsively.' These words merit careful meditation. (*d*)
The depicting of Christ's relationship with the Church in terms of

that between Shepherd and sheep is full of rich suggestiveness for the preacher; it suggests His intimate knowledge of each member (*v.* 14, cf. *v.* 3), His passionate care for each one (*vv.* 12-13), and His concern for their safety and the provision of all their needs. (*e*) These marks of the Good Shepherd are to be reproduced in all His under-shepherds—and that means not only ministers and preachers but also class-leaders, Sunday-school teachers, etc.—who must always be on their guard against the subtle temptation of adopting the mind and outlook of the hireling. (*f*) Verse 16 reveals the universal scope of Christ's mission, and also has a bearing on the question of Christian unity. Christ's will for the unity of His Church is evident in the emphasis on '*one flock, one shepherd*', but it is not without significance that the one flock is not represented as belonging to one fold. This argument is not to be used to justify sectarianism, or to resist attempts to express more fully the visible unity of the Church. But it should help Christians to realize that those who belong to folds other than their own are no less a part of Christ's Church, provided they own and acknowledge Him as the One Shepherd. (*g*) Jesus' vicarious death on behalf of His flock lies at the heart of the gospel message (see commentary on *vv.* 11, 17-18). (*h*) Jesus' act of free obedience (*v.* 18) illustrates the truth of man's relation to God. It is our duty to use our God-given freedom in accordance with His will and not our own; it is by so doing that we become, in the fullest sense, free (cf. 8^{36}). God's service is perfect freedom (cf. *MHB* 596: 'Make me a captive, Lord, and then I shall be free').

10$^{22-42}$: Conflict during the Feast of Dedication

This section records a further debate between Jesus and His opponents, the setting now being Jerusalem during the Feast of Dedication (see on *v.* 22). The subject of controversy is still the question of the Person of Jesus, as in the earlier debates at the Feast of Tabernacles (Chapters 7 and 8); the symbolism of the festival, however, is not reflected in the discussion here as was that of Tabernacles in those chapters.

10^{22}. '*feast of the dedication*', This festival was celebrated in December (hence '*it was winter*'), some two and a half months after Tabernacles. Its purpose was to commemorate the rededication of the Temple in 165 BC after its defilement by the Greeks under Antiochus Epiphanes (for details of its institution and characteristics, see 1 Mac 4$^{36-59}$, 2 Mac 10$^{1-8}$). It was naturally a very joyous festival and lasted for eight days. In a measure the ceremonial resembled that of Tabernacles, the idea of light being prominent (cf. **8¹²**); indeed Dedication was sometimes called 'the Feast of Lights'.

10²³. '*Solomon's porch*' was a cloister or portico on the eastern side of the Temple. In Acts 3¹¹, 5¹², we learn that it became the practice of the early Jerusalem Christians to meet there.

10²⁴. The Jews surround Jesus and seek an unambiguous answer to the question which is puzzling them (see on **10¹⁹⁻²¹**) —whether He is in fact the Messiah or not. The question suggests that hitherto Jesus has not openly claimed—in so many words and in the hearing of the authorities—that He is the Messiah. We have here, more clearly than anywhere else in *Jn*, an echo of the idea which is so prominent in the Synoptics, especially in *Mk*, namely that Jesus deliberately kept the fact of His Messiahship a secret from the people generally, and even from His disciples prior to Peter's confession at Caesarea Philippi. The main reason for this reserve on His part was the vast difference between His own understanding of the Messianic office and ministry and that popularly held by His contemporaries (see on **6¹⁴⁻¹⁵**).

10²⁵. Jesus replies by pointing out that He has in fact told them that He is the Messiah—not in so many words, it is true, but by implication. The claims He has made regarding His unique relationship with God ought to have made this clear beyond doubt. And His words are not the only evidence He has given them; there is also that of His works (cf. **5³⁶**). The Jews' perplexity and unbelief is not due to lack of evidence on which to form a conclusion, but rather to their own stubborn refusal to be convinced.

10²⁶⁻⁹. The echo of the 'Good Shepherd' section (**10¹⁻²¹**) is very prominent in these verses, which can hardly be understood apart from that section. It is because they do not belong to Jesus' flock that the Jews do not know Him. It is only those who are prepared to take the step of faith and self-committal to Jesus who can know the truth about Him (cf. **7¹⁷**). Those who do belong to His flock (like the disciples and the man born blind, cf. **9³⁸**) have believed in Him, and consequently enjoy '*eternal life*' (see on **3¹⁶**). This gives them complete security; no one will ever be able to snatch them out of Christ's hand

—as the wolf, for example, snatches the sheep out of the hireling's hand (cf. *v.* 12). The Good Shepherd's hand is identical with that of God, and God '*is greater than all*', and so able to defeat all. The sheep have been given to Jesus by His Father (cf. **6**³⁹, ⁴⁴). There are variant readings in *v.* 29 (see *NEBm*), but the usual text is to be preferred.

10³⁰. '*I and the Father are one*'. This great pronouncement follows naturally after *vv.* 28-9. Here is stated, briefly and explicitly, the fundamental truth which is implicit throughout the Gospel, namely the perfect unity of the Father and the Son (cf. **5**¹⁹⁻³⁰). It is a unity of will and purpose, of love and trust, of obedience and perfect co-operation. The present verse, however, may contain a more philosophical conception of this unity, namely that Father and Son, though separate Persons, are one as regards their essential nature (cf. **1**¹⁻²).

10³¹. Such a claim is, of course, in Jewish eyes blasphemous, and the Jews react by attempting to kill Jesus (cf. **5**¹⁸ and **8**⁵⁹).

10³²⁻³. Jesus' reply contains a hint of irony. He reminds them of the many good works which He has performed in their presence by His Father's power (cf. *v.* 25), and asks which of these has prompted them to stone Him. The Jews reply that the charge is one of blasphemy, arising out of His claim to equality with God.

10³⁴⁻⁸. Here we have Jesus' reply to the charge of blasphemy. He begins by quoting against them their own scriptures (the word '*law*' in *v.* 34 must refer to the whole OT, since the quotation is from Ps 82⁶). In the Psalm God speaks the words '*Ye are gods*' to those whom He has chosen to be judges in Israel; these were men, called by '*the word of God*' to fulfil, as God's representatives, the divine function of judgement. Thus, says Jesus, the scriptures call such men gods; and He adds the comment, to which no Jew could help agreeing, that '*the scripture cannot be broken*'. In view of this (the argument proceeds) the Jews can hardly accuse Jesus of blasphemy on the ground that He claims to be '*the Son of God*'. The Psalm uses the word 'gods' of mere men who have heard the word of God; Jesus is immeasurably greater than they, being the One consecrated and sent (cf. **9**⁷) by the Father, set apart for a uniquely significant and holy mission. The judges referred to in Ps 82 were men who heard the word of God; Jesus *is* the Word of God Himself, incarnate (cf. 1^{14}). In *v.* 37 Jesus appeals once more to the evidence of His mighty works (cf. *v.* 25); the ultimate proof of the truth of His claim to be the Son of God lies in the fact that He performs the works of deity. If that were not true, the Jews could not be expected to believe; but it *is* true, and this ought to convince them even if Jesus' own words have failed to do so. By perceiving the true significance of Jesus' mighty works, the Jews would come to know and believe the truth about the mutual indwelling of Father and Son (*v.* 38, cf. 14^{10}, 17^{21}).

10^{39}. This self-defence of Jesus incites the Jews to make a further attempt to arrest Him, but this, like all previous attempts, is doomed to failure (cf. 7^{30}, $8^{20, 59}$). Once again 'he escaped from their clutches' (*NEB*).

10^{40-2}. This time Jesus leaves Jerusalem altogether and departs to that part of Perea (Transjordan) which had been the scene of John the Baptist's ministry (cf. 1^{28}). He remains there for a while, and many come to Him; a teaching, and possibly a healing, ministry is implied. There is every reason to believe that this tradition about a ministry in Perea during the latter part of Jesus' life, is a genuinely historical one (cf. Mk 10^1 in *NEB*). The people remember the Baptist's testimony to Jesus (see 1^{29-34}) and voice their conviction that that testimony was true; as always in *Jn*, the Baptist's role is here depicted simply as one of testifying to Jesus, for it is emphasized that '*John indeed did no sign*', i.e. he performed no miracle of the kind Jesus performs. Having seen for themselves that all the Baptist said of Jesus is true, these people who have come to hear and see Jesus in Perea believe in Him.

(*a*) The real reason why the Jews did not believe in Jesus as Messiah was not that the evidence was insufficient but that they themselves were unwilling to consider the evidence with open minds; they make an excuse, however, of the fact that Jesus has not openly claimed to be Messiah. There are many still whose refusal to believe in Christ is really due to a lack of the will to believe, but they excuse their unbelief by claiming that the truth of the Christian faith cannot be *proved*. Perhaps it cannot be proved in the sense in which they look for proof, but the fact is that such people are unwilling even to consider the evidence which for Christians is convincing proof. (*b*) Verse 30 is the clearest expression of the truth which is so basic to the gospel and which for the Christian provides the answer to every question concerning the nature, character and purpose of God. (*c*) Verse 32 points effectively to the tragedy of the misunderstanding and ingratitude which has so often resulted in men persecuting their greatest benefactors, and which in particular brought Jesus to the Cross (cf. *MHB* 144, *v.* 4). (*d*) In a sense it is true of Jesus, as it is of men (cf. Mt 7¹⁶) that they are known by their fruits. He will be known for what He is in His divine Person by a contemplation of His works. This underlines the close relationship between the doctrines of the Person and the Work of Christ; neither can be understood apart from the other. It also suggests that the best way to get people to know and believe in Christ is to point them to His mighty works.

Chapter 11

11¹⁻⁴⁴: The Raising of Lazarus

WHILE Jesus is in Perea (see 10⁴⁰⁻²), news reaches Him from Bethany (see on *v.* 1). The Synoptics tell us that it was at Bethany that Jesus lodged during His final visit to Jerusalem (Mk 11¹¹⁻¹², cf. Lk 21³⁷), but they do not mention, in this connection, the family that plays so important a part in *Jn*. The only synoptic reference to the family—in a quite different context—is at Lk 10³⁸⁻⁴², but there only the two sisters are mentioned and their village is not identified as Bethany. The different characters of the two sisters, as they appear in *Lk* and *Jn* respectively, are consistent, so that there is no reason to doubt that both evangelists are in fact referring to the same family. This coincidence is sometimes adduced as evidence that John knew Luke's Gospel, but it need mean no more than that he was familiar with some of the tradition underlying that Gospel (see Introduction, p. 2). It is not easy to understand why Luke, if he knew that Martha and Mary had a brother named Lazarus, makes no reference to him; on this, and on the whole question of the historicity of the incident, see the *Special Note*, pp. 123-6.

11¹. '*Lazarus*'. The Greek form of the Hebrew name Eleazar, which means 'God helps'. The only other occurrence of the name in the NT is in Lk 16¹⁹⁻³¹; on the significance of this see *Special Note*, p. 125.

'*Bethany*'. See above. The village is situated some two miles from Jerusalem (see *v.* 18), on the farther side of the Mount of Olives. The modern name is El Azariyeh, which derives from the name Lazarus.

11². This parenthesis identifies Lazarus as the brother of Mary and Martha, and Mary as the woman who anointed Jesus—a reference forward to 12¹⁻⁸.

11³. The sisters' message does not explicitly ask Jesus to come to Bethany, but there can be little doubt that such is their desire and hope. They believe that Jesus can heal Lazarus (cf. *vv.* 21, 32), and so naturally turn to Him for help in their distress.

'*he whom thou lovest*'. This and *v.* 5 reveal the particularly intimate friendship between Jesus and the family at Bethany.

11⁴⁻⁶. Urgent as the sisters' request is, Jesus makes a strangely tardy response, and this constitutes one of the chief difficulties of the whole narrative (see *Special Note*). Instead of hurrying to His friend's bedside, He stays where He is for two days. The explanation of this delay appears in *v.* 4, and it is significant that John has inserted *v.* 5 between the two more difficult statements, no doubt in order to emphasize that Jesus' delay is not due to any lack of concern or compassion for His friends. It is simply due to His foreknowledge that 'this sickness will not end in death; it has come for the glory of God, to bring glory to the Son of God' (*NEB*). Jesus' words clearly do not mean that the illness will not prove fatal, since that would imply an error of judgement such as John would never have attributed to Jesus. The clear implication is that Jesus knows that Lazarus will die (cf. *vv.* 11-15), and allows him to die in order that the scene may be set for the greatest of the 'signs' that serve to manifest His glory (cf. 2¹¹). Moreover, the raising of Lazarus will lead directly to the glorifying of Jesus in the special sense which that expression bears in *Jn* (see 12²³, 13³¹, 17¹)—namely, His glorifying by death and resurrection; for it proves to be the direct cause of the Sanhedrin's official decision to bring about His death (see 11⁴⁷⁻⁵³). As has been repeatedly emphasized in the course of the Gospel, the 'hour' of Jesus' glorifying has been fixed in the divine counsels (cf. 2⁴, 7⁶, ³⁰, 8²⁰), and His movements and actions are determined in accordance with that programme. Thus He always acts on His own initiative, at the appropriate time, and not according to the suggestions made to Him (cf. especially 2¹⁻¹¹ and 7¹⁻¹⁰). This idea may account for Jesus' attitude in the present context; whether the report is historically accurate is another matter, which will be discussed later.

11⁷⁻¹⁰. When Jesus does decide to return to Judea, His disciples point out the danger of such a course (cf. 10³¹, ³⁹).

The purport of Jesus' reply (*vv.* 9-10) is to emphasize again that no harm can come to Him until the appointed time arrives. He expresses this idea by means of the familiar figure of day and night. The Jews always divided the day (i.e. the period between sunrise and sunset) into twelve hours. Jesus describes the period of His incarnate life as '*the day*', which must run its course and cannot be terminated until the twelfth hour is completed. Just as a man can walk safely in daylight (which is what '*the light of this world*' means in *v.* 9), but stumbles after darkness descends, so Jesus and the disciples need fear no harm while the appointed '*day*' of His life lasts. This seems to be the primary meaning of *vv.* 9-10, though there may be in John's mind a link between these words and the idea of Jesus as the Light of the world (cf. 8^{12}, 9^5 and 12^{46}), in whose presence the believer cannot come to harm.

11^{11}. Jesus now refers for the first time to Lazarus, informing the disciples that the sick man has died, and that He now intends to raise him. The implication is that Jesus' knowledge of Lazarus' death is supernatural, since no message from Bethany is mentioned after that of *v.* 3.

11^{12-14}. The disciples misunderstand Jesus' words, taking the reference to sleep in a literal rather than a metaphorical sense, and Jesus repeats His statement in plainer terms. The disciples' words in *v.* 12 are probably intended by John to bear a deeper meaning than that a restful sleep will lead to the patient's recovery. The word translated '*will recover*' means literally 'will be saved' (*RVm*), so that the disciples are unwittingly bearing witness to the truth that believers who die will be saved from death by Christ. This, as we shall see, is the great spiritual truth symbolized by the 'sign' of the raising of Lazarus.

11^{15} confirms the explanation given in *v.* 4 of Jesus' delay in going to Bethany, but now the effect of the 'sign' that is to be performed is described, not in terms of the glory of God, but of the faith of the disciples (on the connection between the 'signs' and faith, see 2^{11} and 20^{31}). Jesus' words here also imply that, had He been present, Lazarus would not have died (cf. *vv.* 21, 32).

11¹⁶. '*Thomas .... Didymus*' is here named for the first time in *Jn* (see also 14⁵, 20²⁴⁻⁹, 21²); he is much more prominent in this Gospel than in the Synoptics, where his name appears only in lists of the Twelve. Thomas is a Hebrew name meaning 'twin', the Greek equivalent of which is Didymus; as usual John gives the Greek form for the benefit of Gentile readers (cf. 1³⁸, etc.). Here Thomas urges his fellow-disciples to accompany Jesus to Judea even if to do so should mean death for them as well as for Him. Thomas no more than the others understands the nature of the death that awaits Jesus; it is one that no man can share with Him. Nevertheless his words are those of a courageous and loyal follower and suggest that the traditional estimate of 'doubting Thomas' (based solely on 20²⁴⁻⁹) is not entirely just. Possibly here as in *v.* 12, John perceives in the disciple's words a deeper meaning than that intended by the speaker, for to die with Christ (in a very different sense) came to be regarded in the Early Church as a condition of salvation (cf. Rom 6⁸, etc.).

11¹⁷⁻²⁰. Arriving at Bethany, Jesus finds that Lazarus has been dead and buried for four days. Many people from nearby Jerusalem had already come to Bethany to sympathize with the bereaved sisters ('*the Jews*' in *v.* 19 means simply inhabitants of Jerusalem, and not as so often in *Jn* the official leaders). News having reached the home that Jesus is on His way, Martha goes out to meet Him, leaving Mary at home; Martha here appears, as in Lk 10³⁸⁻⁴², as the more practical and active of the two.

11²¹⁻². Martha's words to Jesus may contain the suggestion of a rebuke for His not having responded earlier to their message (*v.* 3), but they also reveal the sisters' implicit faith in Him and their hope that even now He may be able to obtain divine help for them.

11²³⁻⁴. Jesus' reply is ambiguous. It is meant as a reference to the miracle that is to ensue, but Martha not unnaturally takes it as a reference to the general resurrection at the last day, belief in which was characteristic of Pharisaic Judaism. This 'confession of faith' by Martha prepares the way for the declaration of Jesus which is the climax of the whole story,

I

summing up as it does the fundamental spiritual truth to which the 'sign' points (*vv.* 25-6).

11[25-6]. '*I am the resurrection, and the life*'. Like the other great '*I am*' sayings (see on **6**[35]), this expresses an aspect of the ministry fulfilled by Jesus as Son of God. In **5**[19-47] Jesus explained His relationship with the Father, claiming that the Father has entrusted to Him, the Son, the fulfilment of the two divine functions of life-giving and judgement. Here He repeats that claim so far as the giving of life is concerned; He says nothing here of judgement, since Lazarus symbolizes the believer who is raised to life and not the unbeliever who is raised to judgement. Jesus now, however, goes further than He did in Chapter **5**. He shows that the fact of believers' resurrection to eternal life is inseparable from His own Person. This means not only that Christ alone can impart resurrection and life to men, but also that the way for men to partake of these benefits is to come into personal communion with Christ Himself. In other words, Christ imparts resurrection and life by imparting Himself; we cannot receive these, His greatest gifts, without first receiving Him, the Giver. And the way to receive Him is by faith; to him who '*believeth on me*', the promise is given that '*though he die, yet shall he live*'. '*Die*' here means physical death; the believer is not spared the necessity of dying, but he is assured of resurrection to eternal life. In *v.* 26a there is added a slightly different promise, namely the promise of eternal life to the believer while he still lives in this world. The words '*shall never die*' here cannot (in the light of what has just been said) mean 'shall never experience physical death', but rather 'shall never be deprived of the eternal life which he already enjoys'; i.e. death will not mean for him the end of life. Thus *v.* 25b develops the first half of '*I am the resurrection and the life*', and *v.* 26a the second half; resurrection is something for the believer to look forward confidently to, in spite of death, and life is something for him to enjoy already in the present. Thus the tension between present and future which is so marked a feature of John's eschatology, is prominent here (cf. especially **5**[24-9]).

11[27]. In reply to Jesus' question whether she believes the doctrine He has just outlined to her, Martha replies with the full confession of belief in Him as Messiah. For '*Christ*', cf.

1⁴¹; for '*Son of God*', cf. 1⁴⁹; for '*he that cometh into the world*', cf. 1⁹, 4²⁵, 6¹⁴. Full as this confession is, however, Martha's faith and understanding of Jesus' words are still imperfect, as is witnessed by her doubt expressed in *v.* 39.

11²⁸. Martha now returns home, leaving Jesus still outside the village (see *v.* 30), and calls Mary aside from the crowd of mourners (cf. *v.* 19), who no doubt fill the house, to tell her that Jesus wants her.

'*The Master is here*'. Martha uses the familiar title by which no doubt she is accustomed to speak of Jesus (cf. 1³⁸), though by now she regards Him as more than a mere teacher (see *v.* 27).

11²⁹⁻³². Mary accordingly hurries to Jesus. Her sister's attempt to spare her the attentions of the friends who seek to console her proves unavailing; they follow her, thinking she is going to weep at the tomb. Upon reaching Jesus, Mary falls at His feet (an attitude of devotion which is in harmony with the picture of her given in Lk 10³⁸⁻⁴²) and repeats the words uttered by her sister in *v.* 21.

11³³. The sight of Mary's tears, and those of her fellow-mourners, moves Jesus deeply, and *vv.* 33-8 reveal, perhaps more clearly than any other passage in the Gospels, the tender emotions that were an essential part of His full humanity (cf. Heb 4¹⁵).

'*he groaned in the spirit*'. The verb used here and in *v.* 38 is one that usually implies anger (see *RVm*. The same word occurs in Mk 1⁴³ and 14⁵, on which see *CLM*). Most English versions translate it here, as does *RV*, by a word which does not necessarily imply anger (cf. *NEB*, 'sighed heavily'), on the assumption that the Greek verb could be used to denote emotions other than anger. It is difficult, however, to account for John's use of this particular verb unless he intended to describe a feeling of indignation on Jesus' part. Such an emotion is not inconsistent with His character (cf. 2¹⁵⁻¹⁷), but the object of His anger here cannot be the sorrowing Mary and her companions, for *v.* 35 shows that, far from being angry with them for weeping, He shares the burden of their grief. The best explanation of Jesus' anger (if such is the right interpretation of the verb) is that it is directed at the evil powers which are responsible for the sin and death which bring such sorrows upon mankind.

11³⁴⁻⁷. The Jews interpret Jesus' tears as a sign of His affection for Lazarus and His sense of loss at his passing. His love for Lazarus, however, great as it is (*vv.* 3 and 5), is not the main cause for Jesus' tears—for He knows that Lazarus will soon be restored to life. It is rather His sympathy for the bereaved sisters whose grief is so real and painful. Some of the Jews, however, express surprise that Jesus, who opened the eyes of the man born blind, did not save Lazarus from dying, if He loved him so much.

11³⁸. *'again groaning in himself'*. See on *v.* 33.
   'a cave, and a stone lay against it'. A common Jewish method of arranging burial of the dead (cf. Mk 15⁴⁶).

11³⁹. When Jesus commands the onlookers to remove the stone sealing the tomb, Martha (who has presumably accompanied Mary and the others) reveals her lack of faith and understanding (see on *v.* 27) as well as her eminently practical outlook (cf. Lk 10³⁸⁻⁴²). She reminds Jesus that her brother's corpse has already been entombed for four days and that by now it will be in process of decay. The Jews believed that for three days after death the soul continued to hover about over the dead body in the hope of being able to re-enter it, but that after the third day it was finally separated from the body. Thus by emphasizing that Lazarus has been dead *'four days'*, John reveals that by restoring him to life Jesus is performing a new, creative act of divine power.

11⁴⁰. Jesus gently rebukes Martha for her lack of faith, reminding her of His words in *vv.* 25-6, which should have led her to expect a miracle that would be a signal manifestation of God's glory (cf. *v.* 4). The words *'if thou believedst'*, however, remind us that it is only believers who are able to perceive the divine glory in such a miracle; not all the Jews who will witness the resurrection of Lazarus will recognize the true significance of the incident (cf. *vv.* 45-6).

11⁴¹⁻². When the stone has been removed, Jesus prays to His Father, adopting the familiar Jewish attitude in prayer by lifting up His eyes (cf. Ps 121[1], Mk 6[41], Lk 18[13], and in this Gospel, 17[1]).

'*Father*'. This simple mode of address is typical of Jesus' prayers (cf. 17[1], Mk 14[36] on which see *CLM*, Lk 11[2]). The prayer begins with a thanksgiving, which implies that Jesus has already offered a silent prayer, which His Father has answered. Jesus was in constant and unbroken communion with His Father, and there was no need for His petitions to be expressed in audible words. The words in which the prayer continues, however, imply that on this occasion Jesus has prayed aloud for the benefit of the bystanders. The fear that this might give the appearance of 'praying to the gallery' led some scribes to alter the text of *v.* 42 from '*I said it*' (referring to the prayer) to 'I do it' (referring to the miracle). Such a fear, however, is really unfounded, since the motive of Jesus in letting the crowd for once listen in to His prayer is not to draw attention to His own greatness and power, but to direct attention away from Himself to His Father. He wants to convince the crowd that in performing this, His greatest miracle, He is acting, as always, as the Messenger of God His Father (cf. 5[19-47]).

11[43-4]. The miracle itself is related with great restraint. Jesus utters a loud cry, commanding Lazarus to come out, and the dead man obeys. The description of him, bound in the grave-clothes, is very vivid, but the effect of his appearance upon his sisters and friends is left entirely to the reader's imagination. All that is added is the very practical command of Jesus that Lazarus should be released from the now superfluous grave-clothes. It is impossible not to detect in this description of Lazarus' resurrection a clear echo of Jesus' words in 5[28-9]. The story of Lazarus is in fact the 'sign' which symbolizes the tremendous truth of those verses (so far as the life-giving aspect is concerned, see on 11[25-6]).

Special Note

Before we leave this section some attention must be given to the question which inevitably arises in most thoughtful minds, namely that of the extent to which the account in 11[1-44] may be regarded as a factual report of an actual historical event. The problem of the relationship between fact and interpretation

in *Jn* (see Introduction, pp. 2-4), and that of the historicity of
the Gospel miracle-narratives generally, both appear here in
their acutest form. The question with which we are concerned
is not the *philosophical* question as to whether Jesus could
perform such a miracle. For a person who believes in the
Incarnation such a question ought not to occasion much
difficulty; if we believe that Jesus was the Son of God we shall
be unwilling to set any limit to His power (cf. Mk 10^{27}). We
can believe that He *could* perform any miracle which He *willed*
to perform. To believe this, however, and to believe that Jesus
did, in fact, perform many miracles, still leaves open the
historical question which has to be asked with reference to
each individual miracle-narrative in the Gospels: Is it true that
He performed *this* miracle? The answer, in each case, will
depend partly upon our assessment of the value of the historical evidence for the particular miracle in question, and
partly upon our understanding of Jesus' character, His purpose
and His attitude towards His supernatural powers. Thus we
shall be more disposed to accept as historical a miracle that is
attested independently by two or more witnesses in the Gospels
(e.g. the Feeding of the Multitude) than one which is contained
in a single Gospel (e.g. the Changing of the Water into Wine).
Similarly, we shall find it easier to believe that Jesus healed the
sick than that (for instance) He cursed a barren fig-tree.

The fact that John alone records the raising of Lazarus does
not in itself prove the incident to be unhistorical. We have
repeatedly seen that this evangelist had access to valuable
historical traditions unknown to the Synoptists. The difficulty
in this case is due rather to the important position which the
incident occupies in the development of Jesus' ministry as
depicted in *Jn*. Here the raising of Lazarus is the decisive
turning-point of the later period of the ministry, and leads
directly to the authorities taking action against Jesus (see
11^{45-53}). If this represents the actual course of events, it is
difficult to understand how the Synoptists could have been
ignorant of the incident, and how they could have omitted an
event of such crucial significance. In fact, however, the
Synoptic interpretation of the course of the ministry is quite
different; for them the incident which sets in motion the action
of the authorities against Jesus is the Cleansing of the Temple
(see Mk 11^{18}). As we saw on 2^{12-22}, it is probable that the
Synoptists are right on this point and that John, for theological

reasons of his own, has removed the Cleansing to the beginning of his Gospel. He was accordingly free to use the Lazarus story as the climax of his account of the ministry, and so to interpret it as the decisive turning-point. To this extent we may believe that John's interpretative tendency is at work here, as elsewhere in the Gospel, so that the story as he tells it is not to be regarded as a bare historical record.

Some modern commentators regard the Lazarus story as pure allegory, having no historical basis at all, created for the purpose of conveying, in a vivid and dramatic form, the spiritual truth summarized in *vv.* 25-6. They point out that the figure of Lazarus appears in none of the other Gospels—not even in *Lk*, which does refer to Martha and Mary. Most readers feel, however, that the story contains too many vivid details and life-like touches to enable it to be regarded as an imaginative allegory. Such details are best explained as the recollections of an eye-witness; 'if (the author) is romancing, he is one of the most consummate artists in fiction, for so vivid is the impression he makes of reality' (A. E. Garvie).

Some consider that the story is a legend that grew out of the parable of the Rich Man and Lazarus (Lk 16^{19-31})—in much the same way as the incident of the cursing of the fig-tree (Mk 11^{12-14}) is alleged to have grown out of the parable in Lk 13^{6-9} (see *CLM*, p. 88). It is a striking fact that in the parable the suggestion is made that Lazarus should 'rise from the dead', but Abraham insists that even if that happened the Jews would not repent and believe; whereas in the Johannine narrative one named Lazarus does in fact rise from the dead, but the Jews, far from repenting and believing, take steps to destroy both his saviour and himself (cf. **12^{10}**). This parallel seems too great to be accounted for as mere coincidence, so that it would seem that there must be some connection between the Lukan parable and the incident in *Jn*. Not only are these the only two places in the Bible where the name 'Lazarus' appears, but the poor beggar in the Lukan parable is the only character in all the parables of Jesus to be given a proper name. It may well be that it was His actual experience with Lazarus that led Jesus to give that name to the character in the parable, rather than that a knowledge of the parable led to the composition of a legend of an actual rising from the dead.

There appears, then, to be no good reason for denying that an actual historical incident lies behind the Johannine narrative. John's special source of tradition may have contained a story of the raising by Jesus of a dead man (similar to the stories of Jairus' daughter in Mk 5²¹⁻⁴³ and of the widow's son in Lk 7¹¹⁻¹⁷), and the man so raised may well have been the brother of Martha and Mary, and his name Lazarus. It is unlikely, however, that this incident was the direct cause of the move to arrest and kill Jesus; the incident may in fact have belonged to an earlier period in the ministry. John, however, takes this incident and adapts it to his own purpose, just as he adapted the incident of the Cleansing of the Temple in 2¹³⁻²². His interest is not primarily in bare historical record but in theological truth, and in his masterful hand this incident comes to form a most effective climax to his whole account of Jesus' ministry and a dramatic transition from that account to the story of the Passion of Jesus. This supreme 'sign' of the ministry symbolizes the truth that Jesus is the Resurrection and the Life (see on 11²⁵⁻⁶). It seems likely that in making the incident a vehicle for this teaching John has added to the wonder of the event—e.g. by representing Lazarus as having been in the tomb for four days (see on 11³⁹), and so making Jesus wait two days before responding to the sisters' appeal (see on 11⁴⁻⁶). Thus many of the details of the narrative, as it stands in the Gospel, may be unhistorical, but the narrative as a whole is based on an actual historical incident.

Opinions will inevitably differ on the *historical* question with which this *Note* has been concerned. Nevertheless the essential *value* of the passage, as a glorious means of conveying the theological truth it signifies, should be the same for all Christians. It may be that we can never know precisely in what way Lazarus was raised from death to life in Palestine about the year AD 30. But if we take Jesus at His word in 11²⁵⁻⁶ and believe the truth which it is John's purpose to teach through this section of his Gospel, we may certainly know in what way men can be raised, throughout the world, in 1965 and in every age, from the death of sin to eternal life. And to know that is what matters in the long run.

(*a*) The roles played by Martha and Mary respectively in this story can be used to illustrate their different temperaments as they appear in Lk 10³⁸⁻⁴². (*b*) The sisters' simple appeal in *v.* 3 reveals their implicit trust in, and dependence upon Jesus—a trust and dependence based on their assurance of His love (*v.* 5). His response does not come as promptly as they expect, nor in the manner they expect, and this causes them some disappointment and perplexity (*vv.* 21, 32). Their faith is tested, but it stands the test (*vv.* 22-7, 40), and His final response to their appeal is greater than anything they could have foreseen. This bears upon the problem of a delay on God's part in answering our prayers. (*c*) The supreme manifestation of God's glory is seen in the raising to eternal life of men who are dead in sin, but for this to happen necessitated the 'glorifying' of the Son of God through the Cross (*v.* 4). (*d*) Just as no physical harm comes to the man who walks in daylight, so no spiritual harm will come to the man who walks in the light of Christ; this is suggested by *vv.* 9-10, taken in conjunction with 8¹², etc. (*e*) Thomas's words in *v.* 16 illustrate the courage and loyalty that should mark the true disciple; they also illustrate the misunderstanding of the true nature of Jesus' suffering which was characteristic of the disciples then (and often still is). (*f*) Verses 25-6 summarize unforgettably the glorious promise of the gospel—eternal life here and hereafter—and the condition on which it may be realized. The only fitting response to such a promise is the faith confessed in *v.* 27. (*g*) Martha's hurrying to share the good news with her sister symbolizes the passion of the true evangelist (cf. 1⁴¹), and the words she speaks are words which every evangelist should echo. The Master has indeed come, and His call is to all mankind. (*h*) Verses 33-8 reveal very movingly the intensity of Jesus' compassion and sympathy for suffering humanity. Only here and at Lk 19⁴¹, in the Gospels, is Jesus depicted as weeping. Tears are sometimes regarded as a sign of weakness and sentimentality, but when shed out of genuine feeling for others (as His tears were) they are in reality a sign of great strength and nobility of character. The same verses reveal another aspect of the strength of Jesus' character—His righteous anger. The compassion and the anger are not contradictory. (*i*) The reference to four days underlines the fact that the restoration of Lazarus is a new creative act of God. Such also is the regeneration of man (see on 3¹⁻²¹). (*j*) Verses 41-2 reveal the closeness of Jesus' communion with His Father and His complete submission to Him (cf. 5¹⁹⁻⁴⁷).

11⁴⁵⁻⁵⁷: The Plot to Kill Jesus

This section describes the consequences of the act of raising Lazarus. As on so many other occasions, the work of Jesus has the effect of dividing men into two classes—believers and unbelievers (cf. 1¹⁰⁻¹², 3¹⁹⁻²¹, 7¹², ³⁰⁻¹, ⁴³, 9¹⁶, 10¹⁹).

11⁴⁷⁻⁸. The authorities at Jerusalem lose no time. The Sanhedrin (see on 7³²) is hastily summoned and expresses concern about its own inactivity in face of the obvious danger.

'*all men*' is an obvious exaggeration, but Jesus is attracting too many followers (cf. *v.* 45) for the Sanhedrin's liking. Their fear is that if the masses accept Jesus as Messiah they will attempt a revolt against Roman authority, which Rome will suppress by depriving the Jews of their national and religious institutions.

'*our place*' is a reference to the Temple.

11[49-50]. '*Caiaphas*' appears here for the first time in *Jn*. He was appointed high-priest in A D 18 and held office until A D 36. Thus the phrase '*being high priest that year*' simply underlines the fact that Caiaphas happened to be in office in the fateful year of the crucifixion (cf. *v.* 51, **18**[13]). John dates Caiaphas from Jesus, not *vice versa*. Caiaphas' words here express an astute political judgement; the death of one trouble-maker is a small price to pay for national security. Temple calls it 'a piece of cynical utilitarianism'.

11[51-2]. As is so often the case, John discovers in the words he records a deep symbolical meaning, and it is in this meaning rather than that intended by the original speaker that the evangelist's interest chiefly lies. He clearly regards Caiaphas as an unwitting prophet and unconsciously an instrument in God's hands to express the fundamental truth of the gospel, that in that year of destiny one man, Jesus, is to die on behalf of His nation, and of mankind as a whole.

'*the children of God . . . scattered abroad*', i.e. the Gentiles. John is thinking in terms of the missionary task of gathering together into the one Church which is the Body of Christ both Jews and Gentiles (cf. **7**[35], **10**[16], **17**[21]). He has previously taught (**1**[12-13]) that men become children of God by believing in Christ and being reborn; he now emphasizes that all who thus become children of God are to be united in one fellowship, and that all this is made possible by Jesus' sacrifice on the Cross. The Good Shepherd can only gather His sheep into one flock by laying down His life (cf. **10**[15-17]).

11[53]. The Sanhedrin immediately acts upon Caiaphas' advice and plots the death of Jesus. As we have seen (see *Special Note*, p. 124), the raising of Lazarus is for John the immediate cause of the action against Jesus.

11[54–5]. Jesus, aware of the plot, leaves Bethany with His disciples 'for the country bordering on the desert' (*NEB*)—to the N.E. of Jerusalem. '*Ephraim*' is probably the modern Et-Taiyibeh, on the road from Samaria to Jericho. No crowds follow Him now, as they did on His previous retreat (**10**[41–2]). Alone with the disciples, He awaits His 'hour' (see on **7**[30]); until then His enemies' plot cannot succeed. The 'hour' is to strike during the Passover festival, which is now '*at hand*'; this is the third Passover mentioned in *Jn* (cf. **2**[13], **6**[4]). Many pilgrims are already arriving in Jerusalem '*to purify themselves*' in preparation for celebrating the festival by offering the necessary sacrifices, etc. (cf. Num 9[10], 2 Chron 30[17–18]); such rites sometimes took as long as a week to perform. The Jews must be ceremonially clean before they could keep the Passover (cf. **18**[28]).

11[56–7]. The growing crowd congregates daily '*in the temple*' and speculates as to whether Jesus will dare to show His face in the city. The form of the question asked suggests a negative answer. It is not only the crowd, however, that is on the look-out for Jesus; '*the chief priests and the Pharisees*' (cf. *v.* 47) have sought the co-operation of the public in bringing about His arrest. Jesus is now regarded as a fugitive from justice. Soon, however, He will return to Jerusalem (contrary to the crowd's supposition), not under cover as a fugitive, but in open triumph (see **12**[12–18]).

(*a*) The most fruitful idea in this section is that suggested by the unwitting prophecy of Caiaphas. God can sometimes speak—and act (cf. Cyrus in Isa 44[28])—through those whose purpose it is to oppose Him. (*b*) Caiaphas' policy, taken at its face value, illustrates the perennial tendency to sacrifice what is right to what is expedient. (*c*) The ultimate purpose of Jesus' redemptive ministry comes out in *v.* 52. It is not merely to make men God's children, but to gather all the children into one family community. (*d*) Two familiar attitudes towards Christ appear side-by-side in *vv.* 56-7: that which makes Him a subject for interested speculation, and that which makes Him the object of vindictive attack.

Chapter 12

12^{1-11}: The Anointing at Bethany

SIX days before the Passover Jesus returns to Bethany (see on 11^1). He is once again within reach of His enemies; His 'hour' is at hand. The story of the supper at Bethany is also recorded in Mk 14^{3-9}, on which see *CLM*. Mark gives the impression that the event took place two days before the Passover, but this is due to his desire to include it within the framework of his Passion narrative, which opens with the note of time in Mk 14^1. It is likely, therefore, that John's dating of the incident is the more accurate. The two accounts agree in substance, and in many of the details; indeed the verbal agreement between 12^3 and Mk 14^3 is so striking as to make it almost certain that John knew either Mark's Gospel or the tradition underlying it (see Introduction, p. 2). Some details in John's account, however, are reminiscent of the story of the anointing of Jesus by a sinful woman in Lk 7^{36-50}; this suggests that he also knew Luke's Gospel (or its tradition) and that, consciously or unconsciously, he has combined elements from both Synoptic narratives in order to serve his own symbolical purpose in recording the incident (see on 12^3).

12^{1-2}. John does not name the host, but there is nothing inconsistent with Mark's statement that he was Simon the Leper (see *CLM* on Mk 14^{3-9}). If this is correct, Lazarus and his two sisters were among the guests, and it would be thoroughly in keeping with Martha's practical nature to act as a good neighbour and assist by serving at table.

12^3. Mary's action too is thoroughly 'in character'. In Mark's account the woman who anoints Jesus is not named, but this is not surprising since he shows no knowledge of Mary, Martha or Lazarus. There seems to be no good reason why John's identification of the woman with Mary should not be historical (cf. 11^2).

'*ointment of spikenard*'. The words are identical with those used in Mk 14³, and since they include the very rare Greek word *pistikos* there is obviously some connection between the two accounts (see above). The meaning of *pistikos* is uncertain (see *RVm* on Mk 14³), but the most satisfactory interpretation is that which understands it as meaning 'pure' (*RSV, NEB*). The important point is that the ointment was '*very precious*'. Only John mentions '*a pound*' as the amount of ointment used.

'*anointed the feet . . . wiped . . . with her hair*'. On the correspondence with Lk 7³⁸ see introductory comment. In *Mk* the ointment is poured on Jesus' head—a much more natural act—and the probability is that Mark's is the more accurate report in this respect, and that John, under the influence of the Lukan story, has changed the manner of the anointing for reasons of his own. A possible explanation of the change is provided by a comparison with 13⁸⁻¹⁰: to wash the feet (as appears there) is to wash the whole body, so to anoint the feet is (symbolically) to anoint the whole body (see further on *v.* 7).

'*the house was filled . . .*'. This statement is undoubtedly literally true, as such precious ointment would have a sweet and penetrating scent. John's interest, however, is not so much in the literal fact as in its symbolical significance, suggesting as it does that Mary's beautiful act has a fragrance which pervades the whole Church. It is a different way of expressing the idea contained in Mk 14⁹.

12⁴⁻⁶. As in Mark's account, the woman's act provokes a protest, but only John specifies Judas as the protester. This is the second reference to Judas in *Jn* (see on 6⁷⁰⁻¹). John attributes Judas' protest to dishonest cupidity; from this passage and 13²⁹ it appears that Judas was the 'treasurer' of the little company—a fact which only John mentions but which may well be true. Whether Judas was a pilferer, however, is uncertain; there was a natural and growing tendency in the Early Church to blacken the character of Jesus' betrayer, and the judgement expressed here by John may be due to such a tendency (the fact that Judas received a bribe for betraying Jesus could easily lead to the supposition that he was a common thief).

'*three hundred pence*' agrees with Mk 14⁵ (see *CLM*). It is equivalent to about 'thirty pounds' (*NEB*).

12⁷⁻⁸. The second part of Jesus' reply agrees with Mk 14⁷ (see *CLM*), but the former part is rather different.

'*Suffer her . . . my burying*' is obscure and has been interpreted in many different ways, but the most satisfactory solution is to understand '*it*' as referring, not to the ointment, but to the rite of anointing dead bodies for burial (cf. **19⁴⁰**). Thus the meaning is 'let her keep (i.e. observe) now this ritual of anointing my body, in readiness for the day of my burial'. This brings the meaning of the words into line with that of *Mk*. The obscurity of John's text may be due to his wish to avoid the actual statement 'she hath anointed' (Mk 14⁸), in view of the fact that his account of the burial in **19³⁹⁻⁴⁰** is to include a reference to anointing which is absent from the Synoptic accounts of the burial of Jesus.

12⁹⁻¹¹. News of Jesus' arrival at Bethany spreads, with the result that 'a great number of the Jews' (*NEB*, which is here more accurate than *RV*) hurry thither, intent on seeing not Jesus only but Lazarus also. The chief priests are quick to appreciate the significance of this interest in Lazarus: to get rid of Jesus (cf. **11⁵³**) is not enough, without also destroying the outstanding evidence of His miraculous power (which has already led many Jews to believe in Him, cf. **11⁴⁵**). So they include the death of Lazarus in their programme.

(*a*) The fragrant and pervading influence of every sincere expression of love and devotion to Christ is well illustrated in the closing words of *v.* 3. (*b*) The incident as a whole exemplifies the joyous abandon of a love that knows no bounds and spares no expense. Such is the love with which Christ deserves to be loved. (*c*) The story reveals also how the circumstances of an action and the motive behind it affect its legitimacy and its worth. In other circumstances such a prodigal waste of precious ointment might well have been irresponsible and extravagant. (*d*) Judas' protest reveals the wrong type of utilitarian attitude, which is insensitive to aesthetic and moral values, and often insincere and selfish. There are those who are prepared to talk piously about 'helping the poor' only in order to find fault with the ways in which other people spend their money. (*e*) There is something suggestive in the fact that Mary expresses her respect for Jesus (the anointing of a dead body was a mark of respect for the dead) *before* he died. Too often we wait until a person dies before we give him the respect he deserves. Moreover, help should be given to a person while there is an opportunity to help him. It is possible to be so concerned with the needs of 'men' in the abstract that we neglect the particular man on our doorstep whom we have the opportunity to serve. (*f*) Verses 9-11 point to the evidential value of lives which have been transformed by Jesus. The chief argument for the truth of Christianity is the life of a saint.

12¹²⁻¹⁹: The Entry into Jerusalem

The story of the entry is told in all four Gospels; cf. *CLM* on Mk 11¹⁻¹¹, *AMW* on Mt 21¹⁻¹¹, and Lk 19²⁹⁻⁴⁴. Although John's account is similar in broad outline to that of the Synoptics, the similarity is not so close as to require his direct dependence upon the earlier Gospels. There are also certain significant differences: John says nothing of the elaborate preparations for the entry, which are given prominence in the Synoptics; his interest lies not in such details but in the significance of the manner of the entry and of the crowd's acclamation of Jesus.

12¹²⁻¹³. The Synoptics do not explain where the crowd came from or who it consisted of, but John describes it as consisting of festival pilgrims whose interest has been aroused by the testimony borne to the resurrection of Lazarus (see *vv.* 17-18), and who leave the city to meet Jesus as He journeys from Bethany.

'*branches of the palm trees*'. Only John mentions palms in this connection, presumably in order to underline the royal character of the acclamation—palm branches being traditionally associated with the joy of victory (cf. 1 Mac 13⁵¹, Rev 7⁹).

'*Hosanna . . . King of Israel*'. As in the Synoptics, the crowd greets Jesus in the words of Ps 118²⁶, but John makes the significant addition of the title (not in the Psalm) '*the King of Israel*' (see on 1⁴⁹). This means that the crowd is acclaiming Jesus as the victorious Messiah. The Hebrew word '*Hosanna*' was originally a fervent prayer ('Save now'), but had come to be used as an exultant shout of praise to God.

12¹⁴⁻¹⁵. '*having found a young ass*'. As we have seen, John is not primarily interested in the question where Jesus found the ass, but rather in the way His action fulfils the prophecy of Zech 9⁹. There can be little doubt that it was this prophecy that suggested the course of action to Jesus' mind (see *CLM* on Mk 11¹⁰ and *AMW* on Mt 21¹⁻¹¹), and John has clearly

perceived this. By quoting the OT passage he further underlines the kingship of Jesus (cf. *v.* 13). The choice of a
donkey is not only a sign of humility but also, and more
important, an indication of the peacefulness of Jesus' mission.
An Eastern king rode a horse when going forth to war,
but a donkey when on a peaceful errand. Jesus' action is a
last despairing attempt to convince His people of the true
character of His Messiahship, so different from their expectations (cf. 6[15]).

12[16]. John explains parenthetically (cf. 2[22]) that the full
significance of Jesus' action as fulfilling Zech 9[9] was lost upon
the disciples at the time. They only realized it after the
crucifixion and resurrection, when they had received the Holy
Spirit to enlighten them (cf. 7[39], 16[13-14]). If even the disciples failed to grasp Jesus' message, how much more so the
crowd!

12[19]. Little as the crowd understand, however, their excitement
is evident enough—and not least to the Pharisees, much to their
discomfort. They feel that their plans are misfiring.
  '*the world is gone after him*'. As intended by the speakers,
this is simply a way of describing Jesus' widespread popularity
(cf. 11[48]). But John as usual sees below the surface a prophetic
significance in the words. The '*world*' is indeed to be the scope
of Jesus' mission—as the next section will reveal.

(*a*) The significance of the Entry lies in the light which it throws on
the true nature of Jesus' Messiahship. The tragedy is that the crowd
(and even the disciples at the time), whilst recognizing that Jesus is
the victorious King, fail to appreciate the character of His victory
and reign. This is a tragedy that has been endlessly repeated; so
often we attribute to Christ, and praise Him for, achievements
which are really at variance with His character and purpose. (*b*)
Verse 16 points to the truth that only in the light of the Cross and
Resurrection, and by the illumination of the Holy Spirit, can the
true meaning of Jesus' ministry be understood. (*c*) The 'unconscious
prophecy' of the Pharisees has been fulfilled, and is being fulfilled,
in ever-increasing measure with every new advance in the world-
wide mission of the Church. Ultimately, all the efforts of Christ's
enemies will '*prevail nothing*' against His purpose of world redemption.

12²⁰⁻³⁶: Jesus and the Greeks

The hint of the world-wide scope of Jesus' mission, given at the end of the previous section, is now taken up and developed, being symbolized by the Greeks (i.e. non-Jews, cf. 7³⁵) who desire to see Jesus. John is writing for the Church which is fulfilling its mission in the Hellenistic world, and it is appropriate that before he closes his account of the public ministry in Palestine of the Incarnate Lord, representatives of the wider Gentile world should be brought briefly into the picture. John's interest is not in the details of Jesus' encounter with these Greeks, but rather in the significance of their request. The incident, so briefly related in *vv.* 20-2, merely serves as a setting for the discourse which follows in *vv.* 23-36. It is likely that he deliberately omits any description of the Greeks' actual meeting with Jesus because he wishes to emphasize that the entry into the Church of the Gentiles (of which the approach of the Greeks here is a symbol) cannot actually happen until after Jesus has been glorified. This is the main point of the discourse (see on *v.* 32).

12²⁰⁻². '*to worship at the feast*'. There is nothing unusual here; there were many non-Jews in the early first century who had tired of the degenerate heathen religions and who admired the monotheism and high moral standards of Judaism. Without becoming proselytes, many such people feared and worshipped the God of Israel (cf. Lk 7⁵, Acts 8²⁷, 10¹⁻²).

'*Philip . . . Andrew*'. On these disciples, and their common concern for introducing others to Jesus, see 1⁴⁰⁻⁵, 6⁵⁻⁹. It is significant, in the present context, that they were probably the only two disciples who possessed Greek names.

12²³. Jesus begins His discourse by declaring that '*the hour*', which has been pending throughout the Gospel (see on 2⁴, 7³⁰, 8²⁰) has now arrived. He is about to be '*glorified*' through death and resurrection (cf. 7³⁹, 12¹⁶).

12²⁴. He explains the effect of His impending sacrifice with the aid of a metaphor from nature, which is reminiscent of the 'seed parables' of Mk 4 and Mt 13. The principle of 'life through death' which runs through the world of nature applies also in the spiritual realm. The death of the individual wheat-grain

K

results in the more abundant life of 'the full corn in the ear'. Likewise the death of the historical Jesus results in the more abundant life of the Church which is the Body of the living Christ, into which all men are to be drawn (see *v.* 32). In 1 Cor 15³⁶⁻⁸ Paul applies the same metaphor to show how this principle also applies to the death of the Christian believer.

12²⁵. This saying, which expresses in more general terms the principle of 'life through death', occurs in slightly varying forms in the Synoptics (Mk 8³⁵, Mt 10³⁹, 16²⁵, Lk 9²⁴, 17³³)—usually, as here, in the context of a reference to Jesus' death.

'*hateth*' is a typically Jewish way of saying 'loves less' (cf. Lk 14²⁶ with Mt 10³⁷).

'*his life*' is a Jewish way of saying 'himself' (*NEB*). The way to eternal life is the way of forgetting one's selfish concern for one's own safety and interests in a single-minded devotion to Christ (see *CLM* on Mk 8³⁵).

12²⁶. In the light of the aforementioned principle Jesus challenges the disciples, as His servants, to follow Him—which now means to follow Him along the path that leads to the Cross (cf. Mk 8³⁴). By so following, however, they will have the consolation of knowing that, whether in life or death, they will be with their Lord, and honoured by the Father. True greatness and honour in the Kingdom of God belong to those who give themselves in self-forgetting love and service (cf. Mk 10⁴³⁻⁴⁴).

12²⁷⁻³⁰. Here we see Jesus facing the crisis brought about by the arrival of His '*hour*' (cf. *v.* 23). We catch a glimpse of what the Cross meant for Him, and the only adequate commentary on *vv.* 27-8a is the Synoptic narrative of the Agony in Gethsemane (see *CLM* on Mk 14³²⁻⁴², *AMW* on Mt 26³⁶⁻⁴⁶, and cf. Lk 22³⁹⁻⁴⁶). John does not record the Agony in the Garden as such, but this passage and **18¹¹ᵇ** reveal that He was conversant with the tradition represented in the other Gospels. Probably he wishes to emphasize that the Gethsemane experience was one that was constantly present to Jesus as He approached His decisive hour; 'What took place in the garden was not an isolated crisis; it was the focus of a lifelong temptation and of a lifelong victory over temptation' (W. Temple). He rejects the temptation to pray, '*Father, save me from this* *hour*' (cf. Mk 14$^{35-6}$), realizing that only by enduring the Cross can He fulfil the divine vocation on which He has embarked. So He prays, '*Father, glorify thy name*', knowing that only by His death on the Cross can God's name be fully glorified (cf. 17^1). Here, as throughout *Jn*, the Son's perfect submission and obedience to the Father is seen (cf. Mk 14^{36}). On the address, '*Father*', see comment on 11$^{41-2}$.

'*a voice out of heaven*'. This is not intended for Jesus Himself (*v*. 30); His constant communion with the Father enabled Him to understand instinctively the Father's will (cf. 11$^{41-2}$). It is meant to declare to the bystanders that God's name has already been glorified through Jesus' signs (cf. 11$^{4, 40}$) and that it will be fully glorified through His death and resurrection. The crowd hear a sound but do not grasp its message. Some mistake it for thunder; others, realizing its supernatural origin, yet fail to appreciate its relevance to themselves—they think it is an angel speaking to Jesus.

12^{31}. The effects of Jesus' death are now further specified, the repeated '*now*' referring to the 'hour' of *v*. 23. It will constitute both '*the judgement of this world*' and the overthrow of its ruler. For the meaning of '*world*' in *Jn*, see on 1^{10}; being in revolt against God, its ruler is the devil (see on 8^{44}). The idea of judgement as a present process is a prominent theme in *Jn* (cf. 3$^{17-21}$, 5$^{22-30}$). Men are judged by their attitude to Christ: to reject Him is to be condemned. The world's rejection of Christ is focused at the Cross, which therefore constitutes its judgement. Similarly, the Cross constitutes the decisive encounter between Christ and Satan, and contrary to all appearances at the time the victory was Christ's (cf. 14^{30}, 16^{11}, Lk 10^{18}, Col 2$^{14-15}$).

12$^{32-3}$. Here is revealed a different aspect of the victory of the Cross. Not only is it the means whereby Christ has overthrown the power of evil; it is also the means whereby He will draw all men to Himself. As the parenthesis of *v*. 33 makes clear, the lifting up of Jesus from the earth refers to the crucifixion (on the double meaning of the verb see on 3$^{14-15}$). It is as a result of His being glorified through death and resurrection that the abundant harvest of the Gentile mission will be reaped (cf. *v*. 24). The Crucified draws '*all men*' to Himself (the verb is that used in 6^{44}), but that does not necessarily mean that every individual person will eventually be saved, for men may resist the divine 'pull'.

12³⁴. Jesus' words perplex the crowd. They understand scripture ('*the law*' here, as in **10³⁴**, refers to the OT generally) to teach that the Messiah will never die; presumably they have such passages as Ps 110⁴ and Isa 9⁷ in mind. This accounts for the fact that the idea of a crucified Messiah was such a stumbling-block to the Jews (cf. 1 Cor 1²³). Yet Jesus has been speaking of His own impending death (*v.* 32), and a little earlier He used the title '*Son of man*' (which presumably meant 'Messiah') of Himself.

12³⁵⁻⁶. Jesus does not answer their question directly; instead He issues a solemn warning. Referring to His presence among them as '*the light*' (cf. **8¹²**, **9⁵**), He urges them to avail themselves of the opportunity, before it is too late (for the period of His ministry is drawing to a close) to believe in Him. By so doing they will be saved from wandering aimlessly in the dark and will come to partake of the nature of the light—which is what '*become sons of light*' means in Jewish idiom. This appeal concludes not only the present discourse, but also the whole record of Jesus' public ministry in *Jn*. Having issued it, Jesus withdraws finally from the crowd's presence and again goes into hiding (cf. **11⁵⁴**). The remainder of Chapter **12** forms an epilogue to the Johannine record of the ministry.

(*a*) The Greeks' words in *v.* 21 are words which every congregation should address to every preacher and to which every sermon ought to seek to respond. The preacher's responsibility and privilege, like that of Philip and Andrew, is to lead his hearers to his Lord. The words also remind us of the dreadful possibility of our hiding the real Jesus from men rather than revealing Him to them. Men look at us who bear His name, expecting to see Him; but what a terrible distortion they so often see! More people than we imagine in the modern world are sincerely seeking 'to see Jesus'. The responsibility of all Christians is to seek to reflect a true image of Him. (*b*) The emphasis of this discourse on the fact that the Gentile mission can only begin after Jesus has been glorified reminds us that the only adequate gospel for the salvation of the world is a message centred in the Cross and Resurrection. (*c*) The principle of 'life through death' (*vv.* 24-5) takes us to the heart of the Christian doctrine of salvation; cf. Paul's teaching in such passages as Rom 6¹⁻¹¹, Gal

2²⁰. For wider applications of the principle we are reminded that 'the blood of the martyrs is the seed of the Church', and of the possibility, in the providence of God, that particular ecclesiastical institutions may have to die in order that new and better institutions may be brought to life. (*d*) Verse 27 reveals how mistaken it is to suppose that Jesus faced the Cross with a quiet, undisturbed mind. The thought of it filled Him with 'horror and dismay' (cf. Mk 14³⁴, *NEB*). Here more than anywhere else the full humanity of Jesus stands out, and so does His incomparable heroism. It is not the man who faces danger and pain lightly and insensitively that is the really brave man, but he who, intensely sensitive to its full horror and fearfulness, recoils from it and yet goes forward to endure it. The fact that Jesus experienced such suffering and temptation is full of comfort for His followers (cf. Heb 2¹⁸, 4¹⁵). (*e*) Verses 28-30 reveal vividly how differently people may react to the same phenomenon. Some men's perception is limited to the material or physical; others perceive that the material phenomenon has a spiritual significance, though they do not always realize its full implications. (*f*) Verse 31 presents the Cross as the focal point of Christ's judgement of the world and His victory over evil. The world thought that by crucifying Jesus it had judged and finally overcome Him. How completely has history proved the opposite to be true! (*g*) Verse 32 presents the Cross as the great magnetic power which has drawn, and is drawing, men of every age and place to Christ. The preacher's task is so to lift up Christ Crucified before his hearers' eyes that they may feel, and be compelled, by His drawing power (cf. 3¹⁴⁻¹⁵). (*h*) Verses 35-6 contain a timely warning to men to respond to the gospel in the time of opportunity, which is the present (cf. Isa 55⁶, 2 Cor 6²). They also contain a warning of the consequences of refusing the light of Christ; it means not to know where one is going. Of how many people nowadays is this true?

12³⁷⁻⁵⁰: A Summing-up of Jesus' Public Ministry

This 'epilogue' to the first and longer half of the Gospel falls into two parts. (*i*) John's own comments on the significance of the history he has recorded; (*ii*) a brief anthology of Jesus' own sayings, provided to serve the same purpose.

12³⁷. The main comment concerns the persistent unbelief of the Jews, notwithstanding all the '*signs*' performed in their presence. The proper response to a 'sign' is faith (cf. 2¹¹, 20³¹), but the Jews in general failed to make it. The problem of Israel's rejection of the Messiah, in spite of all her privileges and advantages (see Rom 3$^{1-2}$, 9$^{4-5}$), was a very acute one in the Early Church. Paul wrestles with it in Rom 9-11, and it also underlies Mk 4$^{11-12}$, where it is answered by reference to Isa 6$^{9-10}$. John has the same problem in mind here, and quotes the same passage from Isaiah in *v.* 40, along with Isa 53^1 (*v.* 38).

12$^{38-40}$. Like Paul and Mark, John explains the Jews' unbelief as part of the providential purpose of God, who has '*blinded their eyes*' and '*hardened their hearts*' to prevent them from believing and receiving salvation (Isa 6$^{9-10}$); consequently the question of Isa 53^1 is only too applicable to them. Such an explanation strikes us as bordering on the blasphemous, but we must remember that the Jews' sense of God's sovereignty was such that they must attribute everything that happened directly to the purpose of God. *We* should explain the Jews' blindness and unbelief as due to their own sin and failure to profit from their unique privileges. The man who refuses to use his eyes becomes blind, and Israel, by refusing to listen to the words of God spoken to her through the prophets, made herself incapable of recognizing the Word of God when He came in the flesh (cf. 1$^{10-11, 14}$). It was God who ordained that sin should have such terrible consequences, and to that extent the early Christians were right in attributing Israel's blindness and unbelief to His purpose. But that does not mean that God desired their sin and unbelief. 'God does not cause sin, but He does cause its appropriate consequences to result from it' (W. Temple).

12$^{42-3}$. There were, however, exceptions to this Jewish unbelief (cf. 1$^{12-13}$). Some even of the rulers (i.e. members of the Sanhedrin, cf. 3^1, 7^{48}) believed in Jesus, albeit with a very imperfect faith which was too cowardly to come out into the open, for fear that the Pharisees would have them expelled from the synagogue (cf. 9^{22}). These presumably included Joseph of Arimathea (see 19^{38}), and possibly Nicodemus also (19^{39}). John comments that human approbation meant more to them than divine (cf. 5^{44}). Their faith failed to pass the test indicated in 12^{25}. Thus the evangelist's summing-up of the fruits of Jesus' ministry among the Jews is a sad one. In spite of all His 'signs', the great majority have not believed, and the faith even of the minority who have believed is unconfessed, imperfect and lacking in true conviction.

12⁴⁴⁻⁵. These sayings of Jesus underline one of the most prominent themes of this Gospel, namely the perfect unity of Father and Son, and the Son's perfect submission (cf. **5¹⁹⁻⁴⁷, 7¹⁶, 8¹⁹, ⁴², 10³⁰**, etc.). This means that Christ is the complete and final revelation of God; this is John's fundamental claim regarding the Person of Christ, and upon it depends the whole authority of Jesus' teaching and ministry.

12⁴⁶. This saying repeats one of the chief metaphors Jesus has used to signify His Person and presence in the world (cf. **1⁴⁻⁵, ⁹, 3¹⁹⁻²¹, 8¹², 9⁵, 12³⁵⁻⁶**).

12⁴⁷⁻⁸. The idea of Christ as light is associated with that of judgement (cf. **3¹⁹, 9³⁹**), so the next saying concerns this theme, repeating the thoughts of **3¹⁷⁻¹⁹** (cf. **8¹⁵**) and of **5²⁷⁻³⁰**. Though judgement was not the main purpose of Jesus' ministry, that ministry has set in motion the process of judgement upon unbelievers, and '*in the last day*' the result of that judgement will be pronounced. The '*sayings*' of Jesus are the medium of His '*word*' (His essential message of revelation and salvation), and to ignore them is to be judged by that word.

12⁴⁹⁻⁵⁰ again re-emphasizes that this '*word*' of Jesus is none other than the word of God (cf. *vv.* 44-5), and that its content is '*life eternal*'. The summary of Jesus' teaching in the present paragraph would not be complete without the inclusion of this theme which is so central to His teaching as presented in *Jn* (see on **3¹⁶, 6⁶⁸**). Finally, *v.* 50b yet again underlines Jesus' dependence upon and obedience to His Father. 'In the first part of the Gospel, which here closes, Jesus lives in complete obedience to the Father; in the second part He will die in the same obedience' (C. K. Barrett).

(*a*) Persistent unbelief, in the face of all that Christ has achieved, is still characteristic of men. While we may not accept John's ascription of such unbelief to the direct will and purpose of God, *vv.* 37-40 suggest that it is the fruit of wilful disobedience and sin, and so warn us of the danger of such disobedience. To persist in sin is to make oneself progressively less capable of believing in Christ as Saviour. (*b*) The rulers in *vv.* 42-3 typify the timid Christian who hides his faith from the world for fear of the consequences. Faith which is not openly confessed is of little value; we must be 'not ashamed to own our Lord' (*MHB* 485). These were men who wanted the best of both worlds, but there can be no compromise where loyalty to Christ is in question. Unless He has the first place in our lives, He really has no place in them. (*c*) Verses 47-8 remind us of the awful danger, and consequences, of hearing the sayings of Jesus without ever really acting upon them (cf. Mt 7^{24-7}, Jas 1^{22}). We have had ample opportunities of hearing, and the measure of opportunity is the measure of responsibility. Each opportunity a man has had of hearing the gospel will testify against him at the judgement.

Chapter 13

13$^{1-20}$: The Washing of the Disciples' Feet

WE come now to the second half of the Gospel, which comprises the Passion narrative. From now on Jesus' teaching is reserved for His disciples. The setting for Chapters 13-17 is the Last Supper on the eve of the crucifixion; these chapters consist in the main of what we call 'the Farewell Discourse', in which Jesus reveals to His disciples the significance of the work He is about to accomplish in His death and resurrection, the narrative of which follows in Chapters 18-20. John's account of the Supper omits all reference to the institution of the Eucharist, which is the main feature of the Synoptic records (see *CLM* on Mk 14$^{22-5}$, *AMW* on Mt 26$^{26-9}$, and cf. Lk 22$^{17-20}$). That this is not due to any lack of interest in the Eucharist on John's part is clear from the discourses in 6$^{22-59}$ and 15$^{1-17}$; but his interest is in the spiritual meaning of the sacrament rather than in the manner of its institution and the details of its ritual. He may have considered too that the tradition about the institution was sufficiently well-known to members of the Church, and too sacred to be divulged to outsiders who would read his Gospel. The Farewell Discourse is introduced by a narrative of an incident not included in the Synoptic records of the Last Supper (though there may be a faint echo of it in Lk 22^{27}). There is no need, on this account, to regard the incident of the foot-washing as unhistorical. It could have arisen naturally out of the dispute amongst the disciples as to who was the greatest (Lk 22^{24}); it is not difficult to imagine the disciples all being too proud to stoop to perform the menial task of washing each other's feet. By performing the lowly service Himself Jesus not only gives them a much-needed lesson in the humility of true greatness (embodying in an acted parable the teaching of such sayings as Mk 10$^{42-5}$, Lk 22$^{25-7}$), but also provides a 'sign' of the redemptive ministry which He is about to accomplish on their behalf (see on *vv.* 8-10).

13¹. *'before the feast of the passover'* implies that the Last Supper was not the Passover meal. Here we have one of the main historical differences between *Jn* and the Synoptics, in which the Supper is identified with the Passover (see *CLM*, pp. 112-13). John depicts the Supper as being held the day before Passover and the crucifixion as taking place simultaneously with the killing of the Passover lambs (cf. **13²⁹, 18²⁸, 19¹⁴, ³¹, ⁴²**).

'his hour was come'. Cf. **12²³.** This will mean leaving the world to return to the Father (cf. **6⁶²**).

'his own', i.e. His disciples, are, however, to remain *'in the world'* (cf. **17¹¹**).

'unto the end'. The Greek is ambiguous and can equally well be translated 'to the uttermost' (cf. *NEB*). The ambiguity may be deliberate. All that Jesus says and does in the rest of the Gospel is a manifestation of His limitless love. This opening verse really stands as a kind of title to the whole Passion narrative.

13². Attention is drawn to the fact of Judas' presence at the Supper, thus preparing the way for the references to him in *vv.* 11, 18-19, 21-30. John attributes Judas' impending action to Satanic inspiration (cf. **6⁷⁰⁻¹, 13²⁷**, Lk 22³).

13³⁻⁵. Jesus performs this lowly service (a task normally performed by a slave) in spite of His awareness of His unique dignity and authority as the Son of God, entrusted by His Father with all things (cf. **3³⁵, 5²², ²⁶**), and His knowledge that He is about to return to the exalted position at His Father's side from which He came to earth (cf. **17¹⁻⁵**, Phil 2⁵⁻¹¹).

13⁶⁻⁷. *'dost thou wash my feet?'* The pronouns are very emphatic; Peter is horrified at the thought of the Master's stooping to wash *his* feet. Jesus' reply indicates that His action has a significance as yet unknown to Peter. He will only understand it after Jesus has been glorified (the idea is similar to that at **12¹⁶**). It is with this deeper significance of the incident that John is concerned in the following verses.

13⁸⁻¹¹. After Peter has emphatically repeated his protest Jesus warns him that unless he is washed by Him he cannot have fellowship with Him. The truth symbolized is that fellowship with Christ is only possible for those who accept the redemptive service wrought by Him on the Cross. But Peter does not yet understand this (cf. *v.* 7); foolishly he asks for more than His Lord has offered. Jesus replies that nothing more is necessary; the original text of *v.* 10 is probably that of *RVm* and *NEB*, the longer text of *RV* being due to a mistaken belief that the verse referred to the fact that a guest, having bathed before leaving home, only needed to have his feet washed upon arrival at his host's house. Thus the foot-washing symbolizes the complete cleansing made possible by Jesus' sacrifice (cf. 1 Jn 1⁷) and made effective for the believer in the sacrament of baptism, which no doubt is in the evangelist's mind in *v.* 10. R. H. Lightfoot sees a connection between this passage and 12³, where the anointing of Jesus' feet may be equivalent to the anointing of His body as a whole. Jesus implies that the disciples, having had their feet washed by Him, are '*clean every whit*'—with the exception of Judas. With his heart still set on treachery (cf. *v.* 2), Judas, though he has received the literal washing of his feet, has clearly not received the inward cleansing which it is meant to signify.

13¹²⁻¹⁶. John now turns from the symbolical significance of the foot-washing (which they will only come to understand later, cf. *v.* 7) to its practical significance as an example of the humility expected of Jesus' disciples (which they can be made to appreciate at once). Having fulfilled the humble role of the household slave, Jesus returns to His role as Teacher and begins to explain the bearing of what He has just done upon the disciples' duty to one another. If He, whom they rightly acknowledge as Teacher and Lord, could voluntarily assume the status of a slave for them—without for a moment losing the dignity and authority which belong to Him as Lord and Teacher—they can, and ought to do likewise for each other. They cannot, as His servants and messengers, claim exemption from a task which He Himself is willing to perform. The disciples have been jealously concerned to preserve the dignity and authority of their position, but Jesus has shown them that true dignity and authority is not a matter of status but of service.

13¹⁷. The disciples cannot be in doubt any longer as to the meaning of the lesson they have been taught. But Jesus warns them that to know their duty is not enough; they must fulfil it if they are to find true blessedness (cf. **12**[47-8]).

13[18]. The lesson just given, however, like the reference to cleansing in *v.* 10, does not apply to the betrayer. Jesus knows His chosen disciples through and through—as indeed He knows all men (**2**[25])—and this includes Judas (cf. **6**[70-1]). The scripture quoted is Ps 41[9], which was naturally interpreted in the early Church as a 'proof-text' of Judas' betrayal. The Psalmist, of course, was not consciously predicting Judas' action, but the description fits it perfectly. To share a meal with someone was, for the Jew, a mark of the closest personal fellowship and mutual trust, and to 'lift up the heel at' is an idiomatic expression for turning against someone (cf. *NEB*). That Judas should have partaken of the Last Supper with Jesus while treachery lurked in his heart makes his deed doubly black (cf. *v.* 26).

13[19]. Jesus warns His disciples in advance about the betrayal, lest when it happens it should prove too great a shock to their faith. By remembering what He has just told them—i.e. that the betrayal was foreseen in scripture and so, in some mysterious way, is woven into the pattern of the divine purpose—their faith will be confirmed rather than weakened. The reference, of course, is to their faith in the divine origin and Person of Jesus: '*that I am he*' (cf. **8**[24]).

13[20]. The discourse closes with a further solemn reminder that, as His messengers, the disciples (unlike Judas) are to represent Him as He represents His Father (see on **6**[57]).

(*a*) **13**[1] reveals the love of Jesus for His disciples as one that knows no limits, either in time or in sacrificial service. (*b*) The story of the foot-washing serves as a warning against two kinds of pride: the pride that refuses to stoop to serve (represented by the disciples' failure to wash each other's feet), and the pride that refuses to stoop to accept service (represented by Peter's attitude). The latter is particularly dangerous when it leads to an unwillingness to accept the redemptive service offered by Jesus to men. (*c*) Verses 8-11 reveal both the necessity and the sufficiency of the Cross for man's full salvation. If, as is probable, the passage also implies that Baptism is essential, there is no suggestion that the mere rite auto-

matically effects salvation; the contrary is clear from the fact that
the foot-washing was of no avail for Judas. Baptism is real only
when it is linked to a genuine desire and willingness to receive the
benefits of Christ's Passion. (*d*) The two aspects of the incident—as
a symbol of Christ's redemptive service for men, and as a practical
lesson in humility—are neither inconsistent nor unrelated. Jesus is
more than our Example; He is our Saviour. But that does not mean
that He is not the Example we are to strive to follow. 'The death of
Christ is at once the means by which men are cleansed from sin, and
the example of the new life which they must henceforth follow'
(C. K. Barrett). And it is only those who know Him as Saviour who
can really follow Him as Example. (*e*) The story is, of course, the
classic illustration of that divine humility which characterizes all
that Jesus was and did (cf. Lk 22²⁷, Mk 10⁴⁵, Phil 2⁵⁻¹⁵). It is
because such humility is an attribute of God Himself as revealed in
Jesus that it is a mark of true greatness. For the Christian, dignity
and greatness must always be a matter, not of status and honour, but
of character and service. (*f*) Verse 17 reminds us forcibly that
knowing one's duty is one thing, but doing it a very different thing;
but the former without the latter is of no avail (cf. Jas 1²², Mt 7²⁴⁻⁷).
(*g*) The references to Judas are suggestive. The devil can operate
even through members of the Christian community, and does so
when they are prepared to listen to his voice rather than Christ's
(*v*. 2). Every evil act is inspired by the devil, not by God; yet God
is able to work it into the pattern of His purpose, making even the
wrath of man to praise Him (*vv*. 18-19). To know this helps to
preserve one's faith when God's purposes seem to be defeated.

13²¹⁻³⁰: The Prophecy of the Betrayal

In the previous section hints have been given of the presence
amongst the disciples of a traitor. Jesus now openly predicts
His betrayal. This feature of the Last Supper is present in all
the Gospels (see *CLM* on Mk 14¹⁸⁻²¹, *AMW* on Mt 26²¹⁻⁵,
and cf. Lk 22²¹⁻³), but John's narrative has distinctive marks
of its own and leads up to a highly dramatic climax.

13²¹. '*was troubled in the spirit*'. Cf. 11³³, 12²⁷. Though He
has foreseen Judas' treachery (see 6⁶⁴), and knows it to be
inevitable (cf. 13¹⁸⁻¹⁹), Jesus is deeply distressed by the
thought of it. He partakes fully of natural human emotions.

13²². In Mk 14¹⁹ and Mt 26²² the disciples respond to Jesus'
announcement by asking 'Is it I?' In *Jn* their questioning is
more general (cf. Lk 22²³). Both accounts probably contain

elements of truth. It is clear that none of the others knew as yet that Judas was meant. He had kept his treachery hidden from his fellow-disciples, but not from the Master.

13²³⁻⁵. Here we have the first of the Gospel's five references to the 'beloved disciple' (cf. **19²⁶⁻⁷, 20², 21⁷, ²⁰⁻⁴**). This passage makes it virtually certain that the disciple in question was one of the Twelve, since there is no indication that anyone else was present at the Supper (see Mk 14¹⁷). The probability is that John the son of Zebedee is meant (see Introduction, p. 1). The designation does not, of course, imply that Jesus did not love the others (see **13¹**), but that He had a particular affinity and intimacy with this disciple. This is further indicated by the disciple's position at table, '*reclining in Jesus' bosom*'—i.e. immediately on His right, which was the position of second highest honour at a feast (the position immediately on the host's left being the first). In this position the disciple would be favourably placed to speak privately and confidentially to Jesus. Peter, quick to notice this, signals to him to discover the identity of the traitor.

13²⁶. Jesus indicates—privately to the beloved disciple, as is clear from *v.* 28—that the traitor is the one to whom He is about to give a piece of bread which He has dipped in the dish, and proceeds to hand this bread to Judas. For a host to hand food in this way to a guest was regarded as a mark of special favour. Some, reading between the lines, have also seen here an indication that it was Judas who was sitting in the place of highest honour on Jesus' left. If this were true it would suggest that Jesus was making a last despairing appeal to Judas to reconsider his decision.

13²⁷. If Jesus was in fact appealing to Judas to change his mind, Judas did not respond. He accepts Jesus' favour but rejects Jesus Himself, and by doing so surrenders himself finally to Satan. The name '*Satan*' occurs only here in *Jn*, elsewhere 'the devil' being used. Satan has already put the idea of betrayal into Judas' mind (**13²**); now he takes possession of Judas completely to ensure that he fulfils the task. John, however, represents Jesus as being in control of the situation, so that Judas cannot leave to embark on his fell deed without His consent.

13²⁸⁻⁹. The whole company hears Jesus' command to Judas, but without any suspicion of its true import. They think he is being sent either on a shopping errand or a charitable one.

'Judas had the bag'. See on **12⁴⁻⁶**.

'Buy . . . for the feast'. A hint that the Passover has not yet begun (see on **13¹**).

'to the poor'. Almsgiving was customary at Passover time.

13³⁰. *'and it was night'*. This, of course, is literally true, for the Last Supper was held in the late evening (cf. Mk14¹⁷). But as is so often the case the literal statement contains for John a deep symbolical meaning. Judas is leaving the presence of Him who is the Light of the world (see **8¹²**, etc.) and choosing to walk in darkness rather than light (cf. **3¹⁹, 12³⁵⁻⁶**). And the darkness is doubly dark after one has been in the light.

(*a*) Verse 21 reveals the distress caused to Jesus by the sins of His followers, and the suggestion that He was here making a final appeal to Judas (see on *v.* 26) points to the lengths to which He will go to save men from disaster. Though His insight into the divine purpose told Him that nothing could alter Judas' decision, His love for Judas himself was unwilling to let him go without giving him every possible chance. (*b*) A comparison of *v.* 27 with *v.* 2 is suggestive. Until Satan took complete control of him it was theoretically possible for Judas to turn back (hence Jesus' appeal) . But by rejecting the last appeal Judas surrendered finally to Satan, and now there could be no turning back—hence Jesus' command to go and do his black deed quickly. (*c*) The reference to the night dramatically illustrates the whole symbolism of light and darkness which runs throughout this Gospel.

13³¹⁻⁵: The Beginning of the Farewell Discourse

Following his narrative of the Last Supper, John records a lengthy discourse of Jesus with His disciples (**13³¹-16³³**), culminating in the high-priestly prayer (**17¹⁻²⁶**). It is intrinsically probable that a conversation took place in the Upper Room, and this is confirmed by the fact that Luke too (though not Mark and Matthew) records a conversation (though a much briefer one) following the Supper. The Johannine discourse contains Jesus' private teaching to His true disciples, and so it is appropriate that it should begin only after Judas *'was gone out'* (*v.* 31). In it Jesus reveals the meaning of what He is about to accomplish by His death and resurrection, and frequently speaks, in a manner reminiscent of the prophets, of these imminent events as if they were already past. This is not unnatural, since from the evangelist's own point of view the events are in fact already past, and this discourse of Jesus contains the authoritative interpretation of their significance.

13³¹. *'Now is the Son of man glorified'*. The tense of the verb is past (see *RVm*); on the significance of this see above. Jesus is announcing again that the decisive time has arrived (cf. 12²³, 13¹). The glorifying of the Son of Man is at the same time the glorifying of God: the Son glorifies the Father by His perfect obedience unto death (cf. 17¹⁻⁴).

13³². Consequently the Father will immediately glorify the Son in Himself by exalting Him to His own right hand (cf. 17⁵).

13³³. *'Little children'*. A form of address used by Rabbis to their disciples, and later adopted by Christian teachers (cf. Gal 4¹⁹, 1 Jn 2¹, etc.). Jesus reminds the Eleven that His time with them on earth is almost at an end (cf. 7³³, 12³⁵, 14¹⁹, 16¹⁶⁻¹⁹), and repeats to them what He told the Jews in 8²¹. They, no more than the Jews, can at present follow Him along the path He is to tread. On the contrary, they are to remain in the world as His representatives (cf. 13²⁰).

13³⁴⁻⁵. Accordingly Jesus gives them the commandment which is to be the rule of their life as the community of His disciples. This commandment is *'new'*, not in the sense that men had never been told before to love one another (see Lev 19¹⁸), but because the quality of their love is to be such as had never been known before. It is love of the same quality as His love for them. This is a commandment for the new age which is to be inaugurated by Jesus' death and resurrection, and only by possessing the life of that new age will they be able to fulfil it. This love which they will have for one another as disciples of Christ will mark them out as such before the eyes of the world.

(*a*) The form of the 'new commandment' does not, of course, imply that Christians are to love only their fellow-believers. They are to love all men, even their enemies (Mt 5⁴⁴). But Jesus is here dealing with the relationship that is to exist between members of His Church. The mutual love Christians have for one another must be different from that which they have for their enemies, inasmuch as it is mutual. It should reflect the love that exists between the Father and Son, which again is a different kind of love from that with which God loves sinners. (*b*) Verse 35 presents the Church with an ever-present challenge. 'See how these Christians love one another' was the wondering comment of those who observed the early Church; too often in subsequent ages it has become a sarcastic, contemptuous sneer.

13³⁶⁻⁸: The Prophecy of the Denial

Peter's denial is foretold by Jesus in all the Gospels. In Mk 14²⁹⁻³¹ and Mt 26³³⁻⁵ the prediction is made on the way from the Upper Room to Gethsemane, but Lk 33³¹⁻⁴ agrees with *Jn* in setting it within the context of the Supper. John introduces the section quite naturally into his record of the Farewell Discourse by making Peter take up the saying of Jesus in 13³³ and enquire where He is going.

13³⁶. In reply to Peter's question Jesus repeats to him what He said in *v.* 33, with the significant addition of the word '*now*'. He proceeds to tell Peter that later on he will be able to follow Him. The reference is to the fact (which by John's time was a matter of history) that Peter was eventually martyred. The verb '*follow*' came to be used in the early Church of Christian martyrdom (cf. 21¹⁸⁻¹⁹).

13³⁷. Peter responds with characteristic impulsiveness by declaring his readiness even now to die with Jesus; he even dares to use the same phrase as Jesus used in 10¹¹ of His own death.

13³⁸. This leads Jesus solemnly to warn Peter that before cock-crow he will have denied Him three times. The fulfilment of this prophecy will be recorded in 18¹⁷⁻¹⁸, ²⁵⁻⁷.

(*a*) Peter's bold profession of loyalty is a perfect example of the maxim, 'Pride comes before a fall' (cf. Mk 14²⁹). (*b*) Jesus' words in *v.* 36, however, serve to remind us of the encouraging fact that the denial was not the end of Peter's discipleship. Eventually, after he had learned to trust not in his own resources but in his Lord's, he did indeed lay down his life for Christ.

L

Chapter 14

14¹⁻³¹: The Departure and Return of Jesus

JESUS has already warned His disciples that His departure is imminent (13³³), and it is not difficult to imagine their sorrow and distress, and indeed terror, at the thought of being left in the world without Him. It is to this condition that Jesus speaks in the present chapter, the words of which have remained an incomparable source of comfort and encouragement to Christians in circumstances of sorrow and distress throughout the centuries. He assures them that His separation from them is to be only a temporary one, for He will soon return to them (*vv.* 18-19) in such a way that His departure in fact will prove to have been for their good (*v.* 12, cf. **16⁷**). They may accordingly set their troubled hearts at rest (see *vv.* 1, 27 in *NEB*).

14¹. '*Let not your heart be troubled*'. The verb is the same as was used of Jesus Himself in **11³³, 12²⁷, 13²¹**. He urges them to have complete trust in God and in Himself (the reading of *RVm*, *RSV* and *NEB* is to be preferred here to that of *RV*; the Greek is ambiguous, since the second person plural has the same form in both indicative and imperative moods).

14². The exact meaning of this verse has been endlessly debated. The word translated '*mansions*' is a rare one, occurring in the NT only here and in *v.* 23. The word can be used of a temporary resting place on a journey, and many interpreters from Origen to W. Temple have understood it in that sense here. If this is the right interpretation, '*my Father's house*' probably includes this world and the next, so that death means simply to proceed from one stage to another on the same journey, and the progression will proceed from stage to stage in heaven itself. It is more likely, however, that the word here, as in *v.* 23 (where it certainly cannot mean 'temporary abode'), refers to a permanent dwelling-place (it comes from the same root as the verb which in **15⁴⁻⁷** and elsewhere in *Jn* is translated 'abide'). Moreover, '*my Father's house*' in the present context points clearly to heaven, the place to which Jesus is about to depart (cf. **13¹**). Thus He is saying that heaven is like a great house containing many rooms (cf. *RSV*), and implying that there is room for all and provision for the differing needs and circumstances of all. In the second half of the verse the construction and punctuation are uncertain, but the best sense is given by punctuating the sentence as a question: 'if it were not so, would I have told you that I go to prepare a place for you?' (*RSV*, cf. *NEBm*). It is true that Jesus has not yet in John's narrative explicitly told them that He is going to prepare a place for them, but He does so in the next verse—and may have hinted at the fact earlier, though John has not recorded the fact. Jesus never deceives anyone and raises no hopes that He cannot fulfil. He would not have told the disciples that He would prepare a place for them in heaven were there no room for them there.

14³. Jesus now promises that, having prepared a place for them in heaven, He will return to receive them to Himself. Later, in *vv.* 18-19 (cf. *v.* 23, **16¹⁶⁻²²**), He promises to return to be with His disciples in this world, and this return is clearly connected with the coming of the Holy Spirit (*v.* 16). In the present verse, however, it is a different return that is in mind— namely, the coming of Christ to each disciple at the moment of his death, to take him to Himself.

14⁴⁻⁵. In *v.* 4 the clumsy reading of *RV* is more correct than that of *AV* and *RVm*. Jesus has told them enough to enable them to know the way along which He must travel to heaven— i.e. the way of death and resurrection. The question put to Him by Thomas, however, reveals how imperfectly they have understood. This is the second reference to Thomas in *Jn* (see on **11¹⁶**), and his frank admission of bewilderment is thoroughly characteristic of him (cf. **20²⁴⁻⁹**). It is interesting to note that though several disciples question Jesus in this chapter (see further *vv.* 8, 22), Peter, their usual spokesman, is not one of them; had the dreadful warning of **13³⁸** struck him dumb for the time being?

14⁶. To know Jesus' way to the Father is a matter of the utmost importance to the disciples, for they will have to follow

the same way before they can come to the Father and be with
Jesus in the Father's house. The way is that of death and
resurrection. Jesus is about to tread that way, not for Himself
only, but for His disciples also. The death and resurrection
of every believer is in a real sense included in His death and
resurrection. By ascending to heaven along the path of the
Cross and Resurrection Jesus did more than show His disciples the way thither; He paved the way for them to follow.
In a word, He made Himself '*the way*' whereby they might
come to the Father (cf. Heb 10$^{19-20}$). Thus in reply to Thomas'
question Jesus makes the glorious pronouncement, '*I am the
way*'—the sixth of the seven Johannine similitudes in this
form (cf. 6^{35}, 8^{12}, 10$^{7, 11}$, 11^{25}). To the idea of '*the way*' He
adds those of '*the truth*' and '*the life*', but the words that follow
show that '*the way*' is the governing conception. He is the
Way to God, and no one can come to God except through
Him. But so to come to God is to know the truth (cf. 8^{32}) and
to possess life (i.e. eternal life, cf. 3^{16}, 10^{10}). These two words
'*truth*' (see on 1^{14}) and '*life*' (see on 1^{4}) are central to the
thought of John. What we learn here is that both these divine
attributes are embodied in Jesus, and that He is Himself 'the
Way' through which men may attain them.

14^{7}. The claim just made presupposes Jesus' perfect unity
with the Father, so that to know Him is to know the Father.
This knowledge will be theirs '*from henceforth*', i.e. from the
moment of Jesus' glorifying. That it is not already theirs (in
the historical situation of the Upper Room) is apparent from
Philip's question that follows.

14$^{8-9}$. '*Philip*'. See 1$^{43-6}$, 6$^{5-7}$, 12$^{21-2}$. He declares that all they
ask is this direct knowledge of God. The disappointment is
manifest in Jesus' reply. In spite of all the time they have
spent with Him, they still have not known Him or realized that
to see Him is to see the Father in the only sense in which men
can see God in this life (cf. 1$^{14, 18}$). In view of all that Jesus
has taught them about His relationship with the Father (see
especially 10^{30}), the disciples ought to have known better than
to make the request Philip has just made.

14$^{10-11}$. Jesus goes on to describe His relationship with the
Father as one of mutual indwelling (cf. 10^{38}, 17^{21}) and of

obedient submission and dependence (cf. 5^{19-30}, 12^{49}). In all that He speaks, it is the Father who dwells in Him who is 'doing his own work' (*NEB*). Jesus appeals to them to believe what He is now saying to them; but if they cannot believe it because of His own words, let them accept the evidence of 'the deeds themselves' (*NEB*), i.e. His mighty works, which are also His Father's (cf. 5^{36}, $10^{25, \; 38}$). Here, as in 2^{23-4} and 4^{46-54}, there is a suggestion that faith based on miracles is less valuable than the faith which takes Jesus at His word; but the former is better than no faith at all, and can lead to the higher level.

14^{12}. Here is revealed one sense in which Jesus' departure will benefit His disciples (cf. 16^{7}). His going to the Father, far from bringing His work to a close, will result in a great extension of it. The ministry of His incarnate life will be continued and extended in the ministry of His Church.

'*greater works*' does not mean that believers will perform miracles surpassing Jesus' own, but rather that the glorifying of Jesus by death and resurrection will release a new spiritual power that will make possible achievements greater than anything that could be accomplished were He to remain on earth in His incarnate form. The ministry of the incarnate Lord was confined to Israel (cf. Mt 15^{24}); but when He had exchanged His body of flesh for the Body of His Church the scope of His ministry was no longer limited. Moreover, during the period of the Incarnation His ministry was incomplete until it had been consummated on the Cross (cf. 19^{30}), but the mission of the Church after His death is based on His finished work of redemption.

14^{13-14}. This work that believers are to accomplish, however, is not their own achievement but Christ's, and here He assures them that He will answer any request they may make in His name—i.e. in harmony with His character and purpose (see *GPL* on 1 Jn 5^{14}). Superficially this reference to prayer addressed to the Exalted Christ seems to contradict 15^{16} and 16^{23}, which speak of prayer addressed in Christ's name to the Father. To John, however, the unity of Father and Son is so complete (see 10^{30}, 14^{9}) that the distinction is immaterial. In the event, the Church from its earliest days has addressed prayer to the Father and to the Son. In all that the Son will do in answer to the prayers of believers, the Father will be glorified.

14$^{15-16}$. The thought of prayer addressed by believers *to* the Exalted Christ leads on to that of prayer addressed on their behalf *by* Him to the Father. This promise is made subject to the condition that they reveal their love for Him by obeying His commandments (cf. *vv.* 21, 23, and see *GPL* on 1 Jn 5$^{2-3}$). The purpose of His prayer will be to secure for His disciples the gift of the Holy Spirit. Throughout the Gospel it has been emphasized that the Holy Spirit cannot be given until after Christ has been glorified (cf. 7^{39}). This is underlined here in the fact that the Spirit is given at the request of the glorified Christ.

'*another Comforter*'. This is the first of four references to the Spirit in the Farewell Discourse, in all of which He is designated by the Greek word *Parakletos* (cf. **14^{26}, 15^{26}, 16$^{7-15}$**). The only other occurrence of the word in the NT is in 1 Jn 2^1, where it refers to the Exalted Christ (see *GPL*, pp. 31-2, 96-7). In *Jn*, however, it is clear that Jesus is speaking of someone other than Himself; indeed in this first occurrence of the term He qualifies it by the adjective '*another*'. The translation '*Comforter*' is misleading and inaccurate nowadays, since that word in English has come to mean 'consoler'; in the sense in which it was first used by Wyclif—i.e. 'strengthener'— the word was more adequate. The Greek word literally means 'one called in to help', and was usually used in the context of a law-court—hence the translation 'Advocate' in *RVm* and *NEB*). This special sense is clearly right in 1 Jn 2^1 (see *GPL*), and possibly, in a rather different sense, in **16$^{7-15}$** (see comment thereon). In Chapters **14** and **15,** however, it is better to understand the word in the more general sense of 'Helper' (*RVm* and Moffatt). Jesus' promise is that, after His departure, the Holy Spirit will be given to the disciples as their ever-present Companion to guide, support, strengthen and help them in every possible way.

14^{17}. '*the Spirit of truth*' identifies the Paraclete of the previous verse. He is the Spirit of truth inasmuch as He guides believers into all truth (see **16^{13}**) by bearing witness to Jesus (see **15^{26}**), who Himself is the truth (**14^6**).

'*the world*'. See on **1^{10}**. It cannot receive the Spirit because, ignoring God, it neither sees nor knows Him. Faith and spiritual insight are needed in order to see and know the Spirit (cf. 1 Cor 2^{14}). The disciples on the other hand will know Him because He will be present with them (cf. *v.* 16) and will dwell in them.

14$^{18-19}$. Jesus now promises explicitly to return to His disciples. The word translated '*desolate*' literally means 'orphans' (*RVm*), and could be used of disciples bereaved of their teacher as well as of children bereaved of their parents. The coming envisaged in this verse is primarily that of the post-Resurrection appearances. After His death, which is to happen very soon now, the world will see Jesus no more, but His disciples will—for two reasons: because, in consequence of the Resurrection, He will be alive; and because they too will be alive (the reading of *RVm* is preferable here). They will be spiritually alive, having received the Holy Spirit, and so able to see Him as the unbelieving world cannot. It was, of course, only to the disciples, and never to the world, that Jesus did appear after the Resurrection (cf. Acts 10^{40-1}).

14^{20}. When He has thus returned to them, the disciples will understand the truth about His relationship with the Father (cf. *v.* 11) and the corresponding relationship in which they stand to Him (see on 6^{57}). This idea of mutual indwelling will be developed in 15^{1-11}.

14^{21} repeats the thought of *v.* 15, adding that he who shows, by obedience, his love for Jesus will be the object, in a special sense, of the love of both Father and Son. God's love in a general sense extends, as 3^{16} makes clear, to the whole of mankind, but His love for believers has a special character. It is to the disciples who love Him, and who are loved by Him in this way, that Jesus will manifest Himself.

14^{22}. '*Judas (not Iscariot)*' is mentioned only here in *Jn*; he is presumably the 'Judas the son of James' of Lk 6^{16}, Acts 1^{13}. Like Thomas (*v.* 5) and Philip (*v.* 8), he interrupts the discourse with a question. He cannot understand why Jesus will show Himself only to the disciples, and not to the world; if He is to return after death, surely He might be expected to show the world that He has conquered death. Judas' mistake is that of Jesus' brothers in 7^4.

14²³⁻⁴. In reply Jesus repeats again the substance of *v.* 21, but this time the promise is to the effect that both He and the Father will come and make their abode with the believer. For '*abode*' see comment on *v.* 2. In *v.* 17 the Holy Spirit is said to abide with and indwell the believer; in *vv.* 18-20 the same is said of Christ; now it is the Father and the Son together. This illustrates the impossibility of separating the Persons of the Trinity; where one is they all are. The relationship between love and obedience is repeated in a negative form in *v.* 24a, and *v.* 24b repeats the thought of *v.* 10b.

14²⁵⁻⁶. How little the disciples have understood the full significance of what Jesus has just been telling them has been apparent from the questions of *vv.* 5, 8 and 22. Jesus promises, however, that when the Paraclete comes to help them (see on *vv.* 16-17) He will remind them of all that Jesus said and teach them its true meaning. The Holy Spirit is here described in His capacity as Teacher, continuing the work of Jesus in that respect (cf. 16¹³⁻¹⁵). He comes in Jesus' name, because it is at Jesus' request that He is sent (see *v.* 16), and because His purpose is in perfect harmony with that of Jesus (see on *vv.* 13-14).

14²⁷. Here the farewell note is particularly clear. 'Peace be unto you' was the regular Jewish form of greeting upon arrival (cf. 20¹⁹, ²¹, ²⁶) or departure. But here far more than a polite greeting is involved. Peace is the legacy which Jesus leaves to His disciples. And it is not such peace as the world might be able to give, but the peace which is His own peculiar possession. The world's idea of peace is absence of strife, conflict and peril; such peace never belonged to Jesus, least of all on the eve of the Passion. But He always enjoyed, and now more than ever, that indefinable, positive quality of peace which stems from perfect harmony and communion with God, and which none of life's storms can destroy. Such peace belongs to Jesus alone, for only He enjoys the perfect communion with God which makes it possible. But here He graciously bequeaths it, and by His death makes it available for His disciples. Having promised them such peace, it is natural for Him to repeat the comforting words with which the present chapter opened, and to add the injunction, 'banish your fears' (*NEB*).

14²⁸. There is a note of rebuke in this verse. Jesus reminds them of all He has said about His departure and return (see *vv.* 3, 12, 18-19, 21), and says that if they loved Him they would have rejoiced, since His departure means His glorifying and return to the Father.

'*the Father is greater than I*'. This is no contradiction of such claims as that made in **10³⁰** (cf. **1¹, 5¹⁸**). It simply means that in the humiliation of His earthly life the Son voluntarily accepted a position lower than that which belonged to Him from eternity and which He is now about to resume.

14²⁹. Throughout the discourse Jesus has been preparing His disciples for what is to happen to Him, in order that when it happens their faith may stand the test (cf. **13¹⁹**).

14³⁰⁻¹. These verses have the appearance of a conclusion to the Farewell Discourse, and it is somewhat surprising that after them Jesus continues to talk to His disciples for two whole chapters, and to pray with them for one. This has led many commentators to place Chapters **15-16** before **13³¹-14³¹**. On such theories of transposition see Introduction, p. 4. In the present instance the transposition does not really solve the problem since Chapter **17** still follows **14³¹**, and it raises other difficulties since the sequence of thought is more natural if Chapters **15-16** follow Chapter **14**. A more satisfactory solution is that John has made use of two separate versions of the Farewell Discourse, one represented by **13³¹-14³¹** and the other by **15¹-16³³**; **14³⁰⁻¹** then reads perfectly naturally as the conclusion to one of the two versions.

'*the prince of the world*', i.e. the devil (see on **12³¹**), who has already taken possession of Judas as his instrument (see **13², ²⁷**).

'*he hath nothing in me*' reflects a Hebrew idiom meaning 'has no rights over me' (*NEB*). Jesus does not belong to the devil's 'kingdom', since He is not 'of this world' (cf. **8²³**).

'*that the world may know*'. This clause has no principal clause on which to depend, so we must understand 'this happens' or 'he is coming'. Thus the meaning is that the decisive battle between Jesus and the devil must be joined in order that the world may know that Jesus loves the Father and obeys His commandment (i.e. that of **10¹⁸**). For Jesus, as for the disciples (cf. *v.* 15), love must express itself in obedience.

'*Arise, let us go hence*' could conceivably refer to an advance to meet the enemy (cf. *NEB*) but is more naturally understood literally.

(*a*) **14¹** provides the Christian's 'prescription for anxiety'—an implicit trust in the God revealed in Jesus Christ. (*b*) **14²⁻³** is a golden text for the Christian message concerning the after-life. The NT, it is true, tells us very little about the nature of life in heaven, but it tells us enough to banish all fear of death. Jesus' words here afford a glimpse of the spaciousness and richness of life in the Father's house. It is not a life of static uniformity but of progression and variety. Above all it is life 'with Christ', who has gone ahead to prepare a place for His own; the joy of fellowship with Christ on earth is to be consummated in the eternal blessedness of an infinitely rich fellowship with Him hereafter. And death itself, for the Christian, simply means the coming of Christ to take us to Himself. (*c*) The supreme need of lost and wandering sinners is to know the way home and to be enabled to travel along it. Jesus not only shows us the way; He is Himself the Way, so that to know and follow Him is to travel homewards. It is not for nothing that the early Christians spoke of their new-found faith as 'the Way' (cf. Acts 9², etc.). Moreover to follow Jesus as the Way is to know the Truth and to possess Life. (*d*) Philip's question illustrates the search for God which is the object of man's age-long spiritual quest, to which every religion testifies. Verses 6-9 provide the Christian answer—that God can be found, and known, in Christ. There is also a hint of the tragic possibility for a man to spend years in the presence of Christ (say as a member of the Church) without ever knowing Him in the true sense. (*e*) **14¹²** strikingly reveals the re-lationship between Jesus' ministry and the continuing ministry of the Church, and the cruciality of the Cross for the latter. (*f*) Verses 13-14 teach important truths about prayer: it may be offered to Christ or to God the Father; it must be offered 'in Christ's name'—which is more than a liturgical formula; and if so offered it is assured of an answer. (*g*) Verses 16-17 remind us that the gift of the Holy Spirit to the Church is made available by Christ's death and resur-rection. The Spirit is ever present with the Church, indwelling its members, enlightening them with the knowledge of the truth as it is in Jesus, and supplying all their needs. (*h*) One can imagine the disciples, while taking comfort from all Jesus' promises in *vv.* 1-17, still feeling desolate at the thought that their Master's personal presence is to be taken from them. In *vv.* 18-19 Jesus assures them that this loss will be only temporary. The Resurrection means that believers are never bereft of the presence of Jesus (cf. Mt 28²⁰). (*i*) There are still those who, like Judas in *v.* 22, cannot understand why God does not dramatically assert His authority over the world. His way of achieving His purposes, however, is the slower but surer way of winning men to faith in Christ. (*j*) **14²⁷** reveals the true and positive character of peace, and the fact that it is a gift that Christ alone can give, and that the world, for all its storms and stresses, can never take away. Such peace removes all anxiety and fear. (*k*) Those who love Jesus will rejoice at every occurrence that promotes His glory, even though it has all the appearance of tragedy (*v.* 28). Moreover, the apparent tragedy of the Cross, when viewed in the light of all that Jesus says in this discourse, far from undermining faith, serves to confirm it (*v.* 29). (*l*) The forces of evil, though appearing to triumph, can never prevail against Christ (*v.* 30). Like **12³¹**, this verse represents the Cross as the decisive battle between the devil and Christ, a battle which is won through His perfect obedience to the will of God (*v.* 31, cf. **10¹⁸**).

Chapter 15

15$^{1-17}$: The True Vine

IF Chapters **15-16** are based upon an alternative version of the Farewell Discourse (see on **14$^{30-1}$**), this passage may be read as following immediately upon the account of the Supper. This would be peculiarly appropriate since during this Supper (as the Synoptics tell us) Jesus imparted to His disciples 'the fruit of the vine' (see Mk 14^{25}). It is true that John does not mention the actual institution of the Eucharist (see on **13$^{1-20}$**), but just as **6^{35}** is the Johannine version of Jesus' saying over the bread (Mk 14^{22}), so **15^{1}** may be regarded as the Johannine version of the words 'This is my blood of the covenant' (Mk 14^{24}). The whole passage is concerned with the new covenant-relationship into which believers are brought with Jesus as the result of His sacrificial death on their behalf, and by virtue of which they reproduce His love in their lives.

15^{1}. This is the seventh, and last, of the great '*I am*' similitudes (see on **6^{35}**). The use of the vine or vineyard as a symbol for Israel is common in the OT (cf. Isa 5$^{1-7}$, Jer 2^{21}, Ezek 15$^{1-8}$, 19$^{10-14}$, Ps 80$^{8-16}$) and in rabbinic literature. Israel is repeatedly represented as having become a degenerate and wild vine rather than the 'choice vine wholly of pure seed' which God planted when He elected her as His own people. This theme is prominent in Jesus' teaching in the Synoptics, particularly in the parable of the Vineyard (Mk 12$^{1-12}$ and parallels). It appears here in the fact that Jesus claims to be the true (i.e. real, or genuine, cf. 1^{9}) Vine—as opposed to the false and barren vine, which was Israel. Since the disciples are represented as branches (*v.* 5) incorporated in the vine, the idea of the Church as the New Israel is implicit here (see *CLM* on Mk 12^{9}).

15^{2}. The new Israel, no less than the old, is under the care and control of God who, as the husbandman, removes barren branches and prunes the good so as to ensure their maximum yield. This means that God's judgement rests upon unworthy and unfruitful members of the Church (cf. *v.* 6). They are removed from the Vine; the classic example, of course, is Judas. It also means that good and faithful members must be constantly under the discipline of God if they are to develop and bear fruit.

15³⁻⁵. The disciples are already clean by virtue of their relationship with Jesus (cf. **13¹⁰**), i.e. they are healthy branches of the Vine, capable of bearing fruit. But the fruit will only appear if the branches remain in a living, organic union with the Vine itself, receiving from it the life-giving sap. Thus Jesus expresses the concept of the mutual indwelling of Himself and His disciples (cf. **14²⁰**). They are to live in such close and intimate communion with Him that His life will flow into them and find expression through them (cf. Gal 2²⁰). Only so can they bear fruit.

15⁶. Not to live in this relationship with Christ is to wither like a severed branch and become fit for nothing but firewood. This underlines the warning of judgement already given in *v.* 2.

15⁷. '*my words*' are the specific sayings which together constitute '*the word*' of *v.* 3. The suggestion is that the disciples must treasure in their memory the sayings of Jesus (the Holy Spirit will be with them to make this possible, **14²⁶**), and that this will be one means of maintaining their communion with Christ. Those who thus '*abide in*' Him will desire nothing that is contrary to His mind and will, and accordingly they may ask whatever they will and be sure of receiving it (cf. **14¹³⁻¹⁴**).

15⁸. The Father is glorified by the obedience and fruitfulness of the Church as branches of the true Vine, just as He is glorified by the perfect obedience of the Son Himself (cf. **14¹³, 17⁴**). And it is by their fruitfulness that the disciples will show themselves to be Christ's disciples. This reminds us of **13³⁵**, comparison with which suggests that the fruit which the disciples are to bear as branches of the Vine consists primarily of the quality of love. All that follows in *vv.* 9-17 confirms this.

15⁹⁻¹⁰. Love is the essence of the eternal relationship between the Father and the Son (cf. **3³⁵, 5²⁰, 10¹⁷, 17²⁴, ²⁶**), and on the Son's side this love is expressed in obedience (cf. **14³¹**). In these verses Christ's love for the disciples, and their response in love and obedience (cf. **14**[15, 21, 23]), is shown to reflect the Father-Son relationship (see on **6**[57]).

15[11]. A new quality is now mentioned, namely joy. The implication is that Jesus' perfect relationship of love and obedience with His Father brings Him joy (just as it does peace, **14**[27]). He desires that His disciples may share completely in this joy of His, as in His peace; that is why He has said all He has said about their mutual indwelling.

15[12-13]. Jesus now repeats His fundamental and all-inclusive commandment of love (cf. **13**[34]), and proceeds to show the extent of His own love for them, which is the pattern their love is to follow. It is love which gives of itself—to the point of death—for the sake of its objects. The word translated '*friends*' could mean 'those who are loved', and so does not imply any limitation of the scope of Christ's sacrificial love.

15[14-15]. The same word for '*friends*' occurs here as in *v.* 13, but here it has a more positive meaning and applies specifically to the disciples. They are, of course, objects of Christ's love, but they also love Him in return; *v.* 14 in fact repeats the thought of **14**[15, 21, 23], **15**[9-10]. The word '*friends*' is used of the disciples here, however, to distinguish them from '*servants*' (i.e. slaves). Jesus regards them not as slaves but as friends. This does not mean that they are not to offer Him the complete obedience that is due from a slave to his lord (*v.* 14 reveals that such obedience is required). The difference between a slave and a friend is not that one obeys and serves and the other does not, but rather that the one enjoys his Master's confidences and the other does not. Jesus has revealed to the disciples all that His Father told Him to, thus treating them as friends and not slaves.

15[16-17]. This privileged position is theirs not by their own choice but by His. The initiative is always God's (cf. **6**[37, 44]). Moreover, God's election involves obligation as well as privilege. By choosing His disciples Christ has appointed them to a task—to '*go*' (this probably refers to the apostles' mission in the world) and '*bear fruit*' that will last (i.e. the Church gathered together as the result of the mission). This appointment by Jesus, however, means not only that they have a responsibility to discharge, but also that they have the assurance that every prayer they offer in His name will be answered (cf. 14^{13-14}, 15^7). The section closes with a solemn repetition of the fundamental commandment of *v.* 12.

(*a*) The symbol of the Vine is the classic expression of the organic relationship in which believers stand to Christ. He is the source of their life and apart from Him they are barren and dead. Their concern therefore must always be to '*abide in*' Him and to allow Him to abide in them. One way of ensuring this is by constant and prayerful meditation on His words (*v.* 7). And if we are justified in finding a connection between this section and the Eucharist (see p. 162) we may stress the importance of sacramental worship in this respect; through it believers are enabled to partake of His life which was poured out in sacrifice upon the Cross. (*b*) The Christian Church—the true Vine and its branches—is now the Israel, the elect People of God, enjoying special privileges (*v.* 15) but also charged with a special responsibility (*v.* 16). The whole passage warns us that the true branches will be known by their fruits, and of the consequences for those which prove barren (*vv.* 2, 6). This reveals the possibility of being in the Church, in the formal sense, without being 'in Christ'. (*c*) Verse 7 refers to both Jesus' words and to prayer—a suggestive combination. The words of Christ can only abide in us as we regularly read and meditate upon the scriptures under the guidance of the Holy Spirit (cf. 14^{26}). By so doing we may have the mind of Christ and bring our will into line with His. We shall thus know what to pray for, and be assured of an answer to our prayers. This means that the reading of scripture and prayer should always be closely related to each other in the devotions of a Christian. (*d*) Verse 11 reveals the secret of Christian joy. It is the joy of Christ Himself (who was not *only* a 'Man of sorrows'), and is the fruit of a relationship of perfect love and obedience to God. Contrast the shallow, transient joys of the world. (*e*) Verse 13 has often been applied to the heroism of men who have given their lives on behalf of others. In its original context, however, it refers to the love of Christ manifested on the Cross. Before this all other love pales into insignificance. Christians' love for one another is to be a reflection of His love, and such love can only be ours as we allow His love to possess us and flow through us. It is the fruit which we cannot bear unless we abide in Him. (*f*) The contrast between slave and friend in *v.* 15 is suggestive. What matters is our motive for serving God, and the privileges we enjoy in so doing. 'His service is perfect freedom'. God wants sons, not slaves (cf. 8^{35-6}). (*g*) When a person is converted we often speak of him as

'deciding for Christ', as jf he himself were choosing to follow Him.
Verse 16 points to the important truth that we could never choose
Him as Saviour and Lord unless He first had chosen us (cf. 1^{48}, 6^{44}).
(*h*) The reference to prayer alongside the reference to the disciples'
mission in *v.* 16 suggests the essential connection between the
Church's prayers on the one hand, and the fruitfulness of its mission
on the other.

15^{18-27}: The World's Hatred of Christ and His Church

The previous section was concerned with the relationship of
believers to Christ and to one another within the Christian
fellowship—though in *v.* 16 there was a hint of the Church's
mission to the world. The present section deals with the
world's attitude towards the Church, which is one of hatred.
'*The world*' in *Jn* always stands in opposition to the Church
(see on 1^{10} and cf. 14^{17}, 17^{9-19}). By the time the Gospel was
written the Church had experienced, and was experiencing,
the world's hatred in abundance, and this experience is
reflected in John's record of Jesus' words.

15^{18}. That Jesus predicted the hatred of the Church by the
world is confirmed by such passages as Mk 13^{9-13} and Mt
5^{10-11}. That the world's attitude to the Church is the same as
it was to Christ is only to be expected—and is a source of
strength and comfort to persecuted Christians.

15^{19}. The world can only love '*its own*', i.e. those who conform
to its own manner of life. By virtue of their election by Christ
the disciples no longer belong to the world in this way; they
belong to Him who is 'not of this world' but 'from above'
(see 8^{23}), and have themselves been 'born from above' (see on 3^3).

15^{20}. Jesus reminds them of His words in 13^{16}. The servants
cannot expect to be treated better than the Master. This verse
suggests, however, that just as a small remnant believed in
Jesus when the great majority rejected Him (cf. 1^{11-12}), so
there will be a small remnant which will respond favourably to
the Church's mission.

15^{21}. The world's hatred of the Church is due to its hatred of
Christ, which in turn is due to its ignorance of God. A man's
attitude to Jesus is really his attitude to God (cf. *v.* 23).

15²²⁻⁴. The world's rejection and hatred of Christ and of the Father is here described as '*sin*'. The essence of sin, for John, is unbelief—the deliberate rejection of the light that came into the world in Christ (cf. **3¹⁸⁻²⁰**, **16⁹**). Such sin would not be possible unless men had been given a fair opportunity of seeing the light and believing in Christ. But the Jews have had ample opportunity, by reason of the teaching (*v.* 22) and incomparable works (*v.* 24) of Jesus, and yet their only response has been hatred. Accordingly '*they have no excuse for their sin*'.

15²⁵. The Jews' hatred, like Judas' defection (**13¹⁸**), has been foretold in their own scriptures ('*law*' here, as in **10³⁴**, means the OT generally, the quotation being actually from Ps 35¹⁹ or 69⁴). That their own scriptures characterize their hatred as '*without cause*' makes it all the more inexcusable.

15²⁶. On '*Comforter*' and '*Spirit of truth*' see on **14¹⁵⁻¹⁷**. There the Father is said to send the Paraclete (cf. **14²⁶**). Here Jesus Himself promises to send Him, though He does describe the Spirit as proceeding '*from the Father*'. There is no real inconsistency here (see on **14¹³⁻¹⁴**). The Spirit's role here, as in **14²⁶**, is that of witness to Christ (cf. **16¹³⁻¹⁵**).

15²⁷. With the Spirit's testimony Jesus associates that of His disciples, which will be based on their first-hand experience as His constant companions throughout His ministry on earth. In fact, of course, the apostolic preaching consisted of this combined witness (cf. Acts 5³²). That the disciples could never have borne their witness apart from the Holy Spirit is clear from **14¹⁶, ²⁶**.

(*a*) This section is a salutary reminder that the Church—as long as it remains faithful to its Lord—must always expect to be the object of the world's hatred and opposition. When the Church is popular, or when it is simply ignored as irrelevant, this is probably an indication that it is failing to be the Church. In the face of the world's hatred our consolation is to remember that its attitude to Christ was the same, and our hope lies in the victory which He achieved (cf. **16³³**). (*b*) To have had opportunity to hear Christ's teaching and to know of His works is to be without excuse for sin (*vv.* 22-4). If this was true of Jesus' contemporaries, how much more

M

true is it of our generation! (*c*) The Christian mission depends upon a combined witness of the Holy Spirit and the Church. It is the witness of the Spirit which enables the Church to understand its gospel, and it is by the power which the Spirit provides that the Church is able to bear its witness (*vv.* 26-7).

Chapter 16

16¹⁻³³: The World Judged and Overcome

THE previous section was concerned with the world's rejection and hatred of Jesus. The present chapter shows that the world, by adopting this hostile attitude towards Christ, brings the judgement of God upon itself. This judgement is conceived not in apocalyptic terms, but in terms of the present activity of the Holy Spirit in the life of the Church. Finally the disciples are bidden to take heart, amidst all the tribulations which they have to suffer in a hostile world, in the assurance of Christ's victory over that world.

16¹. Jesus again explains His reason for warning the disciples of the troubles that lie ahead for them (cf. **13¹⁹, 14²⁹**): it is 'to guard you against the breakdown of your faith' (*NEB*).

16²⁻³. Two forms which the world's hatred of Christians will take are here mentioned: excommunication from the synagogue (see on **9²²**) and execution. In so treating them men will think they are serving God. Such perversion reveals how completely ignorant they are of God as He is revealed in Christ (cf. **15²¹**).

16⁴⁻⁵. This warning of Jesus' was not necessary while He was still present with the disciples. While He remained on earth He Himself, rather than they, was the object of the world's attack, so that He stood between them and the enemy (cf. **18⁸**). Now that they are to be deprived of His visible presence they need to be warned. When persecution comes they will remember Jesus' words and take courage.

'*none of you asketh*'. This seems to contradict **13³⁶** (cf. **14⁵**), but the present tense suggests that Jesus is here concerned with their immediate reaction to what He has just said.

16⁶ suggests that they are too overcome with sorrow at the thought of His departure to ask where He is going.

16⁷. Jesus now tells them explicitly '*the truth*' that has been implicit in so much that He has said in the Farewell Discourse: '*It is expedient for you that I go away*'. Only as a result of His going (i.e. His being glorified) can the Paraclete come to them (see on **14¹⁶, ²⁶, 15²⁶**). The earlier references to the Paraclete have mentioned certain aspects of His activity, but the present reference introduces the fullest treatment in this Gospel of the Spirit's work (*vv.* 8-15).

16⁸⁻¹¹. First the Spirit is to '*convict*' the world in a threefold respect. The verb here is the same as that used at **3²⁰** and **8⁴⁶**. Its root meaning is 'to expose' or 'prove guilty', but it can also be used in the more general sense of 'convict' or 'convince' (*RSV*). The problem of this passage is whether the same meaning of the verb applies throughout or whether different meanings apply to the different clauses (as in *NEB*). The latter interpretation makes good sense, but on the whole it is better to keep the same meaning for the verb throughout; in this case the preposition must mean '*in respect of*' (as in *RV*), and the meaning will be that the Spirit convinces the world of the true character of sin, righteousness and judgement (or possibly, exposes the erroneous notions the world holds in regard to these matters). In the case of '*sin*', the convincing amounts to conviction, for the sin is that of the world itself. Sin is defined here as the unbelief in Jesus (cf. **15²²⁻⁴**) which is the final expression of rebellion against God—the refusal to accept His self-revelation, the loving of darkness rather than light (cf. **3¹⁹**). The '*righteousness*' of which the world is to be convinced is that of Christ, and it consists in His departure to the Father, which means His crucifixion and resurrection. In Biblical thought righteousness stands not only for an attribute of God's character, but also for a mighty saving activity of God (see *GPL* on 1 Jn 1⁹). The supreme manifestation of this righteousness is seen in the Cross and Resurrection. The Spirit is to convince the world of this. The '*judgement*' of which the world is to be convinced is God's judgement upon '*the prince of this world*' (cf. **12³¹, 14³⁰⁻¹**), i.e. the devil. The world and its 'prince' thought that the Cross was the execution of its judgement upon Christ, but the exact opposite is the truth; this reveals the extent to which the world needed convincing of the true character of judgement. Throughout this passage the 'legal' sense of the term *parakletos* (see on

14¹⁶) is prominent, but He is here conceived, not as the advocate for the defence pleading on behalf of the Church, but as the prosecuting counsel. This is natural since it is His attitude to the world that is in question. The Advocate who pleads the Church's cause also acts as Prosecutor of the Church's adversary, the world. The question may be asked: if the world cannot receive the Paraclete (see **14¹⁷**), how can it be convicted or convinced by Him? The only possible answer is that the Spirit works upon the world's mind and conscience not directly but through the witness of the Church's preaching and life, which are inspired by the Spirit (cf. **15²⁶⁻⁷**).

16¹²⁻¹⁵. The Spirit is not only to convince the world but also to instruct the Church. This aspect of His ministry, already touched upon in **14²⁶** and **15²⁶**, is now more fully developed. During His incarnate ministry Jesus has instructed His disciples, but there is much that He has not been able to tell them because there were not yet ready for it. The Gospels all show how imperfect was the disciples' understanding, even at the close of the ministry, of the teaching they had received from Jesus (cf. **12¹⁶**, **13⁷**, **14⁴⁻⁹**, etc.). Yet Jesus is able to entrust them with their mission, ignorant and immature as they are, because He knows that they will have the Holy Spirit to complete their instruction. As the Spirit of truth (see on **14¹⁷**) He will guide them into all truth. Like the Son (see **7¹⁶⁻¹⁷**, **12⁴⁹**), the Spirit does not speak on His own authority but in dependence upon and obedience to the Father. There will be a prophetic element in this instruction of the Spirit: '*he shall declare ... things that are to come*', i.e. the eschatological events of the 'last days' (for the traces of futurist eschatology present in *Jn* see **5²⁸⁻⁹**, **6³⁹⁻⁴⁰**, **14³**). The Spirit will reveal to the Church the true meaning of these future events; possibly this involves showing that the eschatological events, such as the enjoyment of eternal life and the process of judgement, are already anticipated in the present (see on **3¹⁶⁻²¹**). His task is not to reveal truths additional to those included in the revelation given in Christ, but to enable the Church to apprehend the truth as it is in Jesus (see **14⁶, ²⁶**). All truth belongs to Jesus as it belongs to God, who shares everything with the Son (cf. **3³⁵**, **5²⁰**, **17¹⁰**). By enabling believers to understand more fully their Lord and His teaching, the Spirit will '*glorify*' Jesus, i.e. enable them to recognize and acknowledge His glory.

16¹⁶⁻¹⁹. After a long monologue by Jesus **(15¹-16¹⁵)** the dialogue style is resumed. After Jesus has again stated the fundamental theme of this Farewell Discourse—His impending departure and subsequent quick return—the disciples are puzzled and ask one another what He means. They hesitate to put the question to Him, but He perceives what is in their mind and proceeds to explain His departure and return in terms of what it will mean to them.

16²⁰⁻². His death, which for the world will be a matter for rejoicing, will be for the disciples an occasion of grief and sorrow. But just as the pains of a woman in childbirth are soon forgotten when she has the joy of seeing her new-born child, so their grief will soon be turned into joy when He returns to them after the Resurrection (cf. **14¹⁸⁻¹⁹**). This joy will be a lasting joy of which no one will be able to deprive them, because His presence will never again be taken from them (cf. **14²³**). It is worth noting that the language in *vv.* 16-22 has a distinct eschatological flavour, and it may be that John is suggesting in this way that what Jesus said to His disciples in the Upper Room—with reference to His death and resurrection—is also applicable to the Church's situation in his own day: it is at present passing through experiences of suffering and persecution, but these will be transformed to eternal joy when Christ returns at the Parousia.

16²³⁻⁴. '*in that day*', though an eschatological expression, refers primarily here to the post-Resurrection period. Two different verbs for '*ask*' are used in these verses. The one in *v.* 23a means to ask questions (cf. *RVm* and *RSV*); the other in *vv.* 23b-4 means to make requests. Hitherto the disciples, owing to their lack of understanding, have repeatedly questioned Jesus, but after He has been glorified this will no longer be necessary, for they will have the Spirit to guide them into all truth (see on *vv.* 12-15). They will still, however, need to make requests to God in prayer, and they are assured of an answer to any prayer offered in Jesus' name (cf. **14¹³⁻¹⁴, 15¹⁶**). Hitherto they have not prayed in His name—such prayer is only possible after His exaltation. The promise of an answer to prayer is repeated in a form reminiscent of that of Mt 7⁷ and Lk 11⁹. The words '*that your joy may be complete*' suggest that the complete and lasting joy promised in **16²⁰⁻²** will only remain theirs as they maintain, by constant prayer, a close communion with their Risen Lord.

16²⁵. '*These things*' refers to the Farewell Discourse generally. '*proverbs*' represents the same word as is translated 'parable' in **10⁶**. Here the meaning is clearly 'figures of speech' (*NEB*), for such a way of speaking is contrasted with speaking '*plainly*' (the adverb is that found in **10²⁴, 11¹⁴**). Jesus' teaching up to now has been clothed in symbolical language, but the time is coming—i.e. after the Resurrection (cf. *v.* 23a)—when they will be taught in plain words.

16²⁶⁻⁷. Then they will pray in Christ's name (cf. *vv.* 23b-4). Jesus adds words which at first sight seem to contradict His promise in **14¹⁶**, but which probably mean that it will not be necessary for the Exalted Christ to pray to the Father on behalf of the disciples since they are already the objects of the Father's love, as those who have responded, in faith and love, to the revelation in Christ (cf. **14²¹, ²³**). Here, as throughout the Gospel, the complete unity of will and purpose between Father and Son is stressed. The idea of a loving, merciful Son pleading for sinners before an angry, offended Father is completely out of harmony with NT teaching.

16²⁸ summarizes the whole truth about Jesus—His divine origin, His incarnation, death and exaltation.

16²⁹. The disciples think that He is now fulfilling His promise in *v.* 25 and speaking plainly. But they deceive themselves, for the language of *v.* 28 is no different from that which Jesus has previously used. As we have seen, it is after the Resurrection and coming of the Spirit that the disciples will understand the plain meaning of His teaching.

16³⁰⁻¹. They claim to understand Jesus' complete knowledge —His ability to read men's thoughts (cf. **2²⁴⁻⁵**) and to answer their questions without their having to ask them (cf. **16¹⁹**)—and on this basis they believe that Jesus has come from God. Their faith, like that of Nathanael (**1⁴⁸⁻⁹**, cf. **4⁴⁸**) is based on Jesus' supernatural knowledge. This, as we have seen, is a low level of faith, which reveals how far they still are from understanding their Lord's teaching. There is therefore a note of disappointment in Jesus' answer, implying as it does that their faith is still immature.

16³². Jesus proceeds to tell them that the inadequacy of their faith will be revealed in the time of testing that is ahead (that has indeed arrived, for the process of His arrest has already been set in motion). The little company will be scattered, each fleeing to his own home and leaving Jesus alone (cf. Mk 14²⁷, where Jesus makes much the same prophecy by quoting Zech 13⁷). He adds that He will not be entirely alone, for the Father is always with Him; as has been repeatedly emphasized throughout the Gospel, the Father and the Son work together in complete unity in everything, and this includes the redemptive act upon the Cross. Whatever may be the meaning of the Cry of Dereliction (see *CLM* on Mk 15³⁴), it cannot mean that Christ was actually forsaken by His Father.

16³³. The long discourse concludes with another reference to the peace which the disciples may find by virtue of their relationship with Christ (cf. **14²⁷**). This peace, they are reminded again, is not an absence of tribulation, of which they will have plenty (cf. **15¹⁸⁻²⁵, 16²⁻³**). They may take courage, however, in the assurance that Christ has conquered the world. The Cross is the focal point of His conflict with the world and its 'prince' (see on **12³¹, 14³⁰⁻¹, 16¹¹**). Here, as He prepares to go to the Cross, Jesus declares prophetically (see p. 150) that His victory is achieved. In that victory believers share by faith (cf. 1 Jn 5⁴⁻⁵, and see *GPL*, pp. 114-16).

(*a*) **16¹** reminds us of the possibility that Christian faith may break down under the stress of trial and persecution. It also points, however, to the secret of avoiding such a breakdown, which is to remember that Jesus both warned us to expect trial and persecution and promised us the resources to endure and conquer (cf. *v.* 33). (*b*) Verses 2-3 remind us of all the injustice and cruelty that can be practised in the name of religion, arising out of the failure to understand God's true nature and purpose. It was the religious authorities that brought about Jesus' death. (*c*) Verse 7 contains the supreme example of the truth that what appears at the time to be stark tragedy and irreparable loss may be seen, in the light of later events, to be the means of infinite gain (cf. **12²⁴**). This verse also witnesses to the truth that there could be no Pentecost without

Calvary (cf. 7^{39}). (*d*) 16^{8-11} is the classic description of the Holy Spirit's working upon the mind and conscience of men. Only He can make sinners aware of their need of salvation and enable them to understand how God fulfils that need; but it is through the Church's prophetic preaching that the Spirit is able to exercise this influence upon men (cf. Acts 2^{37}). (*e*) Verse 12 is suggestive. Just as all education must progress from step to step, so must the instruction of Christian disciples. The elements must be mastered before the more advanced aspects can be approached (cf. Heb 5^{12}). But we do not have to wait until we reach maturity before we can take our place in the fellowship of the Church; there is room in Christ's 'school' for the elementary classes. The disciples' immaturity did not prevent Jesus from entrusting His mission to them. The important thing is that we should continually advance up the school under the guidance of the Spirit. (*f*) Verses 13-15, in addition to developing more fully the teaching of 14^{26} and 15^{26}, bear witness to the perfect unity that exists between the Persons of the Trinity. The Spirit speaks only what He hears from the Father; what He speaks are the things of Christ; and what is Christ's is the Father's. By this ministry of the Spirit the believer has the privilege of being admitted into the riches of the divine mind. (*g*) Verses 20-2 illustrate the gospel's power to transform bitter and sorrowful experiences into occasions of deep and lasting joy. The secret of joy (cf. 15^{11}) is to enjoy Christ's companionship. He draws near to us in all life's storms and distresses (cf. 6^{19-21}) and transforms them by His presence. Verse 24 suggests, however, that this sense of Christ's presence must be nurtured in prayer. (*h*) Verse 28 is a concise summary of the Christian doctrine about Christ, and can be filled out by this Gospel as a whole, or by such a passage as Phil 2^{5-11}. (*i*) Verse 32 presents a vivid picture of Jesus, in His passion and death, forsaken by all His friends but never forsaken by God. He may have *felt*, in the dreadful moment of Mk 15^{34}, as if God had forsaken Him; but 'there never was an utterance that reveals more amazingly the distance between feeling and fact' (T. R. Glover). (*j*) Verse 33 fittingly sums up the fundamental message of the Farewell Discourse. Jesus has warned the disciples of the tribulation that awaits them. He has never promised His followers a life of ease and comfort. But He does promise peace in the midst of distress (cf. 14^{27}) and a share in His own victory. His conquest of the world means that He and not the devil is henceforth its Ruler, and that through His Church's mission His rule over it is being extended.

Chapter 17

17¹⁻²⁶: The Prayer of Jesus

WE come now to one of the most sacred passages in the whole
NT. It is the only lengthy prayer of Jesus to be recorded in
the four Gospels—though they all testify to Jesus' regular
practice of prayer. Only John tells us that Jesus prayed with
and for His disciples in the Upper Room, but that is no reason
for doubting the fact. It is inherently probable that He would
pray in this critical hour of His ministry, and it is reasonable to
suppose that the substance of His prayer on such a solemn
and memorable occasion would remain indelibly stamped
upon the disciples' memory. What we have in this chapter, as
in the discourses of Jesus in *Jn*, may not always represent the
actual words uttered by Jesus but the essential content thereof,
expressed in the language and idiom of the evangelist and
interpreted under the guidance of the Holy Spirit in accordance
with the promise of **16¹³⁻¹⁵**. We may therefore turn to this
chapter confident that in it we find revealed the mind and will
of our Lord as expressed in the most solemn and momentous
hour of His sojourn on earth. The prayer is appropriately
called the 'Prayer of Consecration' because in it Jesus consecrates Himself to the act of sacrifice whereby He is to consummate His own mission, and prays for the consecration of
the disciples to the mission they are to fulfil after His departure
to heaven (*vv.* 17-18). It is also appropriately called the 'High-
priestly Prayer', not only as it is the prayer of the great High-
priest as He consecrates the victim (in this case Himself) for
the atoning sacrifice about to be offered on the Cross, but also
because it foreshadows the continuous intercession at the
throne of grace of the Eternal High-priest on behalf of the
Church (see *GPL* on 1 Jn 2¹, and cf. Rom 8³⁴, Heb 7²⁵). Thus
the prayer not only reveals Jesus' mind at the most solemn
moment of His life on earth; it also reveals the mind and will
of the Eternal Lord for His Church and its mission in the world
in every age. The prayer falls naturally into three parts: (*i*) In

the opening verses Jesus has in mind the fulfilment of the mission of His own incarnate life and death (*vv.* 1-5); (*ii*) He proceeds to think of the needs of the Church which He is leaving behind in the world to fulfil its appointed mission (*vv.* 6-19); (*iii*) Finally His thought moves forward to embrace the world to which that mission is directed (*vv.* 20-6).

17¹⁻². '*These things*' comprise the whole Farewell Discourse from **13³¹**.

'*lifting up his eyes. . . . Father*'. See on **11⁴¹⁻²**.

'*the hour is come*', i.e. the hour of Jesus' glorifying (cf. **12²³**). Acknowledging as always His absolute dependence on the Father, Jesus asks His Father to effect His glorification. The glorifying of the Son by death and resurrection becomes the glorifying of the Father too, not only because it is the supreme revelation of God's character, but also because by it is achieved the Father's purpose of imparting eternal life to men. The right so to impart eternal life belongs to the Son, to whom the Father has given authority over all mankind (cf. **5²⁴⁻⁹**). He is to give this life to those whom God has given Him, i.e. those who in faith have responded to the divine 'pull' (see **6³⁷, ⁴⁴**).

17³ is probably a comment by the evangelist on the meaning of '*eternal life*' rather than part of the actual prayer (Jesus would not need to define the term for the Father's benefit!). The term has been used throughout the Gospel (see on **3¹⁶**), and here we find John's classic definition of it. It means knowing '*the only true God*', who can only be known by knowing the Messiah whom He has sent, namely Jesus (cf. **1¹⁸, 14⁹**, etc.). This knowledge of God is not just an intellectual grasp of truth, but more a matter of personal acquaintance. To have eternal life means to enter into a living personal relationship of intimate communion with God, a real sharing in His own life. As such it is the life of the world to come, though by the gift of Christ it can in some measure be inherited here in this world (cf. **10¹⁰**).

17⁴⁻⁵. Here Jesus speaks of the work entrusted to Him by the Father as already '*accomplished*' (cf. **4³⁴, 19²⁸⁻³⁰**), thus regarding the Cross as already behind Him (see introductory comment on **13³¹⁻⁵**). It is by this perfect fulfilment of the Father's will that He has glorified the Father on earth (cf. *v.* 1); and it is on the basis thereof that He can now confidently ask the Father to glorify Him by exalting Him to the place at His own side which belonged to the Son from eternity (cf. 1¹, 6⁶²) and which He left in order to become incarnate. There is nothing unseemly in Jesus asking for this glorification, because He knows that His path to glory is the way of the Cross.

17⁶⁻⁸. Jesus' thoughts now turn to His disciples, who constitute the nucleus of His Church and the firstfruits of the community of believers which the Father has given Him (cf. *v.* 2). Jesus has prepared them for their all-important task by making known to them the Father's name. A person's '*name*', for the Jew, includes his nature, character and purpose. Jesus has revealed the Father to them by allowing them to be with Himself, seeing and knowing Him intimately—for to see and know Jesus is to see and know the Father (cf. 14⁷⁻⁹). The disciples on their part have received this revelation with obedience and faith and now, having recognized and believed in the divine nature and origin of Jesus and of His mission, they are fully equipped for the part they are to play after He has left them.

17⁹⁻¹⁰. '*not for the world*'. This of course does not mean that Jesus is not concerned for the world (on the meaning of '*world*' see on 1¹⁰); His concern for it is manifest in *vv.* 20-1 and in 3¹⁶⁻¹⁷ and 6⁵¹. In this part of the prayer, however, Jesus' concern is for the needs of the disciples set within the hostile world (cf. 15¹⁸-16³). They belong to the Father and to the Son (cf. 16¹⁵) and in them Jesus is glorified; this latter statement is again an anticipation of what is to become a fact through the Church's witness to Jesus.

17¹¹⁻¹². He continues to speak from the point of view of the post-Ascension Church, when He Himself is no longer in the world but His disciples are.

'*keep them in thy name . . . given me*'. The precise interpretation of this petition is uncertain, as a glance at *NEB* with marginal notes will show, but it probably means that God's name (see on *vv.* 6-8), which is also the Son's name—i.e. all that God is—will be their protection from the hostility of the world. Under such divine protection the disciples will be able to manifest among themselves the same unity as exists between the Father and the Son (this idea is more fully developed in *vv.* 21-3). During the period of the Incarnation Jesus Himself was able to provide this protection for His disciples, and none of them was lost except Judas (here called '*the son of perdition*') —and this loss was inevitable, having been foretold in scripture (cf. **13^{18}**).

17^{13}. Another consequence of their being kept in the divine name will be the possession in their hearts of Jesus' own joy (cf. **16$^{20-4}$**).

17$^{14-16}$. Jesus has delivered to the disciples the Father's word of self-revelation, and they have obeyed it (see *v.* 6). This has taken them out of the world, so that they no longer belong to it, just as Jesus does not belong to it (cf. **8^{23}**). Consequently the world hates them (see **15$^{18-19}$**). Nevertheless the disciples are to remain in the world. Jesus does not pray that they may escape from the world, for if that happened His mission to the world would remain unfulfilled. He prays rather that they may be protected from '*the evil one*', i.e. the devil who is 'the prince of this world' (**12^{31}, 14^{30}, 16^{11}**), and as such inspires and leads the world's attack on the Church.

17$^{17-19}$. Hitherto Jesus has been thinking more of the protection of the Church from the hostility and contamination of the world than of its positive mission to the world. He now prays that the disciples may be consecrated to their mission (*RVm* is to be preferred to *RV* in these verses, cf. *NEB*). They are to be consecrated '*in the truth*', the truth which is the '*word*' of God, i.e. the whole content of the revelation brought by Christ. Their mission is to bear witness to this truth. Jesus' sending of the disciples on this mission to the world corresponds to the Father's sending Him into the world (see on **6^{57}**). Their consecration to their mission, however, is possible only when Jesus' own mission is accomplished, and so He proceeds to consecrate Himself to the consummation of that mission, which is '*for their sakes*' (cf. **10^{36}**, where the Father is said to have consecrated the Son in sending Him into the world). The Church's mission is meaningless except as it depends on the redemptive ministry fulfilled once and for all by Christ Himself in His death and resurrection. The word translated 'consecrate' is one that was often used of the consecration of the victim by the priest for a sacrifice, so that its use by Jesus here may indicate the sacrificial nature of His death (cf. **1**[29]).

17[20-1]. In the closing part of His prayer Jesus' thought extends to include the world into which He is sending His disciples (cf. *v.* 18). It is true that even here He does not pray directly for the world (cf. *v.* 9)—the subject of His intercession is still the Church as the community of those who believe in Him through the witness of the apostles—but His concern for the salvation of the world is clear from His prayer for the success of the Church's mission to it. He desires that the world may come to believe in Him. The content of His prayer for the Church is '*that they may all be one*'. As the Church grows through the apostles' mission and comes to include men of different backgrounds, traditions and temperaments, its essential unity must be preserved if the world is to be won to faith. This unity, as already hinted in *v.* 11, corresponds to the perfect unity between the Father and the Son; *v.* 21, however, suggests, not only that the Church's unity is to be modelled on that of the Godhead, but that it is actually to be included as part of the divine unity: '*that they also may be in us*' (the 'one' included in this clause in *AV* is not part of the original text). This means that the unity of the Church is first a relationship in which the Church as a whole stands to God, and then a relationship in which its members stand to one another. It is as the Church partakes in the very life of the Godhead that the perfect unity which is Christ's will for it can be realized.

17[22]. In order to achieve this unity among His disciples Jesus says that He has given them the glory which the Father has given Him, i.e. a share in the divine character and activity (see note on '*glory*' at **1**[14]).

17[23]. The unity of the Church is perfected as it is indwelt by Christ, who is Himself indwelt by the Father. 'The disciples form a circle of love which includes also both the Father and the Son. The existence of any part of this circle bears witness to the whole' (C. K. Barrett). And the result of this witness of a Church united in God will be to convince the world (cf. *v.* 21) that Jesus is indeed sent by God and that the Church, with Himself, is the object of the Father's love.

17²⁴. Jesus now expresses His desire that the members of His Church, who are God's gift to Him (cf. *v.* 2), may come to be with Him so as to behold the glory which belonged to Him through the Father's love from eternity, and to which He is now to be restored (cf. *v.* 5). There is a sense (see *v.* 22) in which the Church already shares in the glory that is the life of the Godhead. But the ultimate destiny of the Church is to behold the divine glory, and to be with Christ, in a fuller measure than can ever be realized on earth. Hitherto Jesus has been praying for the Church's preservation and unity and for the fulfilment of its mission while it remains in the world as a community that is not 'of the world'. Now, however, He looks forward to the time when the Church, having fulfilled its mission on earth, will follow Him to the place He has gone to prepare for it (cf. **14²⁻³**).

17²⁵⁻⁶. Finally Jesus' thought turns again to the world, whose tragedy is that it has not known God (cf. **1¹⁰**)—in spite of the revelation given in Christ. But if such blindness constitutes the world's tragedy, its hope lies in the fact that there are now within it those whose eyes have been opened by One who has known the Father, and who has imparted His knowledge to them (cf. **1¹⁸, 17⁶**), and who will continue to do so through the Holy Spirit (cf. **14²⁶, 16¹³⁻¹⁴**). As they receive this revelation they will have, within them and amongst them, the love which is the essence of the divine nature. This love will be in them because Christ Himself will be dwelling in them. The prayer ends on this note, which has been so prominent throughout the Farewell Discourse (cf. **14²⁰, ²³, 15¹⁻¹¹**).

(*a*) That the path to glory for Christ was the path of humiliation and sacrificial suffering is a fact which cannot be without significance for the Church. 'It is the way the Master went; should not the servant tread it still?' (*MHB* 589). (*b*) **17³** provides the classic definition of eternal life and is the obvious text for a sermon on this theme. The previous verse reveals that this life can only be obtained as a gift from Christ, and that the gift is made to those whom the Father has enabled to believe in Him. The context in which the reference to eternal life is set suggests that the gift only becomes possible as the result of Jesus' death. (*c*) Verses 6-8 tell us what kind of men they were to whom Jesus was able to entrust His mission to the world. They had been called '*out of the world*' by God; they had been to school with Jesus, learning the truth about God's nature, character and purpose; and they had received the divine revelation with faith and obedience. Ought not the same to be true of Christ's missionaries (i.e. of all Christians) at all times? (*d*) Verses 9-10 contain the assurance that the Church, as it is engaged in its mission in the world, is constantly being prayed for by its exalted Lord (on the high-priestly prayer as the pattern of the High-priest's continuous intercession on high, see p. 176). There is also the hint in *v.* 10b that Christ's glory is to shine through the Church as it fulfils its mission. The tragedy of the Church is that it so often hides rather than reveals His glory. Only as His prayer is answered can this tragedy be avoided. (*e*) To be saved and brought into the Church, far from making us immune from the danger of attack or contamination by the world, exposes us all the more to its hatred and to the enmity of the Evil One (see *vv.* 11-16). Christians are called to live in the world as not belonging to the world, and only the protection and power of God Himself can make this possible. Our comfort is to know that this divine protection and power are ever available and that as Jesus invoked it for His first disciples so He continues to invoke it for His Church at all times. (*f*) The relation of Jesus' own mission to that of the Church comes out clearly in *vv.* 17-19. The Church's mission is an extension of His—He sends them out as the Father sent Him; it is only made possible by the perfect fulfilment of His redemptive ministry; and for it they too have to be consecrated as He was. (*g*) 17^{20-3} is the classic text on the unity of the Church. It reveals that unity is Christ's will for the Church, and that it is a unity grounded in the perfect unity of the Godhead. This means that the only way the unity can be realized is for each of the sundered sections of the Church to realize fully in its own life the indwelling presence of Christ Himself. It is only as we severally draw closer to Him that we shall draw effectively closer to one another. The Church's unity, however, is to be modelled on that of the Godhead, which is one in which personal distinctions find a place (see on 1^{1-5}). The believer, though one with Christ and God, retains his personal identity. The unity of believers with one another must be of the same kind—a unity of love and sympathy and character and purpose, but not necessarily a uniformity in which each member's individuality would be lost. This is true, but 'we cannot suppose that the author of this exalted prayer would have been content with the grudging toleration or even apathetic indifference which sometimes passes for Christian courtesy and charity in relations between the denominations' (A. R. George). Finally this passage, though making clear that Church unity is to be sought as an end in itself, rightly emphasizes that the achievement of true unity becomes an effective means to the fulfilment of the Church's mission to the world. Experience may not suggest that the converting power of the Church's mission is completely nullified by the divisions of Christendom, but that power would undoubtedly be enormously enhanced were the divisions less marked and less bitter. 'It is not our unity as such that has converting power; it is our incorporation into the true Vine as branches in which the divine life is flowing. When all believers are truly "in Christ", then their witness will have its destined effect' (W. Temple). (*h*) Verse 24 points to the Church's ultimate destiny. For it, as for its Lord, the world is not its homeland and there is reserved for it in the end a glorious home-coming. (*i*) Verses 25-6 underline the tragedy of the world and show that its hope lies in the presence within it of the Church. Jesus has not in this chapter prayed directly for the world, but His concern for its salvation is obvious. The only meaningful prayer that can be offered for the world is that it should cease to be '*the world*' in the Johannine sense; and to pray for the success of the Church's mission to it amounts to just that.

Chapter 18

18^{1-11}: The Arrest of Jesus

THE narrative of the events leading up to the crucifixion is now resumed after the long section devoted to the discourse and prayer in the Upper Room (13^{31}-17^{26}). In the sequence of these events John's agreement with the Synoptics is closer than at any other point in his Gospel. There are, however, certain significant differences, some of which are due to the evangelist's symbolical interests, but some of which (particularly details of time, place and personalities, which do not seem to serve any symbolical purpose) are no doubt to be accounted for by John's use of reliable historical traditions independent of those used by the Synoptists.

18^{1-2}. '*the brook Kidron*'. A ravine to the east of Jerusalem (cf. 2 Sam 15^{23}), in which the river flowed only in winter— the word translated 'brook' literally means 'winter-flowing'. Jesus and His disciples leave the city and cross this ravine to a garden which was a frequent rendezvous of theirs. This was undoubtedly the place called Gethsemane in Mk 14^{32} and Mt 26^{36}; neither Luke nor John gives the name, and only John describes the place as a garden.

'*knew the place*'. Presumably Judas also knew of Jesus' intention to visit it, and this was what he betrayed to the priestly authorities (see *CLM* on Mk 14^{10-11}).

18^3. Judas, having left the Upper Room (13^{30}), has meanwhile been busy preparing to execute his plan of betrayal, and now he leads to the garden a company of Roman soldiers and Temple police.

'*the band of soldiers*'. The word used literally means a cohort of six hundred men, but could be used loosely of a smaller detachment. Only John specifically mentions the participation of Roman soldiers in the arrest of Jesus (cf. Mk 14^{43}), but it is quite possible that the Jewish authorities

sought the assistance of the Roman army in this way.
'officers'. See on 7³².

'lanterns and torches'. Only John mentions that these, as
well as weapons, were carried. The detail is no doubt historically accurate, though he may see some symbolical significance
in it as underlining the utter darkness of the night in which
Judas' black deed is accomplished (cf. 13³⁰).

18⁴⁻⁶. The main feature of John's account of the arrest is the
masterful attitude of Jesus, who is presented as being in
complete control of the situation. He appears not as the pitiful
and helpless prey cornered by the huntsmen, but as the
triumphant and completely self-composed Victor. It is not
Judas who takes the initiative, as in the Synoptic accounts, but
Jesus (cf. 6⁵). John does not mention the kiss of betrayal;
Judas' role, after leading the company to the garden, is a
passive one (*v.* 5b). Jesus is fully aware of all that is to happen
(cf. 1⁴⁷⁻⁸, 2²⁴⁻⁵, etc.), and voluntarily gives Himself up (cf.
10¹⁸).

'I am he' need not here mean more than 'I am the man you
seek', but the expression is the same as that used in 6³⁵, 8²⁴,
etc., and it is probable that John wants to suggest its deeper
theological significance. This is confirmed by the soldiers'
dramatic reaction to Jesus' words; the language used here is
probably to be understood figuratively rather than literally
(cf. Ps 27²), but it is easy to believe that the soldiers and
Temple police were taken aback and filled with awe when
confronted by the regal presence and bearing of Jesus (cf. 7⁴⁴⁻⁷).

18⁷⁻⁹. So taken aback are they that the question and answer
have to be repeated, and this time Jesus adds the request that
His disciples be allowed to go free. John comments that this
was to secure the fulfilment of Jesus' words in His prayer
(17¹²). According to the Synoptics the disciples fled of their
own accord (Mk 14⁵⁰), but John wishes to present Jesus as
controlling the whole proceedings; possibly also he wants to
symbolize the truth that by delivering Himself up to death
Jesus secured freedom for His followers (the Good Shepherd
laying down His life for the sheep, 10¹¹, ¹⁵).

18¹⁰⁻¹¹. This incident is included in all the Gospels, but only
John names the attacker and the victim as Simon Peter and

Malchus respectively. There is no reason to doubt the historicity of these details; the act is completely in harmony with Peter's character (cf. **13^{37}**, where he seems to be thinking in terms of the battlefield), and the name Malchus has no symbolical significance. As in all the accounts, Jesus disapproves of this attempt to defend Him by force. He tells Peter to sheathe his sword, but the reason given for this command is rather different from that given in Mt 26^{52} (on which see *AMW*). John is not interested so much in the ethical implications of Jesus' attitude as in the fact that Jesus, realizing that the way of the Cross is the way of His divine vocation, does not allow anyone to prevent Him from walking that way. The reference to the cup is a clear echo of Jesus' prayer in Gethsemane (see *CLM* on Mk 14^{36}, and cf. Mk 10^{38}), and indicates that John knew the tradition of the Agony in the Garden, though he does not record it (see on **12$^{27-8}$**).

(*a*) There is a dramatic contrast between the elaborate preparations for the arrest—the combined force, representing Jewish and Roman authorities, armed with lights and weapons as if setting out to subdue an armed revolt—and Jesus' passive non-resistance. The superior power and authority of spiritual force over physical is suggested by *v.* 6. (*b*) Jesus' masterful attitude throughout this passage strikingly illustrates the truth of His claim in **10^{18}**. The Cross is not just a matter of passive non-resistance to evil; it is positive victory over evil. (*c*) Verses 8-9 point to the vicarious aspect of Jesus' sacrifice. He was taken captive that captives might be set free. (*d*) Verses 10-11 reveal not only that Jesus is not to be defended by violent force, but also that the obedient acceptance of suffering is the divinely appointed means of overcoming the forces of evil.

18$^{12-27}$: The Jewish Trial and Peter's Denial

As in Mk 14$^{53-72}$ and Mt 26$^{57-75}$ these two narratives are interwoven and are set in the courtyard of the high-priest during the night of Jesus' arrest. Both Mark and Matthew imply that the trial before the high-priest Caiaphas during the night was an unofficial preliminary investigation, the results of which were ratified by a brief official gathering of the whole Sanhedrin early the following morning (see *CLM* on Mk 15^1). John's account is rather different: the only interrogation of Jesus he records takes place during the night at the house of Annas (see *v.* 13) and is apparently conducted by the latter—on somewhat different lines from those followed in the Synoptic narrative. There is no mention of an official gathering of the Sanhedrin presided over by the official high-priest, though such a meeting may be implied by *vv.* 24 and 28. The confusion as to whether Annas or Caiaphas is meant by the references to the high-priest (see on *v.* 19) has led to the rearrangement of the order of the verses in this section in some ancient versions and modern translations and commentaries (see *NEBm*).

18¹²⁻¹⁴. '*Annas*' had been high-priest from AD 6-15, being deposed by the Roman authorities. It is not impossible that the Jews refused to recognize Roman authority in religious matters and continued to regard Annas as high-priest in fact if not in name. In Lk 3² and Acts 4⁶ also his name is linked with that of Caiaphas, and put first. Only John describes him as Caiaphas' father-in-law, but there is no reason to doubt the fact.
    '*high priest that year*'. See on 11⁴⁹⁻⁵⁰.

18¹⁵⁻¹⁸. Here we have the first half of the story of Peter's denial. All four Gospels include this, and though differing in details they agree that the denial was threefold (as predicted by Jesus, cf. 13³⁸) and that it took place in the courtyard of the high-priest (whether Annas or Caiaphas), whither Peter had followed Jesus and His captors. Only John, however, mentions the presence with Peter of '*another disciple . . . known unto the high priest*', by whose influence with the woman doorkeeper Peter was admitted to the courtyard. The identity of this other disciple has been much discussed; he has traditionally been identified with the 'beloved disciple' of 13²³, i.e. the apostle John. The word translated '*known*' suggests more than a casual acquaintanceship, and it is unlikely that any Galilean fisherman would be a close friend of the high-priest (the suggestion that the firm of Zebedee and Sons were suppliers of fish to the household of Annas or Caiaphas is somewhat fanciful!). Some think that the evangelist himself is meant, and that here he slips in a passing reference to himself, as Mark may have done in Mk 14⁵¹⁻² (see *CLM* thereon). In any case it is probable that the disciple in question was not one of the twelve (who had all, except Peter, left Jesus and fled, according to Mk 14⁵⁰), but an inhabitant of Jerusalem who had become a follower of Jesus (as had Nicodemus and Joseph of Arimathea, cf. 19³⁸⁻⁹). All the Gospels agree that it was a maid's question that led to Peter's first denial, but only John says that the maid in question was the doorkeeper (this is not unlikely, cf. Acts 12¹³). The '*also*' in her question may suggest that she knew that Peter's companion was a follower of Jesus. There is nothing vicious in the question; at worst it is a provocative taunt, but it is enough to floor Peter. As in Mk 14⁵⁴, Peter is described as standing by the fire, warming himself with the household servants and Temple police. This scene is resumed at **18²⁵**.

18¹⁹. '*The high priest*' would seem at first sight to refer to Caiaphas, but *vv.* 13 and 24 clearly imply that the official high-priest was not present. If Annas was in fact 'the power behind the throne' (see on *vv.* 12-14), there is no reason why John should not refer to him as '*the high priest*' (cf. Lk 3², Acts 4⁶), nor any reason why he should not have conducted the preliminary investigation. Whoever conducted it, the questions concerned Jesus' disciples and teaching, their purpose no doubt being to seek to establish on the one hand that Jesus was inciting a revolt against Roman authority (this would interest Pilate), and on the other hand that He was teaching heretical doctrines (this would interest the Sanhedrin).

18²⁰⁻¹. Jesus' reply exposes the falsity of the former charge, in that His teaching has been delivered '*openly to the world*' in synagogue (cf. 6⁵⁹) and Temple (cf. 7¹⁴, ²⁸, 8²⁰), and not in secret conclaves such as would befit a rebel band. As for the content of His teaching, if the high-priest wishes to learn it, he should ask those who have heard it. There may be in this reply an element of protest, since the proper method of procedure at a trial, according to rabbinical practice, was to call witnesses to testify against the defendant rather than ask him to testify against himself.

18²²⁻³. Regarding Jesus' reply as impertinent, one of the Temple police strikes Him, thus exceeding his powers—his complaint should have been addressed to the presiding high-priest. Jesus reminds him of this, showing a courtesy and dignity in strong contrast to his assailant's callous impetuosity.

18²⁴. After the inconclusive examination, Annas sends Jesus bound to the official high-priest Caiaphas. Presumably there follows a more formal trial, on the lines of the Synoptic accounts, but John has nothing of this, though *v.* 28 implies that the Sanhedrin resolved to take the case before the Roman governor.

18²⁵⁻⁷. The story of the denial is now concluded (cf. *vv.* 15-18). The second denial is here in reply to a question asked by Peter's companions around the fire, and the third in reply to the challenge of one of the high-priest's servants who was a relative of Malchus (see **18¹⁰**) and therefore had good cause for recognizing Peter. Here it is not Peter's Galilean accent that gives him away (cf. *CLM* on Mk 14⁷⁰), but his impetuous act of violence in the garden. There is no reason why both Synoptic and Johannine accounts should not contain an element of truth; Malchus' relative may have recognized Peter, and the reference to his accent may have arisen in the ensuing discussion as corroborative evidence against him. John concludes the narrative with restraint and considerable dramatic effect, with no reference (as in the other Gospels) to the effect of the cockcrow on Peter. Nothing more is heard of Peter in this Gospel until after the Resurrection.

(*a*) The contrast between the two scenes interwoven in this passage is suggestive. Jesus, faced with the whole weight of Jewish authority intent on destroying Him, stands firm—self-possessed and in complete control of the situation; Peter, faced with no more than the mockery of a servant-girl and the suspicion of a slave whose relative he has injured, goes completely to pieces. How often do we see the same great contrast between His steadfastness and our instability and unfaithfulness? (*b*) There is also a striking contrast between Peter's attitude here and that shown by him in the garden (**18¹⁰⁻¹¹**). He was ready to draw his sword to fight an army on behalf of Jesus, but ashamed to confess Him before a servant-girl and a few bystanders. Such instability is characteristic of many Christians. There are some who, if it ever became necessary, would die for their faith in circumstances of religious persecution; but they cannot stand a little mockery of their religious principles and associations. (*c*) The policeman's attitude in *v.* 22 typifies the approach of those who find it easier to answer truth with a blow than with an argument. Jesus' reasoned and dignified reply is in sharp contrast; again we see the triumph of spiritual authority over that of brute force (cf. **18⁶**).

18²⁸⁻⁴⁰: The Trial Before Pilate

John's account of the Roman trial (which continues to **19¹⁶**) is fuller and more dramatic than those of the Synoptics—although it agrees with them on the main outline of the story: the examination by Pilate, the latter's conviction of Jesus' innocence, the Barabbas incident, the scourging and mocking, the crowd's clamouring for His crucifixion and Pilate's ultimate capitulation to their demand. John, in his own characteristic way, expands this narrative by introducing a good deal of conversation between Jesus and Pilate (**18³³⁻⁸, 19⁹⁻¹¹**). According to Mk 15² Pilate's question to Jesus concerned His kingship; in *Jn* this develops into a discussion of the nature of kingship, and it is likely that the evangelist, basing himself on good historical tradition concerning the question at issue before Pilate, has made the history a vehicle for his own interpretation of Jesus' teaching on kingship. On the other hand, the details of time and place which John notes are probably based on his own special historical source, and where they differ from the Synoptics (e.g. at *v.* 28) they may well be more reliable.

18²⁸. '*the palace*' means 'the Praetorium' (*RVm*), as 'the Governor's headquarters' (*NEB*) in a provincial capital was called.

'*that they might not be defiled*'. To enter heathen precincts would defile the Jews, making them unfit to eat the Passover meal. This clearly means that (in contrast to the Synoptic accounts, see on **13¹**) the Passover meal has not yet taken place. According to John the trial takes place in the early morning of Nisan 14th, the day on the afternoon of which the lambs were killed in preparation for the Passover.

18²⁹. '*Pilate*' was Procurator of Judea, AD 26-36. He seems to have been a cruel and oppressive ruler who often clashed with the Jews (cf. Lk 13¹). The Jews, however, were quite prepared to make an ally of him (cf. Lk 23¹²) for the purpose of destroying Jesus. Since the Jews would not enter the praetorium, Pilate had to come out to them to enquire about the charge levelled against Jesus; he would be anxious to respect their religious scruples rather than risk a disturbance during the Passover season.

18³⁰⁻¹. Somewhat insolently the Jews in reply to Pilate's question simply insist that Jesus is a criminal. Pilate, assuming that the offence is a religious one, tells them to judge the case in their own courts (cf. Gallio's attitude in Acts 18¹⁵), whereupon the Jews explain that the charge is one involving capital punishment, which the Sanhedrin has no power to inflict. Whether or not the Sanhedrin at this time in fact lacked the power to deal with capital offences has been, and still is, the subject of much debate (the case of Stephen in Acts 7⁵⁴⁻⁶⁰ seems to point to the opposite conclusion from the present verse). In any case it is clear from all the Gospels that the Sanhedrin, having decided that Jesus was 'worthy of death' (Mk 14⁶⁴), decided to apply to Pilate to pass sentence on Him; even if they were entitled to execute Jesus themselves they may well have preferred to get Him done away with by Rome on a political charge, rather than to have to do so themselves on a religious charge—a course which would perhaps arouse deep feelings amongst the very mixed crowd assembled for the Passover.

18³². Had the Jews executed sentence themselves, the manner of death would have been by stoning (cf. 8^{5, 59}, Acts 7⁵⁴⁻⁶⁰), crucifixion being the Roman method of execution. John believes that Jesus foretold His own death by *crucifixion* (cf. 3¹⁴, 12³²⁻³), and that such a prophecy by Him must of course be fulfilled. Indeed John seems to believe that it was the divine will, not only that Jesus should die, but that He should die in this particular way: He must be 'lifted up' (see on 3¹⁴⁻¹⁵).

18³³. Now that he is aware of the serious nature of the charge, Pilate sees that he must investigate the case further, and takes Jesus inside the praetorium for this purpose. This has the very dramatic effect of giving Jesus and Pilate the stage to themselves, so to speak, for the ensuing dialogue. Pilate's question is the same as in the Synoptics (see *CLM* on Mk 15²), and its form confirms that the charge actually brought against Jesus before Pilate was that specified in Lk 23².

18³⁴⁻⁵. Jesus replies by asking another question, which reveals His knowledge that the governor's question has been prompted by the Jews' allegations. Pilate asks impatiently, '*Am I a Jew?*', indicating that the convictions and claims of a Jew are of no personal interest to him. In his official capacity, however, he has been put into the position of having to investigate the charge against Jesus, so he enquires of Him what He has done to warrant such a charge. John presents Pilate as a judge who wishes to be fair and to give Jesus an opportunity to defend Himself.

18³⁶. Jesus now answers Pilate's original question. In the Synoptics His only reply to this question is a qualified 'Thou sayest' (see *CLM* on Mk 15²); here in *Jn*, however, he answers more fully by explaining that, though He is indeed a king, His kingdom is not '*of this world*'. He is king in a spiritual, not a political sense, so that He constitutes no threat to Roman authority. The fact that His disciples did not resist His arrest by force (though Peter actually tried to do so, 18¹⁰⁻¹¹) is sufficient proof of the fact that His kingdom is not a worldly one. The word translated '*kingdom*' can also mean 'kingship' (*RSV*); *NEB* uses 'kingdom' in *v.* 36a and 'kingly authority' in *v.* 36b. Jesus does not mean that His authority as king does not extend to this world, but that it does not derive '*from hence*'.

18³⁷⁻⁸ᵃ. There is a touch of sarcasm in Pilate's question: 'You are a king, then?' (*NEB*). Jesus now gives the same qualified reply as in the Synoptics (see on *v.* 36), implying that '*king*' is Pilate's word. Then He proceeds to define His kingship further by explaining the purpose of His incarnation, which was to '*bear witness unto the truth*'. He does this, of course, by being Himself the embodiment of the absolute, eternal truth of God (cf. 1¹⁴, 14⁶), and it is in this that His kingship lies. 'The kingship of the Messiah is the sovereignty of the Truth which he reveals and embodies' (C. H. Dodd). Sovereignty belongs to truth in the sense that it demands absolute obedience. Such obedience is what Jesus means by '*heareth my voice*', and it is offered by everyone who is '*of the truth*', i.e. those who have believed in Jesus as 'the Truth'. Pilate is not one of these and cannot conceive what Jesus means by truth. His cynical question, '*What is truth?*', and the fact that he does not stay for an answer, reveal his assumption that such a vague abstraction is beyond man's power to grasp, and that to discuss it is a waste of time.

18³⁸ᵇ⁻⁴⁰. Pilate has seen and heard enough, however, to convince him of Jesus' political innocence, and he goes out to the

Jews to declare his verdict. Realizing, however, that Jewish feeling against Jesus is running high, he seeks a diplomatic way of releasing Him without offending them unduly. He mentions the custom whereby the governor releases a prisoner at Passover time (see *CLM* on Mk 15⁶), and asks whether they wish him to release Jesus in this way. As in the Synoptics, the Jewish crowd vociferously rejects such a suggestion and calls for the release of Barabbas (see *CLM* on Mk 15⁶⁻¹⁵ and *AMW* on Mt 27¹⁵⁻¹⁸).

'*a robber*'. The word probably here means a brigand or armed rebel. This corresponds to the fuller information in the Synoptic accounts, but John probably chooses the single word '*robber*' in order to underline the tragic significance of the Jews' choice—they preferred a robber (cf. the use of the same word in **10¹**) to the Life-giver (cf. **10¹⁰**).

(*a*) Verse 28 reveals John's characteristic irony. The Jews were meticulously careful about observing the ceremonial law but were prepared to resort to deceit and sharp practice in order to rid themselves of an innocent man they regarded as an enemy. There is always a danger for religious people to put trivial ceremonial requirements before vital moral issues of justice and integrity (cf. *AMW* on Mt 23²³⁻⁴). (*b*) There is something suggestive in the way both the Jewish authorities and Pilate try to avoid the responsibility of taking the final decision about Jesus. The Jews, whether or not they had the right to sentence Him to death, prefer to thrust the responsibility on to Pilate, because of their fear of Jesus' popular following. Pilate seeks to thrust the responsibility back on to the Sanhedrin (*v.* 31, cf. Lk 23⁷ where he tries to 'pass the buck' to Herod), because of his fear of offending the Jews and so creating trouble for himself. Men still seek to shelve the responsibility of making their minds up about Christ. (*c*) The scene inside the praetorium dramatically reveals the contrast between Jesus' kingship and that of worldly kings as represented by the Roman governor. The latter is domineering and oppressive, deriving its authority from men and bolstered by physical and armed force; the former is gentle and submissive, deriving its authority from God and unshakeable as truth itself. (*d*) Just as Jesus was, and His disciples are, in the world without being of it, so His kingship is to be exercised *in* the world and *over* it, without being derived *from* it (*v.* 36). (*e*) Verse 37 contains the only explicit reference in *Jn* to the birth of Jesus—and as summarizing in Johannine terms the purpose of the Incarnation it provides a good Christmas text. It reminds us that Jesus' coming into the world, like that of all men, was through the gateway of birth (cf. Gal 4^4); yet, unlike other men's entry into the world, His was a voluntary act, involving the forsaking of His former glory (cf. 1^{1-18}, 3^{13}, 6^{62}, 17^5). (*f*) Pilate's cynical impatience is typical of the attitude of many to the ultimate issues of life. Pilate throughout appears as a man anxious to avoid all responsible decisions. (*g*) The tragedy of the Jews' choice of Barabbas is re-enacted in every age; men choose a principle of life that in the end deprives them of life, and reject the Saviour who has brought eternal life within the reach of all.

Chapter 19

19¹⁻¹⁶: The Trial before Pilate (continued)

See introductory comment on 18²⁸⁻⁴⁰.

19¹. Pilate's attempt to find a way of releasing Jesus without causing undue offence to the Jews fails (18³⁸ᵇ⁻⁴⁰). Now he seeks another compromise by inflicting on Jesus a lesser punishment than death, i.e. scourging. Mark and Matthew record that the scourging took place after the sentence of crucifixion had been pronounced and as a preliminary to the execution, which was the Roman custom (see *CLM* on Mk 15¹⁵). It is possible, however, that Pilate in this case attempted to satisfy the Jews with scourging as a substitute for the extreme penalty (cf. Lk 23¹⁶, ²²).

19²⁻³. After the scourging comes the mockery of Jesus by the soldiers. For them the claim of such a pitiable prisoner to be a king is a great joke, and they make the most of it by dressing Him in royal purple and cruelly crowning Him with a crown of thorns (see *CLM* on Mk 15¹⁶⁻²⁰). One by one they pay Him mock homage, and add injury to the insult with their blows.

19⁴⁻⁵. The scourging and mocking took place within the praetorium (cf. Mk 15¹⁶). Pilate reappears and tells the crowd that he is going to bring Jesus out in order to try to convince them of His innocence. The sight of Jesus, more pitiable than ever after the physical torture He has endured, and clothed in the mock trappings of royalty, ought to show the Jews how ridiculous is their allegation that such a figure represents a political danger to Rome.

'Behold, the man!' Pilate probably pointed to the figure of Jesus in an attitude of sarcastic contempt mingled perhaps with pity. With his characteristic irony, however, John perceives, and intends his readers to perceive, a much deeper significance in the words of the governor. Like Caiaphas in 11⁵⁰, Pilate utters an unconscious prophecy which expresses a fundamental

Christian truth. It is the same truth as is expressed in the title 'Son of Man' (see on 1[51]). The Jewish expression 'Son of Man' would, of course, be out of place on the lips of a Gentile like Pilate, but there was a connection between the Jewish concept and that of the Heavenly Man (a supernatural Redeemer from heaven), which was common in Hellenistic religious thought. Thus by making Pilate refer to Jesus as 'the Man', John makes him an unwitting witness to the true character of Jesus' Person and mission.

19[6]. The Jewish authorities are not to be satisfied with any punishment for Jesus less than crucifixion and they clamour for it. Pilate protests for the third time (cf. 18[38], 19[4]) that he finds no case against Jesus, and again seeks to thrust his responsibility on to the Jews' shoulders. If Pilate actually told them to '*crucify him*', either he did not use the word in its literal sense (even if the Jews could legally have executed Jesus the method would have been by stoning, not by crucifixion, see on 18[30-2]), or he was deliberately taunting them to do what both he and they knew was not possible. By making Pilate use these words, however, John may be underlining the fact that the ultimate responsibility for the crucifixion was not Pilate's but the Jews'.

19[7]. In their reply the Jews introduce a new charge, thus revealing that their real reason for wanting to do away with Jesus is a religious rather than a political one (cf. Mk 14[55-64]). They refer to the law of blasphemy laid down in Lev 24[16] and declare that Jesus is liable to death for having claimed to be Son of God (cf. 5[18], 10[33, 36]).

19[8-9]. This is for Pilate a new aspect of the case, which calls for careful consideration. So he takes Jesus back into the praetorium for further questioning. Pilate has clearly been uneasy about the case from the start—afraid of arousing Jewish feeling that might lead to a disturbance of the peace in Judaea. His earlier clashes with the Jewish leaders have caused him sufficient trouble, and a further disturbance might well mean the end of his procuratorship. His fear now, however, goes deeper; his earlier conversation with Jesus (18[33-8a]) has made him realize that he is dealing with no ordinary prisoner and no ordinary man. And now, hearing of Jesus' claim to be

Son of God, he probably feels something of the awe that men naturally feel in the presence of the supernatural. Legends about sons of the gods visiting the earth were common amongst the Romans, so that Pilate, though far from understanding the true significance of Jesus' claim, may well have had an uneasy sense that He was no mere mortal . So he begins to question Him about His origins. As R. H. Strachan puts it, 'the answer is an imperial silence' (cf. Mk 14⁶⁰⁻¹, 15⁵, Lk 23⁹). We are reminded of the description of the Suffering Servant in Isa 53⁷. Jesus could not answer the question in a way that would be intelligible to one who was unwilling to accept the truth (cf. 18³⁷⁻⁸ᵃ).

19¹⁰⁻¹¹. Jesus' silence only adds to Pilate's bewilderment, and he tries to frighten Him into replying by reminding Him of his authority, as the representative of Imperial Rome, to decide His fate. Jesus replies that the only authority that Pilate (and the State he represents) possesses is that which has been delegated to them by the Ruler of the universe. This doctrine of the State as an ordinance of God is characteristic of NT teaching (cf. Rom 13¹⁻⁷, 1 Pet 2¹³⁻¹⁷). God is the ultimate seat of all authority, and every State is responsible to Him for the way it exercises the authority delegated to it. By crucifying the innocent Jesus, Pilate (and the State he represented) misused his authority and cannot escape responsibility. But Jesus asserts in *v.* 11b that the responsibility of Caiaphas (and the Jewish leaders represented by him) is greater than Pilate's. It was Caiaphas who forced Pilate's hand to condemn Jesus, and his sin is all the greater because it involves inciting the Roman State to misuse the authority entrusted to it by God.

19¹². Jesus' attitude in the foregoing conversation has more than ever convinced Pilate that he ought not to take action against Him. 'From that moment Pilate tried hard to release him' (*NEB*). The Jews, however, now play their 'trump card'; to claim to be a king is an act of treason against Caesar, and for the governor to condone such treason amounts to a betrayal of the Emperor—which can only lead to his dismissal from office. It is true that Jesus' claim, rightly understood, does not involve treason, but the Jewish authorities would have no difficulty in representing it as such to Rome—and their words here amount to a threat to do so.

19¹³⁻¹⁴. Pilate immediately sees the peril of his position. He has been struck at his weakest point, that of his personal ambition. His political career is more important to him than loyalty to what his conscience tells him is right. His period of indecision is now over; however reluctantly, he has decided what to do. He brings Jesus out of the praetorium again and sits down on the judge's tribunal to pronounce sentence. John carefully notes the place and time of this action, giving both Greek and Aramaic forms of the place-name (the Greek word means a stone-paved area, but the meaning and derivation of the Aramaic is obscure). The time is about mid-day (cf. 4⁶) on the day of '*Preparation of the passover*', i.e. Passover-eve (see on 18²⁸). According to Mk 15²⁵ Jesus was crucified at 'the third hour' (about 9 a.m. by our reckoning), but John's timing has the greater probability at this point. With a final touch of sarcasm Pilate presents Jesus to the Jews as '*your King*'; here, as in *v.* 5, John is probably making Pilate voice an unconscious prophecy, bearing witness to the fact of Jesus' kingship.

19¹⁵⁻¹⁶. The Jews angrily repudiate the suggestion that Jesus is their king (cf. *v.* 21) and clamour again for His crucifixion. Pilate provokes them still further with a question that still betrays his reluctance to give in to their demands. In their desire to convince Pilate, the chief priests assert that they recognize no king other than Caesar (thus implying a repetition of the threat in *v.* 12). This is sufficient to prompt Pilate to the decisive step of handing Jesus over to be crucified. Here more than anywhere we see to what depths of deceit and blasphemy the Jewish authorities were prepared to sink in order to get rid of Jesus. The foundation principle of Jewish religion was the conviction that the only king of Israel was God (cf. Judg 8²³, 1 Sam 8⁷). '*We have no king but Caesar*' is a denial of that principle which, on the lips of the chief priests of all people, is nothing short of blasphemy.

(*a*) Ridicule is often harder to endure than physical torture, and the story of what Jesus underwent for our salvation is not complete without reference to the mocking. (*b*) The scene depicted in *vv.* 4-5 is one of the most dramatic in the Bible and has made a deep impression on men's artistic imagination. The regal dignity of Jesus' perfect humanity, His divine authority and His redemptive ministry shine clearly through all the afflictions and indignities that have been heaped upon Him . (*c*) Verses 10-11 reveal how conscious political rulers are of their own authority, and how often they fail to realize that it is not an absolute authority but one that is derived from God, to whom they are responsible for its right exercise. If the Christian's duty is to submit to the authority of the State as ordained by God (Rom 13$^{1-7}$, 1 Pet 2$^{13-17}$), it is also the State's duty to take heed of the words of Jesus that its authority is delegated to it by God. (*d*) Verse 11b suggests that to incite others to sin may be more culpable than to sin oneself. (*e*) Verse 12 pinpoints the dilemma in which Pilate found himself. Ultimately his problem narrows down to a choice between worldly ambition and loyalty to conscience, between what is profitable and what is right. His persistent attempts to release Jesus reveal that he did not want to disobey his conscience. What he wanted was to enjoy the best of both worlds; but ultimately a choice had to be made. It is often possible (as the Covenant Service puts it) to please ourselves and to please Christ, but there always come times when we can only please Him by denying ourselves. This is a choice which continually confronts men, and especially those who occupy positions of authority. (*f*) The depth of shameful betrayal of their fundamental principles shown by the chief priests in *v.* 15 illustrates how hatred and malice can blind men to moral and spiritual values and result in a complete loss of integrity.

19$^{17-30}$: The Crucifixion and Death of Jesus

Here again the sequence of events is substantially the same as in the Synoptics: the journey to Golgotha, the three crosses, the account of the inscription, the soldiers' casting of lots for Jesus' clothing, the women at the Cross, the offer of sour wine to Jesus, followed by His death. John's narrative, however, has certain distinctive features of its own, some of which may be traced to his possession of valuable historical tradition, while others reflect his theological interests. The outstanding feature, as in the account of the trial before Pilate, is the presentation of Jesus as being in complete control of the events —carrying His own cross, arranging for His mother's future, and more or less determining the moment of His death.

19^{17}. '*bearing the cross for himself*'. This was the custom at Roman executions. John does not mention the impressing of Simon of Cyrene to carry the cross for Jesus (no doubt when He showed signs of collapsing under the weight); he omits this detail probably because he wants to emphasize that it was

o

Jesus alone, without help from anyone else, who performed the act upon which depends the salvation of mankind.

'*Golgotha*'. An Aramaic word meaning, '*place of a skull*' (see *CLM* on Mk 15^{22}). The place was probably outside the city walls, as is suggested by '*he went out*' (cf. *v.* 20).

19^{18}. '*they crucified him*'. On crucifixion as a method of execution see *CLM* on Mk 15^{12}. John refers in passing to the two others who were crucified with Jesus, but shows no interest in them save for emphasizing that Jesus was in the centre; it is He who must claim the reader's attention, here as throughout the Gospel.

19$^{19-22}$. All the Gospels describe the inscription which (as was customary) was placed over the cross, indicating the nature of the charge of which the prisoner had been found guilty. All agree that the inscription referred to Jesus as '*the king of the Jews*'. Only John, however, uses the proper technical term '*title*' in this connection, and only he says that Pilate himself was responsible for it. This is not unnatural in view of the interest Pilate has shown, in this Gospel, in the subject of Jesus' kingship (see **18$^{33-40}$, 19$^{14-15}$**), and is another example of his sarcasm directed at the Jewish leaders. To underline this John adds the reference to the latter's request to Pilate to amend the inscription to make it quite clear that Jesus was only king in His own estimation, and to Pilate's refusal to grant this. Here Pilate is once more made the author of an unconscious prophecy (cf. *vv.* 5 and 14); he bears witness not only to the fact of Jesus' kingship but also to the fact that His kingship is a reality that can never be altered. Finally John is alone in mentioning the trilingual form of the inscription and the reading of it by many from the city. It is quite possible that this detail is historically correct (there were many trilingual notices in Jerusalem at that time), but John records it mainly for its symbolical value as signifying the fact that Jesus' kingship is to be proclaimed to the whole world.

19$^{23-4}$. The clothes of a victim were a recognized perquisite of the soldiers who were responsible for the execution. All the Gospels refer to the soldiers' division of Jesus' clothes among themselves by casting lots, but John describes this procedure in much greater detail than the others. He gives the number of soldiers as four and says that they divided the garments into four parts, except for the tunic which was 'seamless, woven in one piece throughout' (*NEB*). Rather than spoil such a valuable garment by tearing it they cast lots for it. In all this John sees a fulfilment of Ps 22^{18} (cf. 13^{18}, 17^{12}); this verse would lend itself to being connected with the soldiers' sharing of Jesus' clothes, and it is likely that it came to influence the form of the tradition concerning the incident. The Psalmist's Hebrew couplet is a good example of the parallelism which is a feature of Hebrew poetry, the second line repeating the first in different words. John may have misunderstood this and concluded that the first line referred to one class of garments and the second to another. This in turn may have led him to visualize the seamless robe—in which, moreover, he would naturally see a valuable symbol of the unity of the Church.

19^{25}. The presence, near the Cross, of women followers of Jesus is recorded in all the Gospels (cf. Mk 15^{40}, Mt 27$^{55-6}$, Lk 23^{55}). Of the four women named by John only Mary Magdalene is named in the Synoptics (the lists there, however, are not exhaustive). This is John's first reference to Mary Magdalene, who appears again in 20$^{1,\ 11-18}$; on her connection with Jesus see *CLM* on Mk 16^1. The important difference between John and the Synoptists is that he mentions the mother of Jesus, and so prepares the way for the beautiful and tender narrative of the following verses.

19$^{26-7}$. Here we have John's second reference to 'the beloved disciple' (see on 13^{23}). He is standing beside Jesus' mother. In His dying moments and amidst His unimaginable suffering Jesus sees and thinks of these two persons who are so dear to Him, and commits them to each other's care. For the address '*Woman*' see on 2^4. John adds the note that in obedience to Jesus' request the beloved disciple from that moment provided a home for His mother. Legally, the responsibility of caring for the mother would be that of Jesus' brothers, in whose company she actually appears in Acts 1^{14}. For this reason, and because of the improbability of friends of Jesus being allowed to stand near the Cross, many doubt the historicity of this tradition. On the other hand, if the beloved disciple is the witness behind the Gospel (see on 19^{35} and 21^{24}) it is difficult not to accept the story as genuine.

19²⁸⁻³⁰. The chief feature of John's account of Jesus' death is that He dies as the Victor who, far from having His life taken from Him, lays it down voluntarily (cf. **10¹⁸**). He Himself is in control, and He does not die until He is ready, knowing that 'all had now come to its appointed end' (*NEB*). Throughout *Jn* it has been emphasized that 'the hour' of Jesus' death has been fixed in the divine counsels (see **2⁴, 7³⁰**, etc.). Now Jesus knows that the hour is striking. That before He died Jesus was offered sour wine, of the kind the soldiers would have with them as refreshment, is recorded in all the Gospels. In *Jn*, unlike the Synoptics, it is Jesus Himself who (always taking the initiative, cf. **6⁵, 18⁴**) draws attention to His thirst and so asks for the drink. John sees in this a fulfilment of Ps 22¹⁵. It also underlines the fulness of Jesus' humanity (cf. **4⁶⁻⁷, 11³⁵**). There is some doubt as to how the sponge soaked in the wine was lifted to Jesus' mouth. The text, in all but one manuscript, reads '*upon hyssop*', but hyssop would be an impossible material for the purpose. One manuscript has the variant 'on a javelin' (*NEB*). The Greek word for javelin is very similar to that for hyssop, and the change could easily have arisen because of the Paschal associations of hyssop and of the whole Johannine Passion narrative (see especially on **19³³**). On the other hand, a reed may have been used (see Mk 15³⁶), and John may have deliberately used the word '*hyssop*' because of its Paschal associations, and a later copyist may have changed it to 'javelin' as being a more suitable instrument for the purpose. The opening words of *v.* 30 suggest that Jesus asked for the drink in order to enable Himself to utter the cry '*It is finished*'. This is not a cry of resignation meaning 'My life is at an end', but a shout of triumph meaning 'My mission is accomplished' (cf. **4³⁴, 17⁴**). Only John records this word from the Cross, though Mark says that Jesus died with a 'loud cry' (see *CLM* on Mk 15³⁷). John may have known from tradition, as Mark did not, the meaning of this dying cry of Jesus; or he may have placed his own interpretation upon it. If the latter, the interpretation is truly inspired for it sums up perfectly the whole teaching of the NT about the mission of Jesus. Having uttered this cry Jesus bows His head and dies. The way in which John describes His death is significant: He '*gave up his spirit*' (cf. Lk 23⁴⁶). The implication is that He voluntarily surrenders His own life; to the very end He is in complete control.

(*a*) The picture of Jesus bearing His own cross it not irreconcilable with that in the Synoptics of Simon of Cyrene carrying it for Him. Together these two pictures symbolize the paradox that, though the redemptive sacrifice on the Cross was one that Jesus alone could offer, it is the privilege and high calling of Christians to share in 'the fellowship of his sufferings' (Phil 3¹⁰, cf. Col 1²⁴). He suffered *for* us, but we may suffer *with* Him. (*b*) Verses 19-22 suggest that the Cross proclaims to all the world (and the reference to the three languages points to the need for presenting the gospel always in language that is intelligible to the hearers) the fact of Jesus' sovereignty—a fact which, however much men may seek to misrepresent it, remains firm and incontrovertible. Jesus 'hath reigned and triumphed from the tree' (*MHB* 184), and He is a King who can never be dethroned. (*c*) The women's presence at the Cross symbolizes the sympathetic and devoted loyalty to Christ and His cause which has always characterized Christian womanhood at its best. (*d*) Verses 26-7 form one of the most tenderly touching narratives in the four Gospels. It reveals that Jesus, in spite of such teaching as is contained in Mk 3³¹⁻⁵, 13¹², Lk 9⁶⁰, 14²⁶, is not insensitive to ties of kith and kin. (*e*) Jesus' final word from the Cross is full of significance and links up with 4³⁴ and 17⁴. The work of redemption wrought in the life and death of Jesus is a finished one. All that needs to be done for man's redemption has been done. It only remains for men to avail themselves of it—by faith. The Cross meant for Jesus the unimaginable desolation expressed in Mk 15³⁴. But this cry in *Jn* suggests that before He died the clouds that had seemed to separate Him from God dispersed, and He knew the satisfaction of having finished the work given Him to perform. Would it be fanciful to suggest that He heard again the Father's voice saying 'Thou art my beloved Son, in thee I am well pleased' (Mk 1¹¹)?

19³¹⁻⁴²: The Burial of Jesus

Jesus' burial by Joseph of Arimathea with Pilate's permission, hurriedly before sunset brought the beginning of the Jewish sabbath, is recorded in all four Gospels. John, unlike the Synoptics, associates Nicodemus with Joseph's action and says that they anointed the body before interring it. The main distinctive feature of John's narrative, however, is that he prefaces it with a paragraph (*vv.* 31-7) which has no parallel in the other Gospels and in which his symbolical interests are very marked.

19³¹⁻². '*the Preparation*'. Cf. **19¹⁴**. It now becomes clear that for John the word has a double sense, for it was the eve of the sabbath (as all the Gospels agree, see *CLM* on Mk 15⁴²) as well as of Passover day. This is why the oncoming sabbath is here called 'a day of great solemnity' (*NEB*). Jewish law forbade that a body should remain on a scaffold overnight (see Deut 21²²⁻³), and this would be especially undesirable in view of the solemnity of the coming day.

'*that their legs might be broken*'—a means of precipitating death. Pilate, unwilling to antagonize the Jews any further, readily grants their request, and the soldiers break the legs of the malefactors on either side of Jesus (cf. 19¹⁸).

19³³. Jesus being already dead, there is no need to break His legs, and John sees in this a fulfilment of Ex 12⁴⁶ (cf. Num 9¹²), which he quotes in *v.* 36. This scripture refers, of course, to the Passover lamb, and John's quoting of it reveals clearly that he regards Jesus as the true Passover Lamb (cf. 1²⁹). Herein lies the theological significance of John's dating of the crucifixion (cf. 18²⁸, 19¹⁴, ³¹), according to which Jesus died at the very time (the afternoon of Nisan 14) when the lambs were being sacrificed in preparation for the Passover feast (Paul's words in 1 Cor 5⁷⁻⁸ may provide independent testimony in support of John's date here).

19³⁴. Instead of breaking Jesus' legs one of the soldiers—presumably either out of sheer callous cruelty or in order to make sure that He was really dead—pierces His side with a spear, whereupon blood and water flow from the wound. Medical evidence indicates that it is not impossible for blood and a colourless fluid, in certain circumstances, to flow from a human body immediately after death. This incident is clearly of outstanding importance for John; in the next verse he goes to pains to establish its historical veracity, but his main interest is in the theological truth or truths symbolized by it. At least three symbolical interpretations are possible, and it may be that they were all, to a greater or lesser extent, present in the evangelist's mind. (*i*) The incident reveals the reality and completeness of Jesus' humanity, for the Rabbis believed that the human body consisted of one half blood and one half water, and therefore consisted that a living personality contained three elements—spirit, blood and water. Jesus has already given up His spirit (*v.* 30), and now blood and water are seen to have been present, so proving that His humanity was real and not false, as the Docetists held (see on 1^{14}). Jesus was perfect man, in His life and in His death. (*ii*) The water may represent the baptism of Jesus and the blood His sacrificial death. The incident then symbolizes the truth that both these events, at the beginning and end of His ministry respectively, are essential to His work as Messiah. (*iii*) It is probable also that a reference to the two sacraments, Baptism and the Eucharist, is to be found here, the meaning being that both of them rest upon the sacrificial and redemptive act of Jesus upon the Cross. This is in keeping with John's teaching about Baptism in 3^{1-21} and about the Eucharist in 6^{22-59}. On the connection between the spear-thrust incident and 1 Jn 5^{6-8}, see *GPL*, pp. 116-7.

19^{35}. John vouches for the historical truth of the incident he has just recorded by appealing to the testimony of an eye-witness. It is probable that by '*he that hath seen*' he means the beloved disciple, who was mentioned in *v.* 26 as being present at the Cross, and who is certainly meant in the similar statement in 21^{24}. If this identification is correct, the use of the third person suggests that the evangelist is referring to someone other than himself, and this means that the beloved disciple is the witness behind the Gospel rather than its actual author (cf. Introduction, p. 1, and on 21^{24}). The second half of the present verse is ambiguous, as it is not clear who it is that is said to know that the witness' testimony is true; '*he*' could be the evangelist himself, or Jesus, or God, but it is more likely that the witness (i.e. the beloved disciple) is meant. In any case the incident so vouched for by first-hand testimony is recorded that the readers may believe (cf. the purpose of the Gospel as indicated in 20^{30-1}).

19^{36-7}. Proof-texts from the OT are provided for both the fact that Jesus' legs were not broken (see above on *v.* 33) and the fact of the spear-thrust (the text in this case is Zech 12^{10}).

19^{38}. '*Joseph of Arimathaea*'. See *CLM* on Mk 15^{43}. John calls him a '*disciple of Jesus*' (cf. Mt 27^{57}), but adds that he kept his connection with Him secret '*for fear of the Jews*' (cf. 12^{42-3}). The sight of Jesus dying on the Cross may have inspired him to forget his fear and show openly his sympathy. He asks, and is granted, Pilate's permission to remove Jesus' body from the cross.

19$^{39-40}$. '*Nicodemus*'. See 3$^{1-12}$, 7$^{50-2}$. All these references to him suggest that he too, like Joseph, was a secret disciple, so that it is not strange to find him joining in ministering these last signs of respect (as they consider them) to Jesus' body. Nicodemus brings a highly extravagant quantity of spices with which to anoint the body; John probably wants to suggest that nothing is too much to do to show one's love and respect for Jesus. The two councillors bury Jesus in accordance with Jewish custom, wrapping the body in linen cloths with the spices (cf. 11^{44}). The Synoptic accounts do not mention any such anointing in connection with the burial (see on 12$^{7-8}$).

19$^{41-2}$. Only John mentions the fact that the tomb was situated in a garden, but it is quite possible that there was a garden on the slopes of Golgotha—as there was on the Mount of Olives (cf. 18^{1})—and that Joseph was its owner. Unlike the Synoptics John neither describes the tomb nor the stone with which it was sealed (but cf. 20^{1}), but he does stress the fact that it was a new and hitherto unused tomb (cf. Mt 27^{60}, Lk 23^{53})—as befitted the burial of Jesus. The proximity of the tomb to the place of crucifixion made it possible for the burial to be completed before the sabbath began; John again draws attention to the date, which for him is so significant (cf. *vv.* 14 and 31).

(*a*) The theme of Jesus as the true Passover lamb, which is implicit throughout John's Passion narrative (cf. 1^{29}), is made explicit in *vv.* 33 and 36. His sacrifice makes possible men's deliverance from a worse bondage than that of Egypt. (*b*) Verse 34 teaches that Jesus' death (*i*) was no sham, but the real death of a real man; (*ii*) was of a piece with the whole of the ministry to which He was 'ordained' at His baptism, and represented the consummation of that ministry; (*iii*) is the event which gives meaning and efficacy to the Church's sacraments. (*c*) Verse 35 contains the theme of witness, which has been prominent throughout *Jn*. Although the verse originally refers only to the spear-thrust incident, it points to the fact that the apostolic gospel is based on authentic eye-witness testimony, that this testimony is '*true*', and that its purpose (as borne out by the Church at all times) is to bring men to faith in Christ. (*d*) The action of Joseph and Nicodemus is a courageous one (cf. Mk 15^{43}), for which they deserve credit (cf. the earlier references to the latter). There is, however, a note of tragedy in that it was only after Jesus' death that they came out into the open as His followers. It illustrates our all-too-common tendency to show to men after their death the respect which we ought to have shown while they lived. (*e*) The extravagant quantity of spices symbolizes the lavishness of the service which the true lover of Jesus should offer Him (cf. **12¹⁻¹¹**). (*f*) The mention of the garden as the place of burial is suggestive. A garden is a place where seeds are buried in order to grow to fuller life (cf. **12²⁴**). So this detail points forward to the Resurrection. There may also be an implied comparison with the Garden of Eden, the scene of man's fall; the present garden is the scene of man's redemption.

Chapter 20

20[1-18]: The Empty Tomb and the Appearance to Mary Magdalene

THE evidence adduced in the NT for the Resurrection of Christ is based on two facts: first the discovery of the empty tomb on the third day, and secondly the appearances of the living Jesus to various individuals and groups of His followers on that and subsequent days. On the relative importance of these two kinds of evidence see *CLM* on Mk 16[1-8]. In the present section of *Jn* the discovery of the empty tomb is combined with the first of the appearances, and the central figure in the narrative is Mary Magdalene (see on 19[25]). All four Gospels describe the discovery of the empty tomb by the women on the first day of the week. How many women were present is not clear (cf. Mk 16[1] with Lk 24[10]), but all the accounts mention Mary Magdalene. John mentions only her, but the '*we*' in *v*. 2 may suggest that she was not alone; that John omits to mention her companions may be due to the fact that Mary has, as *vv*. 11-18 show, a special interest for him. He does not mention the women's intention to anoint Jesus' body—no doubt because in his account the anointing has already taken place (19[39-40]). Only John describes the visit to the tomb of Peter and the beloved disciple after hearing Mary's story (Lk 24[12] is probably not part of the original text, cf. *NEB*). The account of the appearance to Mary Magdalene is very different from that of Mt 28[9-10] (on which see *AMW*).

20[1-2]. '*the first day of the week*', i.e. Sunday, the crucifixion having been on the Friday (see 19[31]) and the Jewish sabbath having intervened; thus by Jewish inclusive reckoning the Sunday was the third day after the crucifixion.

'*Mary Magdalene*'. See on 19[25].

'*while it was yet dark*' emphasizes the earliness of the hour (cf. Mk 16[2]).

'*the stone taken away*'. John has not described the sealing of the tomb in 19⁴¹⁻², but this mention of the stone implies it.

'She runneth. . . .' John does not say that Mary entered the tomb, but her report to the disciples makes it clear that she was fully aware that the body was not there; it also reveals that she assumed that the body had been deliberately removed by some human agent (cf. *vv.* 13-15).

'the other disciple, whom Jesus loved' appears here for the third time in *Jn.* See on 13²³⁻⁵; as there, so here he is associated with Peter.

20³⁻⁸. Both disciples hurry at once to the tomb, the beloved disciple outrunning Peter and arriving first. Stooping to peep inside he notices the linen wrappings in which Jesus' body had been swathed, but hesitates to enter the tomb. Peter arrives and impetuously enters, to see the wrappings and also the napkin which had covered Jesus' head, rolled up and lying separately (cf. 11⁴⁴). The beloved disciple then enters, and John significantly adds that *'he saw, and believed'*. The verb used here for *'saw'* is not the same as that used earlier in *v.* 5; it is the verb used in 1³⁹, ⁵⁰⁻¹, and implies that he not only saw the scene but grasped its meaning and significance—namely, that Jesus had risen from the dead; hence the statement that he believed. The whole narrative vividly depicts the contrast between Peter and the beloved disciple as the two leaders of the band of disciples. Peter is the man of action who first ventures into the tomb; but the beloved disciple is the man of spiritual perception who first realizes the truth of the Resurrection and believes it (the contrast is again brought out in 21⁷, ¹⁸⁻²²). Only John describes the grave-clothes lying in the tomb—doubtless in order to underline the fact that the disappearance of the body is a supernatural event and not due to human agency.

20⁹. John comments that the disciples at the time did not realize that the Resurrection had been foretold in scripture. By the time the Gospel was written this was a common Christian conviction (cf. 1 Cor 15⁴, Acts 2³¹). The implication of the comment is that the faith of the original disciples was based, not on deduction from scripture, but on the evidence of their own experience. Lk 24²⁷, ⁴⁴⁻⁶ indicate that it was the Risen Christ Himself who first opened the disciples' eyes to understand the scriptures which bear witness to Him.

20¹⁰⁻¹⁵. The two disciples return home, no doubt to inform their brethren of what they have seen. Mary Magdalene has apparently followed them to the grave, and stays behind, outside the tomb, after they have left. She has not yet perceived (as the beloved disciple has) the significance of the empty tomb, so that it is natural for her to weep. Stooping to look into the tomb (cf. *v.* 5) she now sees two angels in white sitting there; cf. Lk 24⁴ where the two angels appear to the women when they first arrive at the tomb, as does the one angel in Mk 16⁵ and Mt 28²⁻⁶ (on the discrepancies between the various reports see *CLM* pp. 135-6). In reply to the angels' question Mary explains her weeping in the same terms as she used in *v.* 2. The angels play no further part in John's narrative (contrast the Synoptics), for Mary turns round and sees another figure, whom she takes to be the gardener. When he asks the same question as the angels, adding the further '*whom seekest thou?*' Mary, thinking he may have removed the body, implores him to let her have it; she is still firmly convinced that Jesus is dead and little realizes that she is actually speaking with Him. This failure on the part of Jesus' followers to recognize Him at first when He appears to them is a feature of more than one of the post-Resurrection narratives (cf. **21⁴**, Lk 24¹⁶). It may mean that His outward appearance had in some way been changed by death; it certainly means that they were not expecting to see Him. Their failure to understand His promise to return to them (cf. **14¹⁸**) was complete.

20¹⁶. With powerfully dramatic effect John records that Jesus addressed Mary, simply and tenderly, by her own name, and that she reponded with immediate and raptured recognition. '*Rabboni*' is another form of 'Rabbi' (see on **1³⁸**). He reveals Himself to her in the way He speaks her name—a way, no doubt, which she could associate with no one but Him. We are reminded of **10³⁻⁴**, where Jesus claims that the Good Shepherd's sheep know His voice.

20¹⁷. One can imagine Mary in her joy touching Jesus, or moving to do so (cf. Mt 28⁹). But Jesus forbids her. His words here are difficult to reconcile with **20²⁷** where He invites Thomas to touch Him. Many attempts have been made to overcome this difficulty. Some think that John is implying that the ascension takes place between *v.* 17 and *v.* 27. Others think that 'touch not' is a misunderstanding of another verb (very similar in appearance) meaning 'fear not'. The simplest and best solution, however, is to understand 'touch' in this context as meaning 'cling' (see *NEB*). What is rejected is Mary's attempt to hold on to Jesus' physical form; the relationship of believers to Him is henceforth to be a purely spiritual relationship, and they must learn to be conscious of His presence with them without having to depend on any physical senses such as sight or hearing or touch. The purpose of the Resurrection appearances was to convince the disciples that Jesus was really alive and to prepare them for this new phase in their relationship with Him. Moreover, by seeking to cling to Jesus now, Mary is in effect preventing Him from ascending to the Father, and as John understands it His mission is not complete until He has returned to heaven. Like the disciples in the Upper Room, Mary has failed to recognize that it is expedient for them that Jesus should leave them so far as His visible presence is concerned (cf. **16**[7]).

'*I ascend . . .*'. This message which Mary is told to deliver to the disciples implies that the ascension is about to take place. John does not really distinguish (as does *Lk-Acts*) between the Resurrection and Ascension of Jesus as separate events; as we have repeatedly seen, he thinks of His death and resurrection as constituting His 'glorifying' or 'lifting up' or return to His Father (**3**[13–14], **6**[62], **7**[33, 39], **13**[1, 3], etc.). But in speaking of the Resurrection appearances he is bound to imply an interval, however short, between resurrection and ascension. The form of Jesus' message to the disciples indicates that His God and Father is their God and Father—hence the appropriateness of His calling them His '*brethren*'; this does not mean, however, that their relationship to God as children is the same as His relationship as Son (see on **1**[12]).

20[18]. Mary then goes to the disciples to relate to them her joyous news and to deliver Jesus' message. The next section tells of how they come to share her glorious experience of meeting with the Risen Lord.

(*a*) Mary Magdalene's earlier history is uncertain, but Lk **8**[2] suggests that her life had been (whether physically, mentally, morally, or in all these ways) a sorry and miserable affair from which she had been delivered by Jesus. Thereafter she followed and served Him devotedly, being near the Cross when He died (19²⁵) and eager to reverence His body after burial (20¹). There is something very comforting in the fact that this once poor deranged creature was granted the privilege of being the first witness of the Resurrection. There is no limit to the transformation which Christ can effect in a person's life. (*b*) The discovery of the empty tomb should have been, for anyone who had heard Jesus foretell His resurrection, the most wonderful news. But for Mary it was, and remained for some time, an occasion of bitter grief and disappointment. She wanted to show her reverence for her dead Master, and missed the truth that He was no longer dead. Many still want to pay respect to Jesus as a dead Teacher, and fail to realize that He is the Living Lord. But just as Jesus found a way to reveal Himself to Mary, so He finds an appropriate way to reveal Himself to each of us. (*c*) The contrast between the characters of Peter and the beloved disciple is suggestive. There is room within the fellowship of the Church and among its leaders for both the active and the contemplative types of personality. (*d*) The closing words of *v.* 8 remind us of the essential connection between experience and faith, while *v.* 9 points to the authority of scripture as a basis for faith. These two bases are not contradictory but supplementary. What we believe on the basis of personal experience may be verified by the study of scripture, and *vice versa.* (*e*) Verse 15 suggests the ease with which Jesus may be mistaken for someone quite different. He comes to us in the guise of ordinary persons whom we happen to meet, and we fail to recognize Him (cf. Mt 25³¹⁻⁴⁶). (*f*) Like Mary we often want to cling to the Jesus that we have known (as Teacher, Healer, Friend, Example, Prophet) rather than let Him reveal Himself in His true glory as the Victorious Redeemer and Living Lord. (*g*) The God and Father of our Lord Jesus Christ is *our* God and Father too, and we are Christ's brethren (cf. Heb 2¹¹, Rom 8¹⁶⁻¹⁷). But we need always to remember that our relationship with God is different from His and dependent upon it.

20¹⁹⁻²⁹: The Appearances to the Disciples—without and with Thomas

An appearance of the Risen Lord to His disciples on the evening of the first Easter Day is recorded by both Luke (24³⁶) and John (*vv.* 19-23). According to Luke others besides the Eleven were present (see Lk 24³³), but John mentions no others and points out that of the Eleven, Thomas was absent. Despite this and other differences in the accounts, both may well be based on traditions of the same incident. In both the meeting becomes an occasion for the commissioning of the disciples by Jesus.

20$^{19-20}$. Neither John nor Luke identifies the meeting-place of the disciples, but it may well have been (as traditionally has been assumed) the Upper Room where three nights previously they had eaten the Last Supper (cf. Acts 1^{13}). John suggests that they were in hiding from '*the Jews*', i.e. the enemies of Jesus (see on 1^{19}). This was doubtless true, but John mentions it mainly in order to emphasize the fact that '*the doors were shut*', thus indicating that the body of Jesus passed miraculously through them (the same is implied, though not explicitly stated, in Lk 24^{36}). This suggests that Jesus' Resurrection body was non-material (cf. 1 Cor 15^{44}), though the references to His eating (Lk 24^{43}, Acts 10^{41} and possibly 21$^{12-14}$), and His invitation to Thomas in *v.* 27, seem to point in the opposite direction. On the problem of the nature of the Resurrection body see *CLM*, p. 137. Suddenly Jesus appears in the midst of the company and greets them with the familiar Jewish salutation, '*Peace be unto you*' (cf. Lk 24^{36}). The term '*peace*' on Jesus' lips, however, means more than a mere formal greeting (see on 14^{27}). Immediately afterwards He shows them His hands and side. However different the Resurrection body was from His incarnate body, it is evident that there was an essential connection between them, for He still bears the wounds caused by the nails and the spear (cf. Lk 24$^{37-40}$). John's narrative implies, as does Luke's, that it was these marks of identification that convinced the disciples that it was really Jesus Himself and not an apparition. Their first reaction may have been one of terror (Lk 24^{37}), but the recognition of Jesus transformed this into joy (cf. Lk 24^{41}).

20$^{21-3}$. Jesus now, having repeated His greeting, proceeds to commission the disciples and to impart to them the authority and the resources for the fulfilment of their mission. That this mission is to be an extension of His own, derivative from and dependent upon it, as His was from the Father, is clear from *v.* 21b (cf. 13^{20}, 17^{18}, etc.). The disciples are thus commissioned as apostles; though John does not use this word of them, the essential idea of the word ('one sent to represent the sender') is present in this passage. If they are to fulfil their mission, however, they will have to depend entirely on Christ as He

depended on the Father. The Son was sealed and consecrated
by the Father (6^{27}, 10^{36}) and fulfilled His ministry on earth in
the power of the Spirit who 'abode upon him' (1^{32}). Likewise
the disciples, having already been consecrated by Christ
(17^{17-19}), now receive from Him the gift of the Holy Spirit.

'*he breathed on them*' echoes Gen 2^7; as life was imparted to
man by the divine breath, so new life is imparted to the Church
by the divine breath. Throughout *Jn* it has been emphasized
that the Holy Spirit can only be given as a result of the glorifying of Jesus (7^{39}, 16^7, etc.). Now that that glorifying is an
accomplished fact, the promise (14^{16}, etc.) of the Paraclete is
fulfilled. There is in *Jn* no interval, as in the Lukan writings
(Lk 24-Acts 2), between the Resurrection, Ascension and Gift of
the Holy Spirit (cf. comment on *v.* 17). John's interest is not in
the historical programme (on which Luke may be closer to the
truth) but in the theological truth that it was as a result of the
glorifying of Jesus by death, resurrection and ascension to the
Father that the Church received the Holy Spirit to quicken
and equip it for its mission in the world.

'*whose soever sins . . .*'. Having imparted to them the Holy
Spirit, Jesus gives the disciples the authority to forgive and
retain sins. This means authority to administer discipline in
the Church and corresponds to that of 'binding and loosing'
which in Matthew's Gospel is granted to Peter (Mt 16^{19}) and
to the local Church community as a whole (Mt 18^{18}): to forgive (or loose) is to admit a sinner to communion in the
Church, and to retain (or bind) is to exclude a sinner. This
authority is vested in the Church as a whole (Mt 18^{18}), but is
here imparted by Jesus to His disciples as representing the
original nucleus of the Church. Ultimately, of course, the
authority to forgive sins and to judge sinners belongs to God
Himself (see Mk 2^7) and to Christ (see 5^{27}), but the Church is
charged with the responsibility of pronouncing forgiveness and
judgement in the name of the Lord—a responsibility which it
can only discharge by virtue of its possession of the Holy
Spirit (this is clearly involved in the juxtaposition of *vv.* 22
and 23).

20^{24-5}. On Thomas see 11^{16}, 14^5. His answer to his fellow-
disciples' announcement provides the basis for the traditional
picture of him as an honest doubter. It is not difficult to
sympathize with Thomas' attitude; he was not the only one to

find the news of Jesus' resurrection difficult to believe (cf.
Mt 28[17], Mk 16[14], Lk 24[11, 37, 41]). What he requires is visible
and tangible proof that the Jesus who has appeared to the
disciples is one and the same as He who was crucified. Part of
the reason for John's telling the story in such detail may be to
emphasize this truth in order to refute the Gnostic tendencies
of his own day (see *GPL* p. 69).

20[26]. '*after eight days*', by Jewish inclusive reckoning (see on
20[1]), means the following Sunday. By noting the date so
precisely John indicates that the custom of meeting for worship
on the first day of the week marked the Church from the very
beginning. The meeting-place is no doubt the same as on the
previous Sunday, and this time Thomas is present. Jesus
appears in precisely the same way as before (cf. *v.* 19).

20[27]. Jesus' words to Thomas reveal that He is aware of the
latter's doubts. He offers the very proofs which Thomas has
requested. This offer is not inconsistent with the words
addressed to Mary in *v.* 17. John clearly believes that Jesus'
Resurrection body was real and capable of being touched,
though at the same time capable of passing through locked
doors (cf. Lk 24[37–43], and see comment on *v.* 19).

'*faithless*' means 'unbelieving' (*NEB*).

20[28]. Without availing Himself of the Lord's invitation to
touch His wounds (the evidence of his eyes alone has been
sufficient to scatter all his unbelief, cf. *v.* 29), Thomas replies
with the confession of faith: '*My Lord and my God*'. This
confession of Thomas' constitutes the climax of the whole
Gospel, summing up as it does the truth about the Person of
Christ which has been emphasized throughout. 'Jesus is Lord'
was the earliest form of the Church's confession of faith (see
Rom 10[9], 1 Cor 12[3]) and amounted to an acknowledgment of
Jesus' divinity, since '*Lord*' was a universally recognized divine
title in the first century. The addition of the title '*God*' here
serves to make this meaning more explicit. It is possible that
by John's time this fuller formula of confession was in use in
the Church's liturgy and that this accounts for John's using
it as the vehicle for Thomas' confession. The Gospel opened
with the declaration that 'the Word was God' (**1[1]**) and here
reaches its climax in the confession of Jesus as God.

P

20²⁹. The first half of this verse is better taken as a statement (*RV, NEB*) than as a question (*RVm, RSV*). The beatitude that follows is pronounced upon all Christians of future generations who will believe in Christ without having had the opportunity (now granted to Thomas and his fellow-disciples) of seeing Jesus with their physical eyes (cf 1 Pet 1⁸). By the time John is writing the Church is composed almost entirely of such believers; in using the past tenses here John is thinking of them and speaking from the point of view of his own day. Christians of later generations have often envied those of the first generation whose eyes actually saw Jesus. This beatitude suggests that such envy is not called for; on the contrary those whose faith is not dependent upon the evidence of sight are more truly blessed. This is consistent with the emphasis found throughout *Jn* that faith which depends on 'seeing signs and wonders' is of an inferior kind (cf. 4⁴⁸, etc.).

(*a*) The description of the fear-stricken disciples hiding behind locked doors reveals how completely they had failed to grasp the teaching of Jesus about the significance of His death and resurrection. For them the crucifixion meant that His ministry had ended in tragic and hopeless defeat, and it continued to mean that until they became convinced of the reality and implications of the Resurrection. The beginning of their transformation is seen in the joy that follows their recognition of Jesus (cf. 16²⁰, ²²); its culmination appears in the picture of the fearless witness of the apostles in the early chapters of *Acts.* (*b*) The conventional greeting in *vv.* 19 and 21 is filled with new meaning for the disciples (cf. 14²⁷, 16³³). The experience of these first disciples has been shared by countless groups of Christians throughout the ages; meeting in bewilderment and despair, fear and uncertainty, they have suddenly become aware of Christ's presence among them, and all has immediately become different. (*c*) Verses 21-3 point to the Church's commission as an extension of Christ's own ministry. For its fulfilment the Church is clothed with authority to mediate divine forgiveness and discipline, and with the life and resources of the Holy Spirit. (*d*) Thomas represents the sincere and honest doubter who refuses to commit himself to Christian belief until his own reason has been convinced of its truth. Such an attitude must always be respected, as indeed Jesus does respect Thomas' attitude. Thomas does not doubt for the sake of doubting (as some do), nor out of indifference or disloyalty (cf. 11¹⁶). He dearly wanted to believe, but could not be satisfied with any in-adequate basis for faith. The story also shows that ultimately the only adequate basis for faith is personal experience of encounter with Christ. Thomas longed for such an experience, and did not neglect to seek it where it was most likely to be found—in the fellowship of the Church . He did not stay away the second Sunday. (*e*) The emphasis in this section on the fact that Jesus' body still bore the print of the nails and the wound of the spear underlines the all-important fact that the Risen Lord who appears to His own is one and the same as the Jesus who died on the Cross. We must never forget that the Living Lord is 'the Lamb that was slain'. (*f*) Verse 29 reminds us that the privilege shared by believers of all generations is no less than that enjoyed by those who saw Jesus in the flesh. He belongs to us no less than to them; we too may know Him as Lord and God, and believe in Him and receive all the blessings of the salvation which He achieved for all who will receive Him. For us He is 'unseen but not unknown' (*MHB* 111).

20³⁰⁻¹: The Original Conclusion of the Gospel

These two verses undoubtedly formed the conclusion of the Gospel as originally planned—a conclusion which follows naturally upon the climax reached with Thomas' confession of faith in *v*. 28. Chapter **21,** as we shall see, was added as an Appendix. The conclusion here is entirely fitting: John explains his purpose in writing and compresses into one brief sentence the essential message of his Gospel—that Jesus of Nazareth is the Messiah, Son of God, and that faith in Him as such is the way to eternal life.

20³⁰. '*Many other signs . . . not written in this book*'. This implies that the events recorded in the Gospel are regarded by the author as '*signs*' (see p. 22).

20³¹. '*but these are written*', i.e. these '*signs*' (see above). John has selected, out of the great mass of traditional material available, those events which he regards as specially significant and valuable in promoting faith amongst his readers.

'*that ye may believe*'. The tense of the verb here is uncertain. If the aorist tense is correct (as most manuscripts attest) the meaning is 'that you may come to believe' (*NEBm*), i.e. the Gospel is intended for unbelievers. If the present tense is correct (as a few ancient and valuable manuscripts read) the meaning is 'that you may continue to believe' (cf. *NEB*, 'that you may hold the faith'), i.e. the Gospel is intended for believers. On the whole it seems likely that the latter reading is the original and that the former arose from a later tendency to regard the Gospel as a missionary tract. On the purpose of the Gospel, see Introduction, p. 3. This declaration of the Gospel's purpose should be compared with that of the purpose of the First Epistle (see *GPL* on 1 Jn 5¹³).

(*a*) This passage reminds us that the way to attain to faith is to understand the significance of all that Jesus was and did, i.e. to see and interpret aright the '*signs*' (cf. 2¹¹). This was what the Gospels set out to do, and what the preacher of the gospel must always seek to do. (*b*) The faith which leads to eternal life is of course much more than intellectual belief (see on 3¹⁶). Nevertheless it does involve the grasp of right doctrine, and this comes out in the expression '*believe that Jesus is* . . .'. Before we can believe *in* Jesus as Christ we must believe *that* He is the Christ. Thus, although it is not the whole of faith, right doctrine is not to be despised. It may indeed lead to faith in the more personal sense. When we have become convinced of the truth about Jesus we are more likely to commit ourselves in faith to Him.

Chapter 21

21¹⁻²⁵: Appendix: The Appearance in Galilee

THAT this chapter is an Appendix to the Gospel as originally planned is clear from the natural conclusion in 20³⁰⁻¹. The question is whether it was added by the evangelist himself or by some other person or persons at a later date. The fact that no copy of the Gospel exists from which Chapter 21 is absent suggests that it was never published without the Appendix. This in turn may suggest that the addition was made by the author himself, and there is nothing in the style or content of the chapter (or at least of *vv*. 1-23) to preclude this view. Verse 24 raises a difficulty, however, since it adopts the plural form '*we know*'. Those who regard *vv*. 1-23 as the evangelist's own addition to his original work usually regard *vv*. 24 and 25 as further subsequent additions made by those who wished to commend the Gospel and guarantee its genuineness and value. On the whole, however, it is simpler to suppose that Chapter 21 as a whole was added by a responsible group of Church leaders who published the Gospel some time after its original composition. A point in favour of this view is the fact that the original author, had he wished to add further material, would have been more likely to insert it between 20²⁹ and 20³⁰⁻¹, so as not to destroy the effectiveness of what was such a fitting conclusion to his work. An editor, on the other hand, would hardly feel free to do this. Various reasons probably prompted the addition: (*i*) the desire to add a post-Resurrection appearance in Galilee to those in Jerusalem already recorded (for Galilean appearances cf. Mk 16⁷, Mt 28¹⁶⁻²⁰); (*ii*) the desire to record the story of Peter's restoration; (*iii*) the desire to explain the respective roles that Peter and the beloved disciple were to play in the leadership of the Church.

21¹ introduces the Appendix, indicating that it has to do with a further appearance of the Risen Lord to His disciples (cf. *v*. 14).

'*sea of Tiberias*'. See on 6¹.

21²⁻³. Seven of the disciples, led by Simon Peter, decide to go fishing. They include Thomas (see on **11¹⁶, 14⁵, 20²⁴⁻⁹**), Nathanael (see on **1⁴⁵⁻⁹**), and '*the sons of Zebedee*'. This is the only mention in *Jn* of the latter (cf. Mk 1¹⁹⁻²⁰, etc.), and confirms the view that the beloved disciple (who appears in *v*. 7 as a member of the company) is to be identified with John the son of Zebedee (see Introduction, p. 1 and on **13²³⁻⁵**). The implication is that the disciples, after the events recorded in Chapter **20,** returned to their homes in Galilee; this is quite credible in view of Jesus' promise in Mk 14²⁸ and 16⁷. It is unlikely, however, in view of the commission they received in **20²²⁻³,** that the decision to go fishing involved a permanent return to their former occupation. The incident as recorded here, though possibly based on a genuine historical tradition, has a strong symbolical element. The picture of Peter leading his fellow-disciples on a fishing expedition symbolizes his role as leader of the apostles in their missionary venture as fishers of men (cf. Mk 1¹⁷, Lk 5¹⁰). Their failure to catch any fish that night symbolizes the fruitlessness of missionary activity undertaken without the presence and help of the Lord Himself; the following verses reveal how different things become when Jesus takes control.

21⁴⁻⁶. '*knew not that it was Jesus*'. See on **20¹⁰⁻¹⁵.**

'*Children*'. Cf. **13³³.**

'*aught to eat*'. The word used is one that usually means 'fish' (cf. *NEB*).

'*multitude of fishes*'. The story of the miraculous catch that follows on their obedience to Jesus' command is strikingly similar to that recorded in Lk 5¹⁻¹¹. The most probable explanation of this fact is that Luke knew the same traditional post-Resurrection story as is followed here, but that he used it to describe the original call of the fishermen-disciples (Mk 1¹⁶⁻²⁰ is the more historically accurate account of their original call).

21⁷⁻⁸. With a characteristic flash of insight the beloved disciple recognizes the stranger on the shore as '*the Lord*'. And with equally characteristic impetuosity Peter is the first to act (see on **20³⁻⁸**).

'*he girt his coat about him*'. This seems odd as a prelude to plunging in the sea, but the explanation is to be found in the fact that he is going to meet his Lord, and that to do so in a state of undress would be a mark of disrespect.

'*about two hundred cubits*', i.e. about a hundred yards. It is unlikely that there is any symbolical significance in this reference to the approximate distance.

21⁹⁻¹¹. Meanwhile Jesus has made preparations for a meal of fish and bread, and when the disciples reach the shore He invites them to add some of their own catch of fish. Peter re-embarks to drag the net to land. Two interesting details regarding the catch are now recorded carefully, and it seems clear that the writer sees a symbolical significance in each. (*a*) The number of fish is 153. This symbol is variously interpreted, but the most probable suggestion is that the number symbolizes the universality of the Church's mission, since it was believed that the sea contained a total of 153 species of fish. (*b*) The fact that, despite the great number of fish, the net did not break symbolizes the truth that the Church is one, and capable of containing the whole of mankind.

21¹²⁻¹³. Jesus invites the disciples to join Him at breakfast. None of them dares to ask Him about His identity, of which indeed they are now fully aware. The meal takes place, Jesus acting as host and distributing the bread and fish. Inevitably we are reminded of the similar meal recorded in **6¹⁻¹⁵**, and there can be little doubt that this meal on the lake-shore, like that on the mountainside, is regarded as sacramental—a foretaste of the Messianic banquet in the consummated Kingdom of God.

21¹⁴ rounds off the narrative of the miraculous catch, pointing out that this is the third post-Resurrection appearance to be recorded in this Gospel (cf. *v.* 1).

21¹⁵⁻¹⁷. There follows a private conversation with Peter which is clearly designed to point to his restoration. Corresponding to his threefold denial of Jesus (**18¹⁷, ²⁵, ²⁷**) we have here a threefold declaration of Peter's love and a threefold recommissioning, thus underlining the completeness of his reinstatement. The interpretation of the passage is complicated by the fact that two different words for love are used: *agapan*, the word regularly used in the NT for the distinctively Christian kind of love, and *philein*, which normally means the kind of love that friends have for one another. The former occurs in the first two questions of Jesus, the latter in Jesus' third question and in all three answers of Peter. Some English translations distinguish between the two verbs by using 'love' for the former and 'am your friend' for the latter (cf. *NEBm*). If this is correct, Peter refrains from claiming to love Jesus (*agapan*) but makes the lesser claim to be His friend (*philein*), and Jesus' final question is meant to test whether even this lesser claim is justified. The fact is, however, that the usage elsewhere in *Jn* does not support this distinction between *agapan* and *philein* (the former is used in 14²³ and the latter in 16²⁷, but clearly the meaning is the same in both places). Thus the change from one verb to the other in the present context is probably made simply for stylistic reasons. In the same way some commentators distinguish between the three forms of the commission given to Peter—'*Feed my lambs. . . . Tend my sheep. . . . Feed my sheep*'—as if he were being called successively to the offices of Sunday-school teacher, Class-leader and Preacher! It is likely, however, that here again the change of expression is merely stylistic and that it is one and the same commission that is meant—namely, the commission to fulfil a pastoral ministry in the Church. In *vv.* 1-14 Peter was represented as leading the Church in its mission to the pagan world; here in *vv.* 15-17 he is represented as leading the Church in its pastoral care over its own members. Peter's sorrow at being asked the question the third time is probably not due to a change in the wording (see above) but rather to the fact that the threefold repetition brought vividly home to his mind the painful memory of his threefold denial.

'*more than these*' is ambiguous. It can either mean 'more than these things', i.e. the fishing boat, tackle, etc. (cf. *NEB*), or 'more than these men', i.e. the other disciples (cf. *NEBm*). The latter is more likely in view of Peter's self-confident protestations of loyalty (see 13³⁷ and especially Mk 14²⁹).

21¹⁸⁻¹⁹. By the time this Gospel was published Peter had already proved his worthiness of the confidence reposed in him. *Acts* contains ample evidence of his heroic leadership in the missionary and pastoral work of the Church; and his career was crowned by his martyrdom by crucifixion in Rome about A D 64. The present passage contains valuable and early confirmation of the fact of Peter's martyrdom. The expressions '*stretch forth thy hands*' and '*another shall gird thee*' reflect vocabulary frequently used in connection with crucifixion, and *v.* 19a suggests that they were understood in this sense by the writer (cf. **12³³**). Peter's fate as martyr is contrasted with the freedom he enjoyed in his youth. There may be here an implied hint at the tremendous change that was effected in Peter's character—the fickle and impulsive young man became by his life's end a veritable 'rock' (cf. **1⁴²**) of strength and constancy.

'*Follow me*'. See on **13³⁶**. Clearly the thought of martyrdom is still in mind. In **13³⁷** Peter impulsively declared his readiness to '*follow*' Jesus, and Jesus had to point out that that was impossible at the time, though the time would come when it would be possible. Now that he has been restored after his denial, that time has come and Peter is invited to follow his Lord along the path that for him too will lead to a cross.

21²⁰⁻³. Just as *vv.* 15-19 have been concerned with Peter's future, so the present verses are concerned with the future of the beloved disciple, thus further underlining the contrast between the two (see on **20³⁻⁸**). Peter displays an inquisitive interest in the beloved disciple's future, and is told in effect to mind his own business, which is to follow Jesus in the sense indicated in *vv.* 18-19. If Jesus has something different in mind for the beloved disciple—namely, that he should remain alive until the Parousia, that is no concern of Peter's. The writer explains that Jesus did not actually predict that the beloved disciple *would* in fact survive until the Parousia. This explanation is clearly felt to be necessary in view of the fact that the expectation had become widespread in the Church ('*the brethren*' means Christians, as frequently in *Acts* and the Epistles) that the beloved disciple would not die before the Parousia. The fact that the writer goes to such pains to correct this misunderstanding strongly suggests that at the time of writing the beloved disciple was already dead and that his death (probably as the last survivor of the Twelve) had given rise to considerable concern and perplexity in the Church.

21²⁴. The role of the beloved disciple in the life of the Church is here characterized as one of bearing witness (cf. **19³⁵**) to the truth of the gospel. Peter is to lead the Church in its evangelistic mission, to shepherd the flock and to seal his witness with his own blood. The beloved disciple, on the other hand, is to bear his witness by attesting the truth of the gospel events and providing the Church with an authoritative record thereof. This distinction is thoroughly in harmony with what we have seen in **20⁶⁻⁸** and **21⁷**. The main interest of the present verse is its bearing upon the authorship of the Gospel (see Introduction, p. 1).

'*these things*' is sometimes understood as referring simply to Chapter **21**, or even to *vv.* 15-23 only, but more probably it refers to the whole contents of *Jn*.

'*wrote*' may mean no more than 'caused to be written'; cf. **19¹⁹**, where presumably Pilate did not himself do the actual writing. If so, the statement claims no more than that the beloved disciple (i.e. the Apostle John, see on **13²³**) is the witness whose testimony lies behind the Gospel. It is more natural, however, to interpret '*wrote*' literally and to regard this verse as a 'guarantee of authorship' provided by the Church leaders who were responsible for publishing the Gospel—and for adding the Appendix (see p. 219). The question then arises as to whether this opinion (given no doubt in all good faith) is correct.

21²⁵ simply repeats in more flowery language the point of the original conclusion in **20³⁰⁻¹**. The exaggeration of the expression is natural enough to any one whose conception of the '*things which Jesus did*' is as limitless as was that of the apostolic Church. The subject treated in this Gospel is far too great and glorious for any human literature ever to do it justice. Yet a short Gospel like this and its counterparts contains sufficient (as **20³¹** indicates) to enable men to believe and so obtain eternal life. The use of the first person singular, after the '*we*' of the previous verse, is surprising, but probably indicates that the Appendix as a whole is the work of a single editor who, in the all-important attestation of *v.* 24, associates with himself the whole body of Church leaders in whose name he is fulfilling his task.

(*a*) The picture of Jesus standing on the shore at daybreak, watching the disciples' plight and waiting to come to their aid, is one that has often fired the imagination of preachers. 'And now, as we stand and gaze with our eyes fixed upon the farther shore, a single figure rises from the flood and straightway fills the whole horizon. There is the

Saviour' (A. J. Toynbee). The tragedy is that He so often remains unrecognized. We need both the insight whereby the beloved disciple recognized Him and the enthusiasm with which Peter rushed to greet Him. (*b*) The story of the draught of fishes, symbolically interpreted, has much to teach us about the Church's evangelistic mission. It can succeed only as the Risen Lord takes control and His commands are obeyed. When this happens the most disheartening failure can be transformed into success beyond all expectation. The mission is universal in its scope and there is room in the Church for all. (*c*) The story of Peter's complete reinstatement is full of hope and comfort for all who are conscious of having failed their Master. In spite of our denials and failures He still calls us to Himself and entrusts His work to our unworthy hands. The one qualification that He calls for is that we love Him, genuinely and sincerely. And the way we can prove our love for Him is by showing a pastoral concern for those who belong to His flock (cf. Mt 25[31-46]). (*d*) The references to the futures of Peter and the beloved disciple respectively remind us that there are different ways of bearing witness to Christ. Some are called to pioneer missionary activity and possibly to martyrdom, others to a quiet life of theological study and teaching. It is for each follower of Christ to discover his own vocation and faithfully to follow that, without expecting the vocation of others to follow the same lines and without questioning the validity of other kinds of Christian vocation. If the Lord has something in mind for others of His servants different from what He has in mind for us (whether in the way of responsibility or of privilege), it is not for us to complain or seek to interfere. (*e*) The closing verse vividly expresses the truth (which becomes more forcible with every succeeding generation) that there is no limit to what Jesus has done and can do. It must always 'far outpass the power of human telling' (cf. *MHB* 273, *v.* 4), and eternity itself is far 'too short to utter all' His praise (cf. *MHB* 413, *v.* 6).